Praise for Linda Zercoe's Memoir, *A Kick-Ass Fairy*

"An incredibly moving memoir. Linda Zercoe's book forces us to travel to an intimate and sometimes terrifying world of cancer—but never allows us to lose hope."

> —SIDDHARTHA MUKHERJEE, M.D., assistant professor of medicine, oncologist and researcher at Columbia University Medical Center, NY; author of *The Emperor of All Maladies: A Biography of Cancer*, winner of the 2011 Pulitzer Prize for nonfiction.

"Linda Zercoe describes herself as a Cancerian and a Cancer Warrior and in her memoir, it becomes clear why these are fitting designations for a woman with a hard shell who is soft inside, like her astrological symbol."

> —JEAN SHINODA BOLEN, M.D., author of *Close to the Bone: Life Threatening Illness as a Soul Journey*

"Into each life some suffering comes, but Linda Zercoe has faced with bravery and hope more than her share, leaving the rest of us an awe-inspiring journey of perseverance and grit."

> —KEN BURNS, Award-winning filmmaker of historical documentaries including *The Civil War*, *The Brooklyn Bridge*, *The Dust Bowl*, and *Baseball*. One of his current projects is a six-part series, *Cancer: The Emperor of All Maladies* coming to PBS in the Spring 2015.

"I have learned that there is survival behavior and that a patient who exceeds expectations is not just lucky but has induced the changes and the behavior which led to their survival. Being a good patient means being a submissive sufferer and Linda is what I call a 'respant' or responsible participant who can be a life coach for us all."

> —BERNIE SIEGEL, M.D., author of *A Book of Miracles* and *Faith, Hope & Healing*

"This book will give you a glimpse of what it's like to be affected by cancer and make you aware of how much more needs to be done to support patients and families with cancer and inherited malignancies."

—MARGARET A. TEMPERO, M.D., Director, UCSF Pancreas Center; Leader, Pancreas Cancer Program; Professor of Medicine, Division of Hematology and Oncology;
The Rombauer Family Distinguished Professorship in Pancreas Cancer Clinical and Translational Science

"A one-of-a-kind cancer story ... Zercoe's compassion and humanity shine, and readers can revel in not only her relative health but her ultimate happiness."

—Kirkus Reviews

A KICK-ASS FAIRY

A KICK-ASS FAIRY

A MEMOIR

LINDA ZERCOE

The names and identifying details of some characters in this book
have been changed.

Cover designed by Kimberly Glyder Design
Photo Credit: Larry Washburn / Getty Images
Interior design: Joel Friedlander, Marin Bookworks

Library of Congress Control Number: 2013914529

ISBN: 978-0-9895815-4-7 (Paperback)
ISBN: 978-0-9895815-5-4 (ebook)

696 San Ramon Valley Blvd, Suite #268
Danville, CA 94526

For Doug, Kim and Brad,
who inspire me every day

TABLE OF CONTENTS

IT'S NOT EASY BEING GREEN

I always thought Kermit the Frog's lament was touching. Being different is hard. Being physically different, especially on the inside where no one can see it, is very hard. Particularly when you are a walking time bomb.

My staff and I knew Linda was different from the start. She was too young. She had already had cancer before, a different kind. She was unusually sensitive to radiation. And she was often angry. Why shouldn't she be? Something was wrong and, for a long time, no one could figure it out.

We're all at risk for bad things to happen. A tree might topple over on me. My airplane might not reach its destination. A drunk driver going the wrong way might hit me head on. I might get cancer. But all these things are very rare or at least uncommon, even sporadic cancer. But a patient with an inherited cancer family syndrome faces a nearly inevitable brush with cancer. And, depending on the syndrome, the cancer may be difficult to detect early, making the possibility of a terminal cancer very real.

Right now, we do our best to monitor affected patients but we need better technology and preventive treatment in order to make a bigger impact. Hopefully, this book will give you a glimpse of what it's like to be affected and make you aware of how much more needs to be done to support patients and families with inherited malignancies. With enough focused research in rare diseases, we can transform lives and give everyone a better future.

Margaret Tempero

Margaret A. Tempero, M.D.
Director, UCSF Pancreas Center; Leader, Pancreas Cancer Program; Professor of Medicine, Division of Hematology and Oncology, UCSF; The Rombauer Family Distinguished Professorship in Pancreas Cancer Clinical and Translational Science

A KICK-ASS FAIRY

PROLOGUE

JUNE 12, 2012 JOURNAL

It's 7:20 a.m. on a warm and overcast Monday morning. Doug and I just boarded the shuttle that will transport us from our hotel in Bethesda, Maryland, to the National Institutes of Health, or NIH. We just flew in from California last night and though I'm not normally a morning person, I'm excited and filled with anticipation.

In the Gospel of John, Bethesda is a pool of water near the Sheep Gate in Jerusalem that was used for healing. In the ancient Aramaic language, *Bethesda* means "the house of mercy or grace." Mercy and grace have been part of my prayers for a long time.

Once we arrive at the NIH and get out of the shuttle, we temporarily queue up for a security check with the other passengers and are given badges. Then, back on the shuttle, we drive up the hill to the Mark O. Hatfield Clinical Research Center, where we're scheduled for meetings all day with several researchers in the Clinical Genetics Division. This building is one of many within a large fenced campus that seems to be equivalent in size to a university. Pushing the enormous rotating central door, Doug and I enter the expansive, sunlit atrium.

On our way to registration, we pass the statement in raised silver metal on the light honey-color wood-paneled wall: "The National Institutes of Health is dedicated to fostering discovery at the frontiers of science and medicine... The NIH conducts and supports medical research to uncover new knowledge that will improve the health of all Americans and the human condition throughout the world."

1

I feel like I'm on the edge of the future, arriving here with all of the genetic material in each of my cells, which goes all the way back to the beginning of life. I'm humbled and awed that they want to study me and my story. I'm hoping that my participation will make a difference in their research and in my life. I'm grateful that Doug, my husband of almost twenty-four years, is at my side, and that he also has a significant role in their research.

After registration we step into the south elevator and begin the ascent. Deep in thought, I wonder where my story should begin and how, just a month shy of 55, I tell the story of how I got here. I look over at Doug. Our eyes meet as the door opens, and he squeezes my hand as we step off the elevator into the new frontier—the unknown.

PART 1

CHAPTER 1

EVOLUTION
1901–1957

Giacomo and Frances, my maternal grandparents, were married at a Catholic Mass on November 11, 1923, the fifth anniversary of Armistice Day. Frances, who was an inch taller than Giacomo, was later quoted as saying, "The day of the wedding was the anniversary of one war ending and another beginning." Their marriage was to last 62 years.

Giacomo was 5 years old when the *SS Lombardia* docked at Ellis Island in New York harbor in November 1901. He was the youngest of the eighteen to twenty-one children (depending on the source), of my great grandparents Giocinto and Giovanna. Giacomo and his parents, as well as five of his older siblings, crossed the Atlantic traveling in steerage from Sicily.

Upon arriving, they settled into a one-bedroom tenement apartment on Mulberry Street, in Little Italy. We were told that Giocinto would often say to his children, "The streets aren't just paved with quarry stones or bricks, they are paved with gold." He was employed as a bricklayer.

"If I had a penny for every time [this or that happened], I would be rich" was a favorite expression of my grandfather. We would all be millionaires for the number of times we heard about how he had to sew on buttons on the street corner for pennies to help support the family while he was going to school. His education stopped at the eighth grade.

By 1910, the entire family was working on an assembly line in a garment factory on the Lower East Side. They made pants. One brother was a baster. A sister operated a sewing machine. Another brother was an ironer, one a finisher, and my grandfather, some sort of apprentice.

In 1918, at the end of World War I, my grandfather, then 22, returned from Europe in his doughboy uniform. Although he was known as Jerry, he preferred Giacomo. At about five foot seven, with a full shock of dark hair and a handsome face, he cut quite a figure. He quickly reunited with his brothers and immediately ascended to his rightful place as an equal partner in what was now their own garment factory located on Hart Street in Brooklyn. There they manufactured bathrobes and smoking jackets under contract with West Point, as well as some hospitals and stores.

After a few years, Giacomo met the eye of a young woman named Frances, who worked a sewing machine on the factory floor in close proximity to the woman known as "Fanny Fly," who installed the zippers. For Giacomo, it was love at first sight. Even though he was quite the catch, Frances played hard to get.

Frances was a first-generation Italian American. Her parents, Giuseppe and Marie, had immigrated in the 1870s. Her father had just recently passed away from a heart ailment. Her mother was a seamstress.

During the Depression my grandfather's factory flourished, and they hired many out-of-work family members. By 1940 my grandparents had five children—two boys and three girls. Their fourth, born in 1934, was my mother, also Frances—though she always maintained emphatically that she wasn't named after her mother.

By the time my mother was 5, they had moved to a large Queen Anne Victorian in Richmond Hill, Queens, a house with fifty windows, two kitchens, and multiple cooks and housemaids. As a teenager, her oldest brother, George, was very involved in the Boy Scouts. An 11-year-old boy named Bruce, who would later become my father, would ride his bicycle from his home in Glendale, Queens, to Scout meetings at their house. There were many times when my mother and father were in close proximity during these meetings, not knowing that eventually it would become part of the backstory of their relationship.

Even though my mother was very smart, skipping two grades in school, my grandfather would not pay for her to go to college. He thought that money for college should be spent only on the boys—even though George, a World War II navy veteran, would attend college on the GI

Bill. Since there was only the youngest son left to pay for, my mother felt angry and frustrated by her father's lack of support. To appease her, my grandparents hosted a big party for her "sweet 16" birthday.

Having already graduated from high school, my mother got a job in Manhattan and advanced quickly from the secretarial pool to the post of executive secretary to the president of a nuclear engineering company. She'd proudly tell us stories about the elaborate process for discarding her typewriter rollers because of the secrets they held. She also became a fashion plate, wearing the most current styles either sewn by her own hand or bought at a discount. In every picture of my mother from that time of her life she is striking a pose, as if modeling, while wearing gloves, all manner of hats, purses that matched her shoes, the latest costume jewelry, and often furs.

My mother was beautiful.

My paternal great-grandparents, Heinreich and Auguste, their son Erich, my grandfather, age 3, and their infant son, Adolf, arrived at Ellis Island from Germany in October 1902, on the ship *Pretoria* of the Hamburg-American Line. They settled in Brooklyn.

A few months after arriving, Heinreich went missing. The family soon learned that he was gone for good, never to be seen or heard from again. Rumor had it that he'd eventually settled somewhere in the Midwest and started an entirely new family. Auguste worked as a nurse to support her two sons.

I don't know much more about my grandfather's youth, but in March 1923, Erich, then 24, and my paternal grandmother, May, also of German descent, traveled from their home in Queens to the Eastern District Court of New York in Brooklyn. There, at 22 years old, May was sworn in and became a naturalized citizen of the United States. She was five foot five, and attractive. In a photograph taken that day, she's wearing tight finger waves in her hair, and her flapper-era clothing appears expensive. Erich, at her side in a suit, is tall and lanky, with black hair. He was employed as part of a telephone wire installation crew. Five months later their first son was born, followed six years later, in 1929, by Bruce, my father.

Erich rose through the ranks of the telephone company and in his spare time got together with his male friends to make music, usually in the basement of their Glendale home, where he played Dixieland jazz on a four-string banjo. May, who had asthma, played her piano in the living room and at times she gave lessons to the neighborhood children. Also a very talented artist, she spent many hours indoors sketching portraits of young women using graphite pencils and painting watercolors, mostly of outdoor scenes or flowers.

May's father, having first gone from rags to riches in the first two decades of the century, lost his paint and hardware business during the Depression when his customers couldn't pay their large IOUs. During World War II, May wouldn't leave her house, for fear of what might happen to her because of her German roots.

My father, Bruce, grew up very close to his mother. In addition to being a Boy Scout, he was a good student and was on the safety patrol, where he was assigned to traffic control. When he was a little older, he volunteered on weekends, policing Jamaica Bay as a member of the Junior Coast Guard. He attended a technical high school, where he excelled in math and science. However, his college career ended prematurely, after he supposedly broke both his arms playing football and contracted pneumonia. He spent his mandatory two-year tour of service in the army stationed in Germany. When he had time off from his desk job, he toured the country toting his Leica M3 camera.

My father could play the trumpet pretty well and strum a bit on the guitar, although he wasn't able to keep up with his father and older brother, Eric, who could play a mean clarinet and saxophone. My father wanted to play the trumpet professionally, but also became very enthusiastic about audio electronics and home recording.

My parents were officially introduced at a group gathering hosted by Mom's brother George, Dad's childhood friend from Scouts. They dated for about six months before they became engaged. At the time, Dad was 27, six feet tall and of medium build, with wavy dark brown hair combed back from a high, slightly receding hairline.

By their engagement party on April 1, 1956, an Easter Sunday, he'd given up his mustache, his dreams of being a musician, and his Lutheran faith, as required by the bride to be. He was also receiving instruction in Catholic doctrine. Mom, now 21, wore red lipstick and no other makeup.

She had given up her dreams of marrying a doctor for the handsome man who was "getting frisky with his hands."

The party was at her parents' home, which by this time was downsized to a brick two-story, two-family house in Ozone Park, Queens, near Aqueduct Raceway. The celebration was held in the partially finished basement, replete with knotty pine paneling, linoleum flooring, and ceiling tiles that unfortunately didn't hide the silver-painted plumbing pipes.

Mom wore her hair pulled back in a French twist. Her dress was sleeveless, blush pink chiffon with polka dots, fitted through the bodice with a large full skirt and layers of petticoats. She matched the dress with a darker shade of pink pearl pumps. On her wrist was a corsage of fresh flowers, a gift from my father. Dad wore a suit and a tie. Everyone was dressed up for the occasion, and most of the women wore flowers.

With a cigar clenched in his teeth, my grandfather Erich played his banjo, and my uncle Eric played an assortment of single-reed woodwinds. Their friend Vic played the trumpet, and someone else from their musical troupe played electric guitar. They performed songs named "Allegheny Moon," "Jumpin' with Symphony Sid," "For Me and My Gal," and many others.

Marion, Mom's older sister, sang a soprano version of "Make Believe," modeling her performance on that of Kathryn Grayson, an operatic singer as well as the star of the 1951 movie version of *Show Boat*. Together they all sang "Easter Parade." My grandfather Giacomo, a killer tenor and a hobby opera singer, sang "Song of Songs," written in 1914, a cappella, not a note off key but missing most of the *r*s at the ends of words due to his heavy New York Italian accent. Dad, when not attached to Mom, was busy fussing with his recording equipment, checking microphones and sound levels.

After toasts were given with wishes for the engaged couple, dinner was served. The meal had been laboriously and lovingly prepared by my grandmother Frances, who lived to cook and showed her love with food.

For weeks after the party, Dad spent his free time editing the tape recordings he had made, and then had it all made into a record. The long-play 33 rpm disk also included a later recording of his singing a very bluesy jazz version of "Embrace Me," which featured an entire line of his great whistling.

While on his lunch break at the engineering company where he worked, my father meticulously drew an album cover. In it, a piano holds a drink and a smoking cigarette in an ashtray, while in the foreground, a banjo, a tenor sax, an electric guitar, a trumpet, and a reel-to-reel tape recorder with a microphone attached appear in proper perspective. He mysteriously called the album *Music to Have a Bachelor Party By.*

Instead of going on a honeymoon after their wedding, my parents settled into their new home in Levittown, New York, a one and a half-story gray-shingled Cape Cod with white shutters. They furnished it in the latest modern décor with a palette of turquoise, gold, and black, peppered with some African accents. Parked in the driveway was their 1953 Plymouth Cranbrook, a large, dark green sedan with a white roof and wide whitewall tires.

Within months of the wedding my mother was pregnant, though at work she hid the fact under a girdle for as long as possible. After the first trimester, Dad's mother, May, who had been diagnosed with some type of pelvic cancer, died after the radioactive implants with which the doctors had tried to treat her proved ineffective.

Grieving quietly, every morning Dad would drive Mom—who had no reason to have a license—to the train station, and then head to his job on Long Island. Mom took the train to Pennsylvania Station in midtown Manhattan, and from there walked the few blocks to her office near the Empire State Building. About halfway through her pregnancy, when her feet and ankles started to swell and she was too exhausted to continue working, she quit her job. In photos from her baby shower toward the end of her pregnancy, she still is not wearing maternity clothes.

A month later, my parents hosted an afternoon barbeque on a hot weekend in July. Family and friends, including Mom's former boss and his wife, made up the party. All the usual musicians were there, and after a few beers Dad, slumped in a lawn chair, started improvisational tooting on his trumpet with his eyes closed. The festivities wound down in the evening, and while Mom was standing on a stool putting away plates, she started having contractions.

"I think I'm in labor."

"It is too early for the baby!" my grandmother said. "It's not due for another four weeks."

My mother sat on the couch as ordered, but couldn't stay still. She told my father to get ready since she thought the baby would arrive imminently. Dad calmly showered, slowly shaved, carefully dressed, and methodically gathered the newspapers. Mom was frantic.

Finally in the car, Dad drove deliberately, while Mom, well into labor, moaned and screamed that she was going to have the baby at any moment. The elder Frances slapped her daughter on the face and told her, "Cross your legs and act like a lady."

When they reached the hospital, Mom was quickly put onto a gurney. In the elevator on the way to Labor and Delivery, she gave birth to a five-pound baby girl. Though small, I arrived with ten fingers and ten toes.

A few days later, my mother and I were discharged from the hospital. I was swaddled in a striped flannel receiving blanket. My mother looked like a movie star in a fashionable, tightly belted light blue accordion-pleated dress with turquoise-colored beads and matching high-heeled shoes. Her hair was pulled back in a youthful ponytail, and she was wearing sunglasses like Marilyn Monroe's. After only a few days, she looked like she had never been pregnant.

I was born a month prematurely, under the sign of Cancer, a water sign, ruled by the moon, possessing the tides of emotions, sentimental, and a lover of home. But I should have been a Leo, a fire sign, ruled by the sun, a thinker, impulsive, a leader, someone who follows her intuition.

CHAPTER 2

A SECRET STORM
1958–1965

Apparently my mother and father never expected that their natural family planning method would fail. When I was 16 months old, my sister Alane was born, and then eighteen months later, my sister Diane. By the time I was 3, my mother was 25 and already had three children.

Soon after Diane was born, or maybe because of it, I ate most of a bottle of St. Joseph's baby aspirin that had been left on the toy box in my room. My mother realized I had consumed a huge quantity of pills, so I was rushed to the hospital. After the tube had been forced down my throat in the black room with the bright light in my face, my mother was very angry at me, especially since my father was so mad at her.

Shortly after the arrival of Diane, who was annoying and cried all the time, our family moved into the other half of my mother's parents' house in Queens. As a toddler, Alane, whose nose was always running, looked perpetually sad as she dragged around her blanket and her thumb-sucking stuffed bear, Boo-Boo. The sight apparently bugged my mother, who later nicknamed her Sarah Bernhardt, not meaning anything good.

After Diane was born, my mother was always yelling and for some unknown reason put Alane and her bear out on the front stoop and told her she had to leave and find another home. Both were rescued by my grandmother. My grandparents were always talking to my mother about her parenting skills. Alane became my playmate, my sister-in-arms. I was her overseer and protector. I was underweight for my age and had curly light chestnut hair. Alane was chubby at the time, with dark brown hair.

One night when Diane was about a year old and I was 4, my parents went out for a rare evening as a couple. Our grandparents babysat us upstairs in their apartment, which was decorated in heavy mahogany furniture and smelled like mothballs mixed with whatever was on the stove or in the oven at the moment. Not being closely watched, Alane and I scribbled with crayons all over the marble bathroom floor. When our parents returned home, Grandpa had to show them what we'd been up to. I knew we were in big trouble when the crayon wouldn't come off the marble. Dad told us to get to bed in Grandma's spare room with the twin beds and shut the door of the bedroom.

This was the first time we were left in the dark. Alane was very afraid and started crying. By the light of the moon, which was coming through the open venetian blinds and the gossamer white sheers hanging over the window, I began jumping on the bed, and soon Alane started giggling. Dad opened the door, poked his head in, scolded us, and shut the door.

I said, "Boinga-boinga," and we started giggling all over again.

Later that same year at my prekindergarten physical, Dr. Cushing, a double-chinned, fat-handed, lady doctor with a white coat, glasses, and very ugly shoes, told my mother that I had two "beauty marks" or moles that were a little enlarged and might need to be removed some day to avoid any trouble, like cancer. One was on my shoulder, where she reasoned that it could be irritated by a bra, the other on my upper back.

The next thing I knew, I was in a children's ward, in a hospital gown with a cap on my head. Then the bed was being wheeled through the crowded halls. They tried to suffocate me with a mask and this gross sickly smelling gas called "ether" that made me want to vomit. I think I did. I remember being scared and all alone, trapped within the bars of the bed, tied down.

That summer, right before I turned 5, it was time to go back to the doctor to have the stitches removed from the surgery. I was all excited because Uncle Joey, Mom's baby brother and my godfather, was coming with me and Mom to the doctor. He was home from college for the summer. During the summer he also drove a Bungalow Bar ice cream truck and would swing by and give us ice cream or frozen rocket pops, which we all loved to eat while singing, "Bungalow Bar tastes like tar. The more you eat it, the sicker you are." Also, Uncle Joey was cute.

I remember sitting in the back seat of my parents' old green Plymouth. There was no seat belt. The velvet-velour of the seat was made of horse hair–like material that was scratchy on the back of my legs. Up in front, Mom and Uncle Joey were talking, laughing. I was alone in the back, ignored, rolling around and trying to stay seated. If I sat cross-legged, more of my legs got scratchy, but when my legs were out straight, I had to brace myself with both arms out to either side, and they got tired. It was hot, so hot that the air seemed orange, and my sweaty legs really itched.

Finally, when we were all at the doctor's office and I was stripped down to my underpants, in walked a monster. An old gray-haired man with spots all over his face started talking to my mother, telling her that the other doctor was on vacation. I was really scared. He started chinking and clinking some metal things on a tray, and next I saw scissors and other sharp things. I started crying and then screaming.

The doctor told my mother that it was very important that I stay still. I didn't want to do it.

"Stop it! You are wasting the doctor's time," my mother yelled at me. I didn't care. Then she called out to the waiting room for Uncle Joey. "Joey, hold her down."

The two of them pushed me down onto my stomach on the counter. I was being squished to death. I could hear my mother and Uncle Joey laughing and whispering to each other through the pounding of my heart in my ears. I couldn't move. I couldn't breathe. I closed my eyes.

I heard my mother say, "It's all over." I didn't like her anymore, ever again. I opened my eyes. But for some reason I knew I wasn't me anymore.

That same summer, we moved to a new home on Long Island, in Farmingdale, across the street from Bethpage State Park. A few short weeks later, I was on my way to kindergarten wearing a new outfit, a swirling gray skirt with suspenders that had a wooly French poodle appliqué and a turquoise blouse, and a matching headband holding back my long banana curls. My mother walked with me to school, just her and me. She held my hand the whole way, and after she dropped me off for my first day, I felt like I was in heaven. I felt free and I loved school.

On a pre-Christmas trip to the new Walt Whitman Mall in Huntington to see Santa Claus, Grandma slipped in the parking lot on the ice, tripped over a parking stop, and fell and broke her teeth. Her face was all cut up. Grandma, who already suffered chronic migraines, convalesced at our house. During her recovery over the holidays, my mother dressed me as a nurse, using my starched, embroidered child-size apron and wrapping my head in dishtowels. I was sent into Grandma's room with trays of food to help her eat, keep her company, and hold her hand. I loved Grandma, but she was very scary looking in bed with her cut-up face. I remember my mother proclaiming that she was too busy and, "I always retch at sight of blood or vomit anyway." Grandma was very appreciative of my attention and kind to me. I was forever more called Linda, the nurse.

Shortly after the start of the new year, my grandfather Erich bled to death on the operating table while surgeons were trying to remove a cancerous laryngeal tumor. I had hardly known him since he had moved to Florida after his wife's death. Now we had only one set of grandparents, the Italian ones.

The next summer I packed up my little, round white-plastic valise with the long looped handle and a picture of Barbie on the front to spend a week with Grandma and Grandpa in Queens. They picked me up, and Grandpa drove his new turquoise Chevrolet Impala *very slowly*. During the week, Grandpa, no longer a company owner, worked at a garment firm. Spending time with Grandma was special and very different. She was usually happy, especially when her women friends came over during the week to play cards, eat cake, and drink some clear liquid that smelled of licorice out of very small glasses. She introduced me to her friends as her nurse and gave me some soda in my little glass.

One of the days during my visit, Grandma pulled scarves out of her bureau and said, "Let's be gypsies." We danced ourselves into a frenzy to the music on the record player until Grandma got sweaty and flopped on the chair saying, all out of breath, "I want to just watch you." Every day we'd go shopping, walking at times under noisy trains to get to the stores while dragging a wire shopping basket. I saw things like tongue, brains, and pickled things in jars at her favorite butcher. She'd buy pig knuckles and other assorted grossities that wound up in that night's spaghetti sauce or the stew. Back in her kitchen, I stood on a chair next to her, wearing a makeshift apron, and helped her cook while listening to music and singing, while also receiving cooking instruction that I didn't understand. As much as Grandma liked to cook, she loved to bake, and I got to sample everything. I especially liked the jelly or cinnamon-and-sugar rolls she made with leftovers from the pie crusts that she made with flour and lard. In the afternoons I would draw while Grandma watched her "stories" on the black-and-white television.

Too soon, it was time to go home. I knew my mother was expecting a baby, but now her stomach was really big. One hot, humid afternoon, while sitting in a lounge chair under the large oak tree in the yard, Mom called Alane and me over from playing on the swings to look at the ashtray on her belly. We could see it popping up and down as the baby inside kicked.

First grade started a few weeks later. Dad took Mom to the hospital to have the baby, but they came home the same day with a box of Dunkin' Donuts instead. A week later, my mother really gave birth to our brother, Bruce. While she was in the hospital, my art class at school made congratulations cards for my mother with construction paper and crayons. Shortly after my parents arrived home, after warning my sisters and me that we could look but not touch him, my mother changed baby Bruce's diaper on the dining room table. He wee-weed like a geyser, even getting some in my mother's mouth.

We giggled. Mom yelled.

Dad was so very happy. He whistled while walking us to the bus stop, where he gave the bus driver a cigar with a blue ribbon that said, "It's a boy." I wondered to myself, *Was Dad this excited when I was born?* When Bruce was a little bit older, he became partly my baby, while my sisters practiced being mothers with their Thumbelina dolls.

In the wintertime, I complained to Mom of a sore throat.

"Hmm," she said.

Eventually, Dr. Cushing came to the house. Alane and I were quarantined for scarlet fever that developed from untreated strep throat. We weren't allowed out of our room except to go to the bathroom. Mom would bring us food, and Dad set up a television that we'd watch all day once the fever broke.

Once in a while we were allowed to stay up until 7:30 p.m. and watch *The Flintstones.* Against my mother's protests, Dad, who was now working two jobs, allowed me to stay up late to see the Beatles on *The Ed*

Sullivan Show. Shortly after this, Dad brought home the 45 record of "I Want to Hold Your Hand." Dad was my hero.

After months of Mom's furious sewing, we all had matching clothes for Christmas. This was the trend for all the holidays and events for the next few years. No longer believing in Santa, I had to pretend for everyone else. The magic was gone, except that for Christmas I got a rose-pink–and-white portable record player.

In the fall of 1964, I was seven years old. On the school bus on the way home from school, I was kneeling on the seat with the emergency exit window, three rows from the back. I was leading all the other kids that would be the kind to sit in the back of the bus in singing at the top of our lungs:

> Great, green, globs of greasy grimy gopher guts,
> Mutilated monkey meat, little birdies' bloody feet.
> All these things are very good for you to eat.
> The bus driver forgot his spoon!

Then, in the drizzle of a dreary afternoon, the driver took a curve too fast and I went hurtling out the window. Outside the bus, I was hovering up in the trees above somebody's front lawn looking down at my body curled up on the strip of grass between the sidewalk and the curb, then watching as the bus continued down the street with my pea-soup colored beret that my mother had just crocheted hanging from the bus window, caught by the pompom. I don't remember how I reentered my body. I just remember hearing my 6-year-old sister Alane screaming in the distance, "Stop the bus! My sister Linda just fell out the window!"

The bus driver came back for me. I could walk back onto the bus. He dropped off all the other children before he personally escorted my sister and me to the door of our home. All I could think about was how much trouble I was going to be in if anything happened to that pea-soup-green beret hat that I didn't like but had to wear anyway. It was still hanging out the window, getting all wet and dirty.

I stared down at the milk crate on the stoop as the bus driver, with my hat in his hand, told my mother what happened. He was later fired and I inconvenienced my mother and my poor father with a wasted trip to the hospital to check for injuries. Other than a few scrapes and bruises, I was just fine.

The bills were not. I remember being asked, "How could you be so stupid?" and being punished for not being more careful and sitting properly on the bus. "Well, we'll have to do without now, to pay the hospital bills. Money doesn't grow on trees, you know." The fact that I was alive didn't seem to matter. When I tried to talk about what happened, especially the part about being in the tree and looking down at my body, which I didn't understand, Mom said, "You're fine. Stop feeling sorry for yourself."

One morning I woke up before school and, instead of just getting the usual kinks in my neck that felt like fire and would sometimes cause me to see stars, I couldn't move my head. My neck was frozen.

When Mom saw me she said, "What's wrong with you?"

After Alane got on the bus for school, she drove me, my brother, Bruce—now over a year old—and Diane to the doctor. Dr. Cushing sprayed something smelly on my neck, pushed down hard on the top of my head, and tried to twist it back and forth. It barely moved. She told my mother that I needed rest and that it was from stress and not related to the school bus incident. On the way home Mom pulled into the parking lot at the butcher to buy pounded veal. She was going to make my favorite, breaded and fried veal cutlets for dinner. As another special treat for me, she signed up to come with my class to the Museum of Natural History in New York City the following week.

The kinks in my neck continued for years.

Most Sunday mornings we were free until around 11 a.m. Diane, Alane, and I, charged with watching Bruce, ate out of cereal boxes while watching episodes of *David and Goliath, Gumby,* and *Wonderama.* But, eventually, we got bored. Out of the dressers came all the petticoats and we'd all get dressed up, which included dressing Bruce. Then we'd all jump on the twin beds, bed to bed, bed to floor, then the floor to the bed. Occasionally, Dad would emerge from their room wearing a bathrobe and slippers, his hair all messed up. He would tell us to knock it off and we'd sit down quietly, hands folded across our laps. Then he went back to their room and closed the bifold door. I led the pack and started more jumping after a while. I wondered what they did in there all morning. Eventually Dad would come out and make us pancakes with sausage, or waffles with fried corn beef hash, or bacon and eggs, and then he disappeared to mow the lawn and nap in the afternoon while listening to music with his headphones on.

After the bus incident I needed glasses. When selecting frames I wanted the pink or blue ones "just like the other girls." My mother would only get the ugly kind, brown with pointed tips. Then my hair started to go from curly to frizz. My new nickname became The Four-Eyed Frizz Bomb.

Something happened to my mother in the years after Bruce was born. She started getting big bumpy pimples on her face that she would pick at all the time with her fingernails. She spent a lot of time in her room, and when she wasn't in her room she'd yell, hit Alane and me, and say crazy things that didn't make sense like, "If I say white is black, then black is white." Sometimes I would see her crying and try to hug her, but she would just say, "Leave me alone." One day I found a package of twenty-eight little pills in her room that years later she claimed were for her pimples. I think she was also on Valium.

Saturday mornings were spent in Catechism class, where I had to memorize the mortal and venial sins and also learn by heart many prayers—all of which caused me great stress. I wondered what the point to all of this was. It wasn't like we ever went to church or prayed for anything except to be forgiven for the sins we committed and asking for help to be better behaved.

"God is everywhere," Mom told us, "and even if *I* don't know what you are doing, God can see *everything*!"

She told us God could even read our minds! In a symbol of make-pretend purity, I received First Holy Communion in a sinless white dress. After that, we had to start going to church on Sundays and there was no more jumping on the bed. I was dropped off for confession every week, and sometimes midweek—for what I didn't know.

Sometimes on Sunday afternoon we would all go to our grandparents' house for dinner, where the entire family would gather—aunts, uncles, great-aunts, great-uncles, and, my favorite, cousins. It was here that we would hear my grandfather say things like, "Children should be seen and not heard" or "Who asked for your two cents'?" These sayings were repeated often by my mother, who added "Go tell it to Sweeney" anytime we had any news. Then my father loved to say to each of us at dinner, "You have diarrhea of the mouth and constipation of the brain." We learned not to say much and to disappear as much as possible.

By the summer of 1965, between second and third grade, I was allowed more freedom. We all had to spend most of the day outside in the yard. Out of boredom, we started digging a hole to China in the back corner next to the fence. I remember the smell and sweet taste of the nectar of the blossoms of the honeysuckle bush, since I was now allowed in the front yard. I made friends with a schoolmate named Jeannie, who lived around the corner. I was allowed to go to her house, where her little brother had a box turtle that I would watch for hours.

One day Jeannie and I walked down to the end of her street. Boys not much older than we were gathered in front of the last house on the left. They noticed us and started teasing us, taunting us, inviting us inside the open garage.

Not one for passing a dare, I told Jeannie, "Let's go." Once we were inside the garage, one of the boys told us to take off our underpants. We did. They just looked. Nothing happened. But we ran back up the street anyway, our hearts thumping in our chests, swearing not to tell anyone. I knew before we reached Jeannie's house, all out of breath, that nothing good would come from telling my mother. It didn't matter that I would have no way of knowing, at 8 years old, that it *wasn't* my fault. I felt stupid now anyway. Jeannie and I didn't play again for rest of the summer and were never close again. Years later I thought maybe she told her mother and wasn't allowed to play with me.

CHAPTER 3

THE *STAR TREK* YEARS
1966–1971

On Thursday, September 8, 1966, my relationship with my father changed. That evening, Dad and I began watching *Star Trek* on a little portable color TV while sitting on the foot of my parents' bed. This was a weekly ritual for most of the next three years, unless I was being punished.

For me, Dad was a cross between Captain Kirk, Spock, and Dr. McCoy, with a little bit of Scotty thrown in. When Dad missed *Star Trek* because of a trip to Houston or Cape Kennedy, I would pay extra special attention to the show and then eagerly recount the latest episode when he returned.

Dad was working at Grumman Aircraft on the space program. He sometimes escorted rockets for NASA, and later we would learn of his involvement in the Apollo lunar module project and how he helped the astronauts go to the moon. *Star Trek* helped me understand why he was never home. It was also about this time that Dad gave me a brand new AM transistor radio, and I started listening to WABC, especially *The Cousin Brucie Show* using the tiny ear plug. *Star Trek* and the latest rock-and-roll music formed the cement of our bond.

Mom and Dad would have cocktails almost every night. I really didn't know what Mom did all day, but she sure did complain, especially about us. And after a couple of cocktails Dad, too, could turn on us on a dime.

One day Mom asked us all into the kitchen, where she showed us a large chart she'd made that listed the days of the week across the top and our names down the side. Assigned chores for each day filled up the middle, with room for her checkmark below. Along with this she came up with the idea for us to receive an allowance. I would make twenty-five cents per week, Alane twenty, and Diane fifteen. At 9 years old, I was to bathe my brother every day, and either set the table, clear the table, or do the dishes. (These chores rotated among us sisters, even though we couldn't quite reach the sink.) I had to vacuum all the house carpets on Saturday after Catechism class and grocery shopping with Mom and, of course, bring in all the grocery bags. I also needed to brush the fringe on carpets.

We also had to take cod liver oil every morning. Mom warned us, "If any attitude is displayed while taking the tablespoon of cod liver oil, it will result in allowance deductions."

On the chart, deductions were also listed for answering back, not doing chores, etc. Each infraction I committed, as determined by my mother, resulted in a nickel deduction.

I owed more money than I'd earned long before the week was out.

One morning Alane, now around 8 years old, gagged as usual on the tablespoon of oil, which incidentally smelled rotten as soon as the bottle was opened. But this time it sprayed out of her mouth all over my mother. In an instant, Mom smacked Alane across the face. Alane got on the bus that morning with red-rimmed eyes, red cheeks, a nasty scrape, and the imprint of the stars from mother's wide wedding ring. We knew not to talk about it. Mom had already told us, "Nobody is to know our business." But later that night I overheard Dad yelling at Mom. From then on, Dad started sticking up for Alane.

Most days after school, I skipped any snack and rushed to barricade the door of Alane's and my room at top of stairs in the event that Mom announced that she was "on the warpath" again. Alane and I might have done something while we were at school—or not. The warpath usually started with the banging of pots, slamming down the phone, or slamming a door shut. Then we would hear her feet pounding up the carpeted stairs and the clickity-clack of my mother's slippers heading down the hall to our room. The warpath resulted in the emptying of drawers or the contents of our closet on the floor and then being told, "Now, clean it up." Other times it meant getting something taken away, having our hair pulled, or if we were rolled up in a ball while covering our heads with our hands, getting hit in the back, sometimes using the same hairbrush that I used to brush the fringe or the nap of the carpet.

Mom was acting especially weird. One time I overheard her on the telephone saying, "You know now I am 33. This is exactly the same age as Jesus was when he died." I pondered whether she was afraid she would die, or maybe go to hell, or both.

We usually had roast beef for dinner on Sundays, but one week we were going to have a pot roast. After all taking our assigned seats around the breakfast nook, Mom got mad about something involving Dad, stuck a large serving fork into the roast and hurled it against the wall next to the window over the sink. It landed with a thud on the counter, leaving a trail of gravy dripping down the wall. At least this time, since Dad was home, the food wasn't thrown at one of us.

Mom started crying, stormed out of house, fired up the car, threw it into reverse, then careened into the busy street, and took off with a screech and smell of scorched rubber. Without turning our heads we all looked at each other out of the corners of our eyes and shrugged. Dad got up and opened the cabinet doors. He handed us pots, lids, and spoons and said "Let's go!"

We followed him, marching around the house singing, "Ding dong, the witch is dead. Which old witch? The wicked witch," to which he added in a crazy tone, "If she isn't yet, she soon will be." I was exhilarated to be part of the "getting Mom" band, and even happier that Dad was our leader.

During the fifth grade I experienced a series of calamities. First, Gary Hatch, who sat right next to me at school, was killed in a hit-and-run while riding his bike. Then Dad had a car accident and flipped the car. He was all right but had to wear a cervical collar. Then, to prepare us for a nuclear attack, we had duck-and-cover exercises in school, curled up against the wall of the hall in an attitude similar to the hair brush position. The death of Martin Luther King, in April 1968, was followed by the assassination of Bobby Kennedy in June. Meanwhile, the kinks in my neck continued. The school year culminated with my breaking my foot after jumping down an entire flight of stairs during a fire drill the last week of school, which meant I missed all the field day games. By the end of fifth grade, I had learned that threats and scary stuff also happened to other people outside of our house.

Early in the summer, Grandpa had gall bladder surgery. With Grandpa in recovery and me on crutches, we watched TV most of the summer, especially the ABC 4:30 movie. As soon as I could walk again, I finally got a bra, after months of pleading and my mother telling me I didn't need one.

"Your sister Diane"—who was three years younger than me—"is the one that really needs one," my Mom said.

In November that year we had an early, heavy snowfall. School was cancelled and Dad couldn't get out of the driveway to go to work. Dressed in a winter coat, hat, and mittens I went outside to the driveway to help Dad. All morning we scraped and heaved the snow. Since I didn't have windshield wipers for my glasses, I had to open my jacket and use my clothing to wipe them dry. Stopping to do this made me realize I had a stomach ache. As the morning wore on, my stomach continued to feel worse as I kept trying to keep up with the snow. I went inside to the bathroom and saw a big red-brown stain in my underwear. I thought I might be dying, and it was only because of that that I asked my mother what she thought was going on. She took a look and told me I'd gotten my first period. Mortified and confused, I asked her not to say anything to Dad. My older cousins Christine and Claudia had told me that a "period," also known as "the curse," was getting two blisters on your belly that popped and bled every month. Kotex was worn as a belt over the blisters. But I had no blisters that I could see.

As soon as I was cleaned up and she'd given me supplies, Mom blasted out the front door and shouted to my father, still shoveling in the quiet of the falling snow, and to anyone else in the neighborhood within earshot, "Bruce, our daughter is a woman!" Within a few months, Alane was moved into Diane's room and Mom made a lavender-and-white canopy that matched the girly-girl bedding in my own new room.

By the time it was the summer after seventh grade, the Beatles had broken up. On top of that Dad had left Grumman after the moon landing to open an electronics and music store in Chatham, New Jersey. During the week he lived in New Jersey with my mother's older sister, Aunt Marion, her husband, Uncle Bob, and their children, Christine, Claudia, and Robert. Even though he came home on Sundays, I missed him.

My mother decided to allow me to spend a couple of weeks in New Jersey for a visit. They lived up on Mooney Mountain in Randolph. Uncle Bob picked me up from my father's store and drove me the 15 miles or so to their town. At the bottom of the mountain we had to take the narrow, winding, tree-lined road to get to their house at the top. The excitement of Uncle Bob's casual swaying to and fro of the Pinto's steering wheel up the mountain was the beginning of the adventure.

Soon after arriving, I knew that the place where I'd been living up to now was not where I belonged. Up on Mooney Mountain, my Aunt Marion was always singing, whatever song was in her heart at the moment. Many a morning was spent by me in adoration as my Uncle Bob tinkered in the driveway with the old VW he was restoring for my cousin to eventually drive. He loved Johnny Cash and would be singing along in his low timbre while Claudia and I dutifully handed him the tools he requested, one after the other. He called Claudia "Sam"— "Hey, Sam, would you go inside and ask Mom for a drink?" Then as she went scampering through the garage to the kitchen, he would call out, "Thanks, and don't forget ice!" I wanted to be Sam. My cousin Claudia, a.k.a. Sam, was four years older than I.

In the afternoons, after lunch out on the redwood picnic table in the yard—no fuss, no muss—Uncle Bob would say, "Who wants to go water skiing?" And just like that, no planning, no preparation other than putting on a bathing suit, we piled in the car, making the wild roller coaster descent down the mountain to Lake Hopatcong.

One, two, three—the boat was put in the water and off we went. All of my cousins were great water skiers. They could slalom ski, turn, and do all sorts of tricks. I thought about my family. We had a boat as well. We were not allowed out of the cabin in Long Island Sound unless we were trolling the canal, so we spent most of the time swatting biting green flies while we tried to have fun singing rounds of "You're a Grand Old Flag" or "Yankee Doodle"—interrupted by my mother screaming, "Bruuuce, slowww dowwn!" Life preservers were required at all times, adding a thick blanket to the sweltering heat of the cabin.

I was awakened from my musing when Uncle Bob slowed the boat down, turned to me and said, "OK, kiddo, now it's your turn."

Huh? I thought, already afraid.

On went the ski belt. Sensing my apprehension, my uncle said, "Just jump over the side. Sam will show you how to do it." Into the cool, fresh lake I tumbled, tasting for the first time the lake water that tastes like nothing else.

Over and over for the next few hours, I would try to get up and stay up, then fall, drinking in gulps of that lake. Finally, when I realized that Uncle Bob wasn't in any rush, he had all day, I was able to stay up and really ski. Later, exhausted but equally triumphant, when I climbed back in the boat, Uncle Bob said, "There you go." Then, he revved the motor and turned toward home. He smiled the whole way back.

After that, when my father joined us for dinners during rest of the week, and though I knew I loved Dad, I still wanted to be Sam. Dad was not my hero anymore. I loved him and I felt protective or sorry for him because of "her." When someone egged our house on Long Island that fall, it was like someone had egged Dad. I was very confused.

Perhaps it was natural, then, for me to start acting out in eighth grade at Weldon E. Howitt Jr. High. Following many trips to the principal, I was just sent to detention after holding a "protest" in the stairwell over Mrs. Duncan's latest unfair decree in Spanish class. My mother wasn't called, so I told her I was doing an afterschool sport.

During detention, right after attendance was taken, I climbed out the window of the first-floor classroom and fell into the bushes, cutting the back of my leg and bleeding through my stockings. I left to go hang out with the other "no gooders" until my mother pulled up to school to pick me up. The last day of school I bought two "uppers" that turned out to be Tic Tacs.

After school was out that summer of 1971, our family moved to a rented home in Florham Park, New Jersey, about 15 miles from Aunt Marion and Uncle Bob—worlds away. All of us except Dad, who was already living there, piled into the 1968 green Impala convertible shortly after the moving truck left our house in Long Island with all of our belongings. Mom put the top down and told us to buckle up. It seemed like the beginning of an adventure pulling out of the driveway, but then I noticed Mom was crying. Driving with the top down across the Throgs Neck Bridge and then the George Washington Bridge to New Jersey made me feel small, though I was excited about starting high school and a new life. Being allowed to sit in the front seat, I looked over to Mom with her kerchief and sunglasses on. She was very quiet, lost in her own thoughts, I guessed. But then I noticed her intermittently blowing her red nose. *We're all tired*, I thought, and then my excitement waned.

CHAPTER 4

SEPARATION

1971–1981

Within a day of arriving at our new home I met Nancy, who lived catty-corner to our house through our adjoining backyards. Nancy was tall and had the long, straight hair then in fashion. In that pre-mousse era, my curly-frizzy hair simply couldn't compete with just Dippity-Do. Nancy also had long skinny legs, her own bedroom filled with the girly white furniture, and parents who were nice. She didn't have to ask permission for every breath. She also didn't have a chores list that took hours out of every day. She was free to be 14 and, as far as I could see, was probably free just to be.

Shortly after meeting Nancy, I stepped on a bee, which stung the bottom of my foot while I was walking barefoot on her front lawn. I hit the ground, rolling back and forth holding my foot, screaming in pain. Nancy laughed so hard that she joined me on the ground, rolling on the lawn as well. We became fast friends, spending what time I was allowed going to the town pool, hanging out at her house, or sneaking down to the creek, where we soon became addicted to Tareyton cigarettes as we shared the secrets of our souls and then laughed ourselves to tears.

When high school started we would talk on the telephone every day. She always asked the same question, "What should I wear tomorrow?" This was followed by my daily inquiry, "Do I look fatter?" We had pretend boyfriends, George and Harry, until shortly into the school year when I got a real boyfriend, a trumpet player from the marching band named Glen. After football games I learned to French kiss adeptly, though at first I just slobbered all over his face—not that he was much better. Just like band, it was all about practice.

I thought the Hanover Park Hornets' Gun Squad was cooler than being in the band, and you could wear a dress uniform instead of the high suspender pants. So, without my mother's knowing, I started to practice the drills in front of Nancy's house using her sister's wooden rifle. One afternoon though—*whomp!*—the gun hit my octagonal wire-rimmed glasses, popped the lens out, and cut a gash in my eyebrow that bled down my face. Nancy ran to get my mother, who eventually came around the corner hell bent to fury. She dragged me by the ear to the doctor for a butterfly bandage (in lieu of stitches), followed up with the requisite grounding and being held hostage for a weekend of verbal thrashing and chores.

"Why do you want to be on the gun squad and not play the piccolo in the marching band?" What I wanted or thought didn't matter. By then all questions were rhetorical except for "Where were you?" while she pointed a finger in my face.

Throughout the winter I complained of a sore throat. When I was finally taken to the doctor I had a severe case of mononucleosis and an enlarged spleen. The doctor said I was not to go to school for two months, and arrangements were made to send all my schoolwork home. I wasn't allowed to do any physical activities; we were told that my spleen could rupture. According to my mother, however, "He didn't say you couldn't do your chores."

Soon after my delayed diagnosis, my boyfriend Glen wound up in the hospital with the other half of the "kissing disease." I was forbidden to see him, and that was the end of him and me.

Nancy hung in through my times with a Tom, Chad, a real George, and Bradley, who spanned the next year and a half. She had a few boyfriends as well—one gave her a hickey in the center of her forehead. When my mother saw Nancy and asked her what happened, she didn't answer. Later my mother snickered, "You kids think I was born yesterday." As I rolled my eyes, she went on, saying that Nancy was bad news and I was forbidden to see her anymore. I didn't listen.

In between boyfriend dramas, Nancy and I practiced line dancing. We howled the songs of Carole King's *Tapestry* album, songs of Jethro Tull, Elton John, or Carly Simon's *Anticipation* album as we walked to the creek to smoke or to the Jack in the Box in town after school, where I forced her to try a burger with cheese. Sometimes at my urging we stomped on several to-go ketchup packets I had previously thrown on the floor. It was just like bloody firecrackers. Nancy was the "good girl"—the one without the rules. I was the troublemaker, breaking all my mother's rules and then some.

Beginning in the fall of my sophomore year I learned to sew. I started by making hot pants, then vests, dresses, and eventually whole outfits, using my babysitting money to buy the patterns and fabric. I also began to excel in school. At the end of a quarter I would share my excitement with my mother, proudly showing mostly As, but of course she would focus on the one B I got in physics. Most of the time, though, thankfully, Mom was out, working at Dad's store all day.

One day after the mono and the ho-hum report card reaction, I drank a ten-ounce glass of mixed rum and whiskey. Not yet a drinker, I vomited all over the turquoise-blue nylon pile carpeting in my parents' room. Alane found me there, passed out in a puddle of puke. She helped me clean it all up, being very motherly. We finished up just as Mom pulled into the driveway. I didn't know whether she suspected anything, nor did I care.

Every Saturday I would dress up and then would have to wait for Dad to drive to open the store—and it wasn't even my store. There I worked as a salesgirl and ran the cash register for $1.65 an hour. At lunch, Dad would give me money to go across the street to the Hickory Tree deli and buy sandwiches. Once I caught someone stealing a record album, hiding it under his coat, stealing from Dad. When I said, "Hey, what are you doing?" he dropped the loot and ran out.

By then, though, I wasn't an angel either. Before this, one Saturday night Nancy and I were nabbed by store security for shoplifting in the Two Guys department store while my parents were in the store shopping. After a verbal lashing, including threats of having my parents paged and being turned over to the police and charged with a crime—and the resulting explosion of tears and pleading—we were let go. After being on both sides of the crime, I vowed to myself, no more shoplifting.

In early March of 1973, our family finally moved to our newly built home in New Vernon, part of Harding Township. Nancy and I were tearful about the move but vowed to stay best friends. Dad's business was doing all right, he said, but on Saturdays I noticed the traffic into the store had started dwindling. The receipt of my little pay envelope became erratic. I didn't think about it too much, since I was absorbed in adjusting to a new school in the middle of the tenth grade.

The first time I noticed Dave was on the abbreviated school bus, the short one, I took to Morristown High School. Harding Township didn't have a high school, so I had to be bused to Morristown. After about a week of riding the bus I noticed the mirror above the bus driver Mabel's head, which she used to monitor the activities of the rowdy horde of pimply teenagers on the way to and from school. I could see this guy with long, straight, thick brown hair staring at me in the mirror while chatting with Mabel like they knew each other. Who, I wondered, was this guy sitting behind the driver, leaning over the round silver bar, practically hanging off of her—the woman I thought looked like a *witch*. I immediately looked away, but occasionally my eyes drifted back, only to see the same eyes staring at me. This guy was creepy; in my head I called him *Witch Boy*.

I had already set my sights on Cuffy Coutts, the cute blond guy that played the trumpet in the band. (I was still just a piccolo player.) It was just a matter of time before he would ask me out, since we had spent the whole bus ride home sitting together in our Morristown Colonial uniforms after marching in the St. Patrick's Day parade in New York City. We talked and laughed. He touched my arm. He asked for my phone number.

At school the next week, while thinking about Cuffy, I noticed "Witch Boy" casually leaning on the wall next to my locker between classes. Thank God, he didn't say anything. The next day I was excited because Cuffy and I had band class together. Then I noticed Witch Boy waiting for me outside the band room. *This is crazy*, I thought, *does he know my whole schedule?* Meanwhile, Cuffy never called.

It eventually registered that the guy who seemed to be the son of a witch was at least six feet tall. His long, thick hair parted down the middle. He had turquoise-blue eyes with long eyelashes. He had a cleft in his chin and big arm muscles, and he wore biker boots. Still, he was definitely not my type. It was easy to dismiss him without even one word spoken to each other.

After Cuffy failed to call, my sights were set on some football player in my English class.

As the school year drew to a close, Witch Boy was still staring and following me around like a puppy. One day he smiled, and I smiled back. He moved closer. He talked! I laughed and laughed and laughed. He was so funny. Some little comment like "So" could cause a burp of mysterious chuckles in me for the rest of the day. Jokes turned into little paper notes—scribbles of "Hi" with a doodle or whatever.

It turned out his name was Dave and the bus-driving witch was his aunt. On the last day of school, Mabel announced that the Barkmann Bus Company was offering its annual trip down to Seaside Heights on the Jersey shore in a few days. I didn't really think about it, but someone else did, figuring it was now or never, time to make the move. Dave asked me if I wanted to go. I told him I had to think about it and would let him know. I had to ask my parents.

They said OK, so on June 23, 1973, I was wooed into a first kiss on the boardwalk. We played the machines in the penny arcade, games of chance, did the cliché photo booth shots, went on the scary rides, and kissed well and often.

Dave and I started dating. Living out in the middle of nowhere, that summer I read *Gone with the Wind*. Scarlett became my role model for her strength and perseverance. I saw how she used her feminine ways to her advantage and how she was different from her mother, who was different from my mother. I definitely preferred Rhett over Ashley. Dave was more like Rhett.

Dave loved to work on cars and had a motorcycle and a snowmobile. He fished and hunted deer and pheasant. He had many friends. He had everything my mother hated, and I loved him for it. For some reason my troublemaking stopped.

Deer hunting season was during the first week of December our first year together. At the end of the week, after the hunting was over, Dave picked me up at home. We drove to his parents' house, a converted barn which was part of the salary his father received as the grounds manager for a wealthy family's estate. Their home seemed comfortable enough, though you had to open the sliding barn door to enter. Inside, I met Dave's uncles, all unshaven with cigarettes hanging out of their mouths. After they said hello, they continued recounting their hunting stories and guffawing about the success of this season's deer haul. Everyone was happy.

The men then left to butcher the deer meat, coming back with roasts, legs, and other cuts, some with hair, some sprinkled with shot. Dave's mother led the wives in wrapping the meat and marking up the packages, which were then put in boxes for each family to take home. The women talked and I sat and embroidered between meat boxes while hearing booms of laughter rising through the floorboards from the basement. After the butchering was done, there were toasts and shots of the hard stuff. They were all manly men, rugged.

After drinking a beer from a bottle and taking a bath, as there was no shower, Dave took me home in the light blue metallic 1963 Nova SS with "three on the tree" that he had just finished restoring. Along the way, we parked on the side of the road and steamed up the windows, necking. I decided then I was falling in love.

One weekend during my senior year, Mom was sitting in her usual post in the kitchen when I arrived home from a Friday night date. As I climbed the two sets of stairs in our split level, Mom spit out venomously, "Get in here!" She was sitting at the table in her black negligee with a carafe of wine and an empty glass, her face all red and splotched from picking the hairs out of her face. As I approached, she snarled, "Sit down," and smacked the table while flipping her solitaire cards. Then she looked up at me and started going off about Dave and how I was getting too serious with him. Receiving no response, she stood up and pointed that finger at my face and snarled, "I didn't move here for my daughters to marry the help of the millionaires." She abruptly stated, "You are nothing but a tramp *and* a slut."

I stood up to leave. She erupted, "I didn't say you could get up." I got up and left anyway. As I made my way down the hall she screamed, "You're grounded." *Yeah, right,* I thought.

I didn't know at the time that Dad was losing his business and our family was in financial trouble. On my Saturdays at the store, I had seen that customers would come in and pick my father's brain about the audio equipment he sold, but they wouldn't buy. Apparently they'd go to a warehouse store like Crazy Eddie's down on Route 22 and buy their equipment for less.

Dad was heartbroken.

"We would be rich if you didn't throw our inheritance away on that damn store!" my mother would constantly remind him.

When I shared this turn of events with Dave on the phone, he went to my father's store the next day and bought an eight-track player and speakers for his car.

Shortly after the "slut incident," Mom went back to work as a secretary at a chemical company down the road. I got a job after school at a puzzle factory as a clerk typist in the business office five days a week, and was soon told I had to pay my mother board.

College was never discussed until the day my mother shoved in my face a tear-off application to William Paterson College, a state college located in Wayne, while I was sitting in the kitchen under the large portable hair dryer with my big smooth-out rollers. I looked at the application for this school that I had never heard of and noticed that the deadline had passed more than a month before. Earlier in high school, I had taken a career-interest personality test and it showed that my top two careers were either a fighter pilot in the Air Force or something to do with home economics. I'd given some thought to becoming a nurse in a branch of the service, and traveling, but then there was Dave.

I opted to apply to County College of Morris (CCM), the local community college, and was accepted into the nursing program. I could get an associate's degree and become a licensed registered nurse in two years, after passing the state boards.

Soon after starting college, I got a big abscess in the crack of my backside. I shared this with Mom, who told me I should wait until it exploded before going to the doctor. She explained that Dad had a pilonidal cyst early in their marriage and this was what I had, in her opinion. A few weeks went by. I had to take a bed pillow with me everywhere just to sit half-assed. Finally, belatedly remembering that I was now 18 and unable to bear the pain one more second, I made a doctor's appointment.

The evening of the appointment, I announced that I would be taking the car. Mom asked me where I was going.

"To the doctor," I said, grabbing the keys, going out to the driveway, and starting the car. As I was pulling out of the driveway, Mom ran out of the house and threw herself on the hood of the car.

"You're not going anywhere without me!"

Just to piss her off, I lit a cigarette as soon as she got into the car. Even though she'd never seen me smoke before, somehow she knew now better than to mess with me. Reaching around while backing out of the driveway, I told her, "Keep your mouth shut!" As I shifted the car from reverse to drive to go up the hill, the ash fell off the cigarette that was clenched between my teeth and burned a hole in my white pantyhose. I was still in my nursing school uniform.

The doctor said I had a perirectal abscess and had to take care of it immediately. The next day I was admitted to the hospital for emergency surgery, involving an incision and drainage of the abscess, which was about the size of a banana. My white blood cell count was so high I was in the hospital for a week on antibiotics.

Dave visited every day, sitting at my bedside with his blue puppy dog eyes. He brought flowers, teddy bears, candy, and a different card each time he came. I wondered if he was afraid he was going to lose me. Mom said nothing. I expected nothing good from her anyway. I had Dave.

Dave was my best friend, funny and easygoing. He was the knight who rescued me every weekend in his shiny muscle car. He loved me. The summer before I graduated from nursing school, he proposed, and we made our plans to be married in a year. We smooched like crazy but never went all the way, saving ourselves. I knew God was watching and I didn't want to deal with an accidental pregnancy—and worse than that, Mom.

On the night before our wedding, Dad knocked at my bedroom door. He kissed me goodnight and said "I love you" for the first time. The little girl in me cried all night thinking, *I don't need to get married—Daddy loves me.* The next day Dad walked me down the aisle of the Church of Christ the King in a pure white gown. There I met Dave standing tall in his powder blue tuxedo, so handsome with his dark hair now cut in a sexy style and his incredible blue eyes. So at age 20 we were married. The reception was at a mansion. Nancy, with whom I had remained friends, was a bridesmaid, as were my sisters. I was truly happy. The wedding night was worth waiting for. And after four years of waiting, we could have sex anytime, and it was free, especially free of head garbage.

The next day we left for Cape Cod and Martha's Vineyard in our 1973 Firebird Formula 400. When we weren't coupling, seeing the sights, or listening to the nonstop radio and television reporting on the death of "the King"—Elvis—I was battling a raging urinary tract infection, the notorious "bride's cystitis." It involved spending excessive amounts of time in the bathroom and trying to get an antibiotic prescription from another state over the telephone.

We rented from Dave's parents an old farmhouse, in Harding Township, that had been in his family since the 1800s, and furnished it from top to bottom like a doll house. I started working as a registered nurse. I started as a general medical/surgical nurse but soon progressed to neonatal intensive care, the newborn nursery, and postpartum. I really enjoyed the challenge of being a nurse, the problem solving, prioritizing, constant learning, and connecting with my patients. But my favorite part of the experience was being part of the patient care team and the camaraderie of that.

Dave was a professional landscaper, welder, and heavy machinery operator. Our life was simple, very provincial. For me contentment came from cooking, doing laundry, the silkiness of my legs after shaving them, tending the vegetable garden, sewing, doing crafts, Wilton cake decorating for every occasion, going for walks or bike rides. After work, Dave was on call as a volunteer fireman in our little unincorporated village. For him, there was also hunting season—shotgun, doe season and bow season, fishing season, motorcycles, snowmobiles, trucks, reloading shotgun shells, painting cars. Typically, on Friday nights we went out for pizza or McDonald's, picking up this or that at Bradlees or the mall after driving to the bank to deposit our paychecks using the pneumatic tube at the drive-up window. Saturday, I wrote checks to pay our bills. We had no credit cards.

In the late summer of 1980, after three years of marriage, we went to have a Sunday barbeque at my parents' house. Dad and Mom were having their usual pre-dinner cocktails out on the second-floor back deck off the kitchen. Dad fired up the barbeque, and as we were waiting for the grill to heat up I announced, "We are going to have a baby!"

Mom choked on her cocktail. After catching her breath she shrieked, "I'm too young to be a grandmother! You have ruined your life—it will never be the same!"

Dave and I held hands, taking turns staring off into the yard while I tried to bite back the tears that brimmed if our eyes met. Dad waited until Mom went inside, congratulated Dave, shook his hand, and gave both of us a big hug.

When we told Dave's mother the following week, she shrieked too, but with delight. She giggled with excitement for the rest of the day. After dinner she brought out bags of baby afghan patterns and set out wool to begin crocheting the first baby blanket. Dave's father gently whacked Dave on the back saying, "Way to go, Buck!"

Kimberly was born after the New Year. Dave and I were a little overwhelmed but still in baby heaven. One afternoon, after finally getting her down for a nap in the port-a-crib we kept in the living room, I got cozy on the sofa with relief. I was just starting to fall asleep after being up all night when my mother abruptly flew through the back door, having left work at lunch for a visit without calling to let me know.

Startled, I said that I just got Kim to sleep.

"I didn't come here to watch her sleep."

She picked her up, and immediately Kimberly started fussing. I'd been having difficulty breast feeding, but I tried to feed her. My mother, watching me struggle, said, "Nursing is barbaric. Why don't you just feed her the bottle? After all it worked fine for me."

I gave up breast feeding a couple of days later.

After taking off a year when Kim was born, I went back to work part time while taking a couple of classes at the state university to earn credits toward my bachelor of science in nursing, the BSN. My mother-in-law was very happy to watch Kim for the times I was away. We had it all, love, a beautiful daughter, enough creature comforts, friends, a simple but fulfilling life for a young married couple.

CHAPTER 5

BLACKOUT

1983—1984

I t was Saturday, a sunny but not overly warm day for the later part of August, and my biweekly cleaning and laundry day. I was still glowing with the tan I'd developed on our weeklong vacation on Long Beach Island at the Jersey shore a couple of weeks before. Dave and I had just celebrated our sixth wedding anniversary. It was a good time and I was very content.

After breakfast, Dave had gone out to work on some of his side jobs of mowing lawns and doing gardening for his own clients. Since Kim had been born, he kept busy working to earn extra money as the sole provider for the family. He wasn't exactly happy that I was going to start a new full-time job in a few days, working the evening shift in Labor and Delivery at Morristown Memorial, but he knew this was my dream position and supported my decision to return to work.

He came home for lunch smelling musky and sweaty, but he was animated and got right down on the floor to begin playing with Kim, now 2½. I made our lunches, bologna and cheese with mayo on white bread, served with potato chips and a pickle. The laughter and playing ended when I called out, "Lunch is ready!"

While we were eating, and in between entertaining Kim, we talked about how excited we were that we were going on a rare date that night. His mother was going to babysit Kim. We were going to see the new movie *Mr. Mom* with Michael Keaton. Then the harvest gold wall telephone rang.

"Hi, Dad! Yep, he's here, just a second." I handed the phone to Dave. In a few minutes he was off the phone.

"I'm going to meet the old man after lunch. Ned needs some help with some tree or something." Ned was a realtor that Dave did some work for on the side.

"OK, be careful," I said.

He brushed me with a kiss and off he went.

After lunch I put Kim down for her nap, hung the laundry out on the line that ran from the porch to the horse barn, put another load in the washer, and turned on the stereo. Dancing to Kajagoogoo, the Police, and Dexys Midnight Runners, I vacuumed the downstairs in my cut-off jean shorts, a pastel-striped terry shirt, and flip-flops. When I began to feel hot, I blew away the strands of curly hair that hung and stuck to my face, shut off the vacuum, and walked to the mirror to reclip my hair back. Noticing the beads of sweat on my face, I removed my glasses and wiped my face with my shirt. I headed back to work, but the vacuum abruptly shut off, the music stopped, and in a moment I realized all the power was off. There wasn't a cloud in the sky and no chance of a thunderstorm, so I thought a power failure was odd.

I sat down in the kitchen, phoned up my mom, and while half listening to her going on and on about something, drinking a coke, and smoking a cigarette, I flipped through the newspaper. Skimming down the local activities and clubs page in the paper, I noticed "W.O.W." the young widows and widowers club. *Wow, how sad,* I thought to myself, *a club for people who've lost their husbands or wives.* In another few minutes, the power came back on, so I hung up and went back to vacuuming.

Still cleaning, I heard someone come in the back door. Expecting to see Dave, I saw Bill, my brother-in-law, instead. The look on his face was very determined.

"There's been an accident," he said.

I was speechless.

He continued, "The ambulance is taking Dave to the hospital right now. I need you to come with me."

"Is he OK? What happened? OK. Kim's napping, I'll get her."

"No, leave her. Karen is on her way over to watch her."

"Oh my God," I said.

That was the first of a million times I cried out to God that day.

On the way to the hospital, I asked Bill all manner of questions to try to get an idea of what happened. He didn't really know much. He knew that Dave hit a power line with the chain saw and was alive when the ambulance took him away. *Oh my God,* I thought. I started crying. *Please, God let him be OK. Please ... God.*

We arrived at the emergency room entrance. I looked like such a slob, no make-up, hair a mess, crappy clothes. Who cared, I was so worried. I just wanted to see Dave. The emergency room personnel escorted me to a "family room." They told me the doctors were with Dave and would come by as soon as they could tell me anything. My body starting shaking so violently, I could barely walk. They had me sit down on the sofa.

It was then that I noticed Dave's mother, his father's boss, and my mother were there. What were they doing there? How did they get there? My father-in-law's *boss* was there. *Why,* I wondered. My mother-in-law was moaning. *None of this looked good.* My mother tried to put her hand on my leg, but I swept it away. *Please, God, let him be OK.* A thousand people could have been in the room, it didn't matter. I was getting my first taste of true horror in that family room that day. I was so cold, so worried. My lips and front teeth were numb.

It seemed like hours went by. I couldn't stop quaking. Finally, two doctors walked in. Addressing my mother-in-law, one of them said, "We're sorry, your son didn't make it. We tried everything, but he didn't make it."

The cleaver came down and the world became black. The only way I knew I was still alive was the heaving sobs that came from the depths of my being, making my throat sore, gobs of snot running down my nose. An outpouring of support was circling my bereft mother-in-law, who'd just learned that she had lost her second son. My mother was there telling me, "It's OK. It's going to be OK." I recoiled at her attempts at giving any comfort.

I asked and they let me into the ER treatment room to see him, my love, my sweetheart. He was lying on a stretcher covered in those green-colored scrub drapes. He had a tube hanging out of his mouth. His head was turned to one side. His eyes were closed but had the look of pain around them. I didn't uncover him but instead threw myself over his body. It didn't move. He wasn't exactly warm. He didn't breathe. He didn't tell me it was going to be OK. Then I was escorted out. I may as well have been dead, too.

Eventually someone brought me home with a bag of his clothes. I don't remember seeing or hearing anything about Dave's father other than I knew he was with him when it happened. Time slowed to a crawl. I knew time had passed when I needed a new box of tissues. I was there but not there. People were coming in and out of my house speaking in hushed tones. Kim was talking to me. People were taking Kim away. People were touching me. Food began appearing. People were eating. I could hear my breathing.

Someone put me to bed that night. I fell asleep curled up with Dave's musky, dirty work clothes, my heart hollowed out like an avocado. The next morning I woke up—it wasn't a nightmare. Hell was here, on earth.

Death is so disorienting, just like the act of a cruel magician, and this time the joke is on you. There were arrangements to be made. Kim wandering and wondering where was her daddy? My crying never ceased, to the point where fissures like paper cuts, appeared next to my eyes and around my nose. Horror was the reality of every second. A fifty-pill prescription for Valium showed up.

"Take a pill," someone said.

A few hours later, someone else said, "Take a pill."

Calls were made, and somehow the day of the funeral arrived. With my box of tissues, wearing black polyester, I was held up through a service at the United Methodist Church, where Father Charles, the priest who had married us just six years before was commenting about some tapestry we weave. Everyone filed out to follow the hearse containing my husband in a top-of-the-line walnut box. It was followed by the New Vernon, Green Village, and Chatham Township fire departments and numerous police cars. It was a parade, a spectacle that went on and on, all the way to Somerset Hills Cemetery in Basking Ridge.

He was only 26, not famous for anything. He didn't work at a big company. He loved me. He loved Kim. But, oh, I learned then, was he loved! He was the good guy, the guy that would give you the shirt off his back, stop to help someone with a flat tire. So many friends, some I knew, many I didn't. And how was that? I'd been with him since we were 16. Who were all these people? Back at *our* house someone fashioned some sort of banquet potluck of deli meat, some bowls of mayonnaise-y salads. Kids were running all around the yard. Dave's German shorthair pointer, Rocky, was barking from all the fuss, as if asking the same question as me. *Where is Dave?*

People say stupid things. They don't mean to.

"I'm so sorry for your loss." I thought, *What does that mean?*

"So, what are you going to do now?" I thought, *Kill myself.*

"Let me know if you need help with anything." *Can you bring Dave back?*

"He was such a great guy." *I was lucky to have him, and now he's dead and I have no one.*

"He's in a better place." *And where exactly is that, in a box at Somerset Hills? That's his dead body, stupid. Where is my Dave?*

"God must have really wanted him," someone else said. I thought, *You are absurd. Just go away—leave me alone.*

My maternal grandmother, Frances, had become a widow six months earlier when my 86-year-old grandfather died of a heart attack after sixty-plus years of marriage. She came over to me, fresh with tears, put her arm around me, and pulled me close.

"Well, honey," she said. "This should be the worst thing that should ever happen to you."

She paused. "You're young, and you'll marry again."

Finally adding, "I'm old, my life is over."

At 26, I didn't know any other widows. Although I remembered Scarlett O'Hara, my heroine from *Gone with the Wind*, who upon being newly widowed said, "My life is over. Nothing will ever happen to me anymore." Grandma, age 82, was now my widow pal.

Six months later, Grandma died, on Valentine's Day, from aggressive ovarian cancer. Then it was just me and Scarlett.

In the weeks that followed the funeral, I was able to patch together the events that led to Dave's death. Dave and his father's friend Ned, a realtor from a family of realtors, some of whom were our close neighbors in our small town, had phoned Dave saying that his client was supposed to close escrow on a house. There was a fallen tree and some limbs encroaching across the long driveway approach to the house, which was just down the street. The soon-to-be new owners wouldn't close on the house until this matter was resolved.

Dave had left a message for his dad, who'd called back during lunch. They met at the property and, after assessing the situation, determined that the cable in the midst of these branches was too low and unshielded to be the main power line and therefore must be some sort of guide wire or possibly the ground. Dave's father thought that they shouldn't be messing around with this and that Ned should call the power company. Still, Dave somehow wound up on the ladder. The chainsaw jammed in a limb and when he wrenched it out, it hit the wire. There was a popping sound and black smoke rose from the line. Dave turned, his face covered with black soot, and said "Oh, shit!" He started coming down. After about three or four rungs, he started to get wobbly and jumped to the ground, landing on his feet. Then he collapsed. His eyes were closed, his head moving from side to side. According to Jersey Central Power he was electrocuted with between 7,200 and 12,000 volts of electricity.

Electricity traveled from the road transformer through that power line to several homes. When the chainsaw nicked the wire, the electricity traveled from the line to the chainsaw, through Dave, and down the ladder to the ground. This is what caused the transformer to blow. While this was going on, all I knew was that the power failed on a sunny day when I was vacuuming.

I learned from the police report later that Dave had agreed to take $100 for the job.

Apparently Bill, my brother-in-law, was also there that day. It was he who called for the ambulance while my father-in-law gave his son CPR waiting for the ambulance to arrive. After attempts at rescue were made at the scene, Dave was taken to the emergency room, still alive. The doctors attempted to insert a pacemaker. But, though he was strong, a "buck" as his father fondly called him, he died anyway.

It was classified as a violent death, requiring an autopsy, and since he had taken out a term life insurance policy less than two years before, it was investigated as a possible suicide. Neither Ned, the realtor, nor any of his family attended any of the wakes, the funeral, the burial, or even sent a card. My father-in-law took to his bottle with renewed vigor.

The days and weeks went by. The casseroles stopped. The phone calls slowed to a trickle. I ventured out to do errands. When friends at the ShopRite saw me coming toward them down the aisle with my cart, they turned and walked away as fast as they could. That really hurt. I was so young and so alone. I thought of Dave every second. The grief was inescapable. I began to imagine all the ways that I could kill myself just to make it stop.

I wrung my hands thinking, *Why did he have to die? Wasn't I the bad person?* Just the previous spring semester, I'd written a paper in philosophy class on why God didn't exist. Maybe this was the ultimate punishment—living, living without Dave.

During the winter months of 1984 I started dancing to ease the feeling of despair. Every day while Kim was napping I would dance to "Wanna to Be Startin' Somethin'" from Michael Jackson's *Thriller*. Soon I could do Jennifer Beals's "Maniac" dance from the recent movie *Flashdance*. Then I stopped getting my period. I went to the doctor and learned that because I now weighed less than 110 pounds, my periods had stopped. He said I didn't have enough body fat and should dance less. A few months later they returned.

Then, in another attempt to feel better, I decided to try smoking marijuana.

I called my cousin Tim and asked him to come over and bring some pot. He came over with his wife and we sat down in the living room. Kim was already asleep for the night. I hadn't smoked pot before. He brought out the joint and lit it up. I liked the smell and recognized it from rock concerts.

Soon I was laughing, but then something happened. The television was on in the background with some show about firemen fighting an apartment fire, which got my attention. In addition to the apartment fire, there was a loose power line with sparks flying everywhere. Then I faintly remember wondering if I was saying what I was thinking and trying to test my theory by thinking of sex, sex with Dave, how this or that would never happen again. And then I began sobbing uncontrollably. They put me in the shower with my clothes on. My sister Diane was called to spend the night.

At some point, hours or days later, I woke up on the floor of the kitchen with little Kimberly shaking me saying, "Mommy, wake up. Wake up, Mommy." That incident helped me to realize that I had to live, even if I didn't want to. I had to go on for Kim.

At this point, Kim had been told that her dad was in heaven. Kim thought heaven was in the sky, so every time she saw a plane she would ask, "Is that where Daddy is?" Not really knowing where her daddy was, as if anyone did, I called up my friend Beverly, who had lost her dad when she was little, and asked her how she was told. She gave me an idea.

Fortunately, that night the sky was clear. I bundled Kim up and we went outside to look at the stars. Together we found the brightest star in the sky. I pointed to it and made sure that she could see it.

I told her, "That star is where your daddy is."

"Even during the day," I continued, "Daddy's star is still there, but hidden by the daylight. Even then, day or night, Daddy can see you and hear you."

There were no stars in my sky, though. I was still walking around in the dark with the wind knocked out of me. I saw Dave's ghost in every room. Every corner was filled with memories of stripping wallpaper, painting, laughing, crying, making love. In my nights of insomnia, I poured through a chain-reference Bible, looking for clues about what happens to us when we die.

Finally, on a mid-autumn day while hanging out the laundry, after pleading with the God that I didn't necessarily believe in that I needed a sign that my Dave was OK, I looked out to the Great Swamp National Wildlife Refuge across the street from our house, and for the first time in my life saw a double rainbow. I was so excited I grabbed Kim to show her, hysterical that this was the sign, the sign that he was not just OK, he was great. She didn't understand. I called my mother and told her breathlessly about what had just happened. She responded, "Whatever you need to believe." She didn't believe me. Deflated, as I had been so many times by her, I still held some modicum of excitement and a renewed commitment to forge ahead.

My parents kept asking me what I was going to do and why didn't I move back to their house. I began taking stock of my situation. I finally threw out the rancid clothes I'd slept with and the toothbrush I had contemplated for weeks. But the rest? What was I going to do with a brand new 1983 Silverado three-quarter ton truck, a restored 1953 Chevy pickup in candy apple red, and a 1968 Chevy Camaro SS souped up for racing, not to mention two motorcycles and assorted guns and fishing equipment, a log splitter, and a neglected German short-haired pointer? How was I going to care for three acres and pay rent to my dead husband's parents?

Somehow, my father-in-law got wind of the fact that I was considering what to do with his son's stuff, and came to the conclusion that I was preparing to pack up and move on. One Saturday afternoon he stormed into my house without knocking, drunk and raging like a bull.

"My son isn't even cold in the ground," he thundered. "You are not going anywhere, and I'll be damned if you think you are getting rid of any of my son's stuff," he exploded like a rapid-fire cannon. "Over my dead body, goddamn it," he grumbled with the low rumble of a three-pack-a-day smoker.

What seemed to me like an eternity since I last held Dave was only an instant to him. He really scared me. I grabbed Kim and ran upstairs to my room, sitting against the closed door for further protection until I could hear his truck backing out of the driveway, spraying fans of gravel all over the lawn.

My own father suggested that I might want to see a lawyer to determine if I could sue the realtor, the power company, the property owner, the chainsaw manufacturer, and so on.

"After all," he rationalized, "you're a widow with a small child to support."

I think we went to see two lawyers. We learned that the case would be on a contingency basis, where they would take a percentage of any settlement or court award. However, they warned that there was this thing called contributory negligence, where the defendants would try to prove that Dave had some sliding scale of responsibility for his death. They further warned that we would be going after powerful people and companies.

"They'll try to rip your late husband's reputation to shreds." When my in-laws heard of this, they went ballistic.

"You cannot sue the realtor!" screeched my mother-in-law.

"Dad has known Ned his whole life, since grade school in fact, and that is just not the way we do things. You can go anywhere you want, but we still have to live in this town."

Sometime after the holidays, my mother-in-law commented that I was just like my mother, always concerned about money, and that I pushed Dave too hard. If I hadn't pushed him so hard, he wouldn't have taken that job and died.

I was completely crushed. That was it, I realized. I had to get out of there, and get everyone out of my business, and get away from all the pain. Me and Kim, Kim and me—that was all that mattered to me now.

CHAPTER 6

A CAVALIER
1985–1987

My new life began while I was crossing McCormick Road after getting off the campus bus between Brown College and Monroe Hall. Just like Dorothy's landing in Oz, in one instant the world became living color again.

It was spring of 1985—a non-particular day, late in the morning, more than a year and half after Dave had died.

Looking around I noticed the light that sparkled through the canopy of old-growth trees. Everything was illuminated. While shielding my eyes, I could hear the birds singing and the wind rustling the new leaves in the trees. There were beautiful flowering trees all around me—dogwoods, pears, cherries, and magnolias. I hadn't realized that I'd lost the brilliance of my senses for so long, but I was happy for their return.

I continued walking toward the central grounds at the University of Virginia. The distinctive sharp green smell of the boxwoods permeated the air. I inhaled deeply. Having a bit of time before class, I sat down on a bench on the lawn. I looked left up the lawn toward the far end where the Rotunda stood, panning right were five of the pavilions and the many lawn rooms cascading down each side of the great expanse of grass. I had read that the Rotunda, designed by UVA's founder, Thomas Jefferson, was the cranium, the brain. Back in the early days of the college it housed the library—the repository of accumulated knowledge. As in the beginning, the upper floors of the pavilions were living quarters for some of the professors. The lower floors were originally the classrooms. The lawn rooms in between the architecturally distinct pavilions were for fourth-year students who had applied and were deemed worthy by

49

nature of their leadership skills and contributions to the school. Living on the lawn was considered an honor—even though it meant doing without heat or running water. The University of Virginia was all about tradition and honor.

Behind the five pavilions on each side of the lawn there were the gardens, each unique, flanked by high serpentine brick walls, which were tended by garden societies and clubs. Beyond the gardens were the range rooms for more students, one of which had hosted Edgar Allan Poe as its resident.

This was Jefferson's academical village. And as of that moment, I was *really* there.

I saw a young lady in a white bathrobe carrying a towel and a small basket emerging from one of the lawn room doors, which was cluttered with notices. She scurried off around the corner to what I could only assume was a shower.

I couldn't imagine life in that little lawn room. I lived off campus in a rented three-bedroom townhouse in North Charlottesville with my daughter. Kim attended the Montessori School in town during the day while I took my classes. After class I took the campus bus to the commuter parking lot at Scott Stadium, drove to Kim's school, volunteered for a few hours to reduce the cost of her tuition, did errands, went home, cooked dinner, did laundry, got her bath ready, read her a story, and then began my homework. I learned to like instant coffee—Taster's Choice or Folgers in a microwaved cup of hot water. Caffeine was my drug to get through the day, and a half bottle of French cabernet helped me get through the night.

I was excited by the return of my senses, but I was also very tired both physically and mentally. If I'd had someone to catch me, I would have just collapsed. Before the first anniversary of Dave's death I had decided to get out of Dodge and start over, where no one knew me. I applied to two colleges, and by the anniversary date we had moved and were living in Charlottesville. There was no time to think about the past.

I had originally been admitted to the School of Nursing at the university as an RN BSN candidate. I had accomplished the requirement of 1½ years of their nursing classes by taking the final exam for each class during the summer after we arrived in Charlottesville. I had gotten the payout from Dave's life insurance policy, but I wanted to maintain the nut of the principal for the future. So I looked into getting a part-time job as a nurse at the hospital to supplement the survivor's benefit Kim and I got from Social Security. But I calculated that, after paying for a babysitter, my take-home pay would have been about two dollars an hour. So nursing wasn't going to cut it. I was going to have to figure out a different career, one that let me support my daughter. I researched pre-med programs and medical school and concluded that I wouldn't be finished until my early forties. I'd also be carrying a lot of debt, and not around enough in the meantime to be my idea of a good single mother.

I dropped my Teaching in Nursing Practice course and switched to the Personal Investing at McIntire, the undergraduate business school at the university. When I first walked into the small, vintage amphitheater for the investing class, it was already in session. The teacher was dressed in khaki trousers, a blue button-down shirt with a diagonally striped tie, and a blazer with brass buttons. He had such a southern accent that at times it was hard to understand him. But he had such an air of old world charm, the appearance of an old southern gentleman, truly a Virginia Cavalier in his modern-day uniform. He reminded me of a smaller version of Colonel Sanders of Kentucky Fried Chicken fame, with his impeccably groomed snow-white hair and beard.

Over the semester I learned he was still working at an old southern institution, the brokerage firm of Scott and Stringfellow. From him, we learned about the stock market, the bond market, put and call options, how to read the stock section of the paper, the role of the specialist, the market maker, the risk arbitrage play, investing in commodities, and everything you could want to know about forward contracts. Our semester assignment was to get and read *Barron's* and *The Wall Street Journal* and to create a mock portfolio of investments using $2,000 in Monopoly money. I was up to close to $20,000 by the end of the semester and kicking myself for not being willing to risk real money.

The investment class was such a gas that I began taking classes that were prerequisites for the business school—Economics with the legendary Mr. Elzinger, Calculus, Accounting 101 and 102, and Rhetoric.

The day I got my senses back, sitting on that bench, I suddenly realized I would have to rush to Rhetoric—and I was speaking. I ran, seeing all the colors in a blur through teary eyes as I made my way to class.

My persuasive speech that day was on "The Necessity of Seatbelts on School Buses." This topic was important to me—given that I had miraculously not died after flying out of a moving school bus window at the age of seven. But as I stuttered and *umm*-ed my way through the argument and supporting data, I paused and noticed most of the class was asleep anyway. So I relaxed.

Later that same spring I was one of the students accepted into the McIntire School of Commerce, the university's undergraduate business school, from an ocean of applicants. Now I knew I was accepted not because I was already a nurse or a widow. I was actually qualified.

The following fall, moving between classes in the storied old Monroe Hall, I was walking lighter but still felt out of place, being seven or eight years older than the other students. None of them seemed to notice a difference in our ages, although my body language, among other things, indicated I was not dating material.

Over time I became more confident and more assertive, and let my male side run free. In the classroom, the environment fostered competitive teamwork, and I was there to win. The professors welcomed interaction with the students and preferred to be called Mr. or Ms. rather than Professor or Doctor. All classes were geared toward working in groups, giving presentations, and analyzing different business-case scenarios, which seemed impossible at first but then became solvable.

As Kim moved from toddlerhood to preschool she became more and more feminine. She wanted her straight, long hair done up with curls, bows, jeweled barrettes, and ribbons. She insisted on wearing dresses, of which she had quite a supply from Grandma, Dave's mother—the Polly Flinders smocked kind with embroidery, ruffles, and petticoats. Her patent leather Mary Janes completed the look. She twirled around the house pretending to be Angelina Ballerina, holding her sparkle wand, making magic with every step.

On weekends she had her little friends over. With my help they took blankets and made a house within the bunk beds, where they played with My Little Pony or Thumbelina or Rainbow Bright for hours. She was a normal, well-adjusted, beautiful little girl of sugar, spice, and everything nice.

I bought a Sony Betamax shortly after we moved in, and we had movie night as, one by one, the classic children's movies were released on video. Kim started ballet classes, began to read alone with gusto, and created imaginary friends. As time went on, she learned to eat cereal out of the box and watch Saturday morning television while I caught up on some sleep.

When she was old enough, I finally gave in, and we got a kitten—an adorable little black-and-white one that she carried around constantly, swaddled in dish towels when she wasn't trying to feed it with a fake doll bottle. One weekend, while I was washing my bedroom windows on the second floor of the townhouse, I could hear Kim and Rhyannon, her friend who lived next door, burst into uproarious laughter, the kind that makes you laugh even though you don't know what's funny.

I climbed back in the window and walked toward the girls.

"What's so funny?"

I saw Kim throwing her new kitten down the flight of stairs where it smacked into the wall on the bottom landing. This was what the two four-year-olds were laughing about. I sent Rhyannon home after picking up the kitten, which miraculously seemed to be uninjured (though it was soon given away).

I scheduled Kim to see a child psychologist, thinking this was not normal. After the second meeting, he came out to the waiting room with Kim and asked her to play while he spoke with Mommy. He thought her acting-out behavior was her testing whether she had any control over death. He went on to explain that she thought if she could make me mad enough, maybe I would die, and then she would know why her daddy died. On some level, he continued, she thought he died because of something she did. She would have really killed the kitten.

Her daddy's death was still on her mind, but he told me not to make a big deal of it. So I did my best to assure Kim that I wasn't going anywhere and put some pictures of her dad into frames for her room.

Kim didn't ask about Dave anymore after that. I was busy with school, busy being a mom. I was lonely and grieving, but now I was more angry than sad. I did my best to channel this into my studies.

I was in Mr. Pettit's Finance class in January of 1986 when we heard that the Space Shuttle *Challenger* had exploded. Students in the classroom were sobbing, stunned into silence, overcome with the instantaneous horror of loss, whispering how could something like this happen, asking what happens now. I already knew the answer. Fortunately for them, this happened on television, to others. They would grieve until the next headline. Mr. Pettit handed out the next Harvard Business case study for our assignment and started discussing the Pettit Finance Invitational, which would be held at the end of the semester. Then he dismissed the class early.

In a vivid dream one night, Kim and I went back to New Jersey for a visit. My in-laws were living in my old house. I was confused; I thought my sister-in-law was living there. My in-laws were acting very strange, nervous. Their dialogue was a little cryptic, and I sensed something was up. After visiting for a while in the house I told them that I was taking Kim outside to see the horses. My father-in-law became noticeably upset.

My mother-in-law spoke up. "Lin, we didn't want to tell you this, but now we have no choice," she trailed off. "Come with me."

We went outside and around the back of the old horse barn that stood separate from the house at the end of the driveway. She opened up the side door where the horse stalls were. Her demeanor of mystery lent a sense of dread. It was dark inside. There was a door that looked like it led to a small room I had never noticed. She tapped the door with her knuckles. The door opened.

Standing just inside the room was Dave, still alive. I couldn't understand how this could be. He looked the same but acted as if he didn't really recognize me. He looked afraid and looked from me to his mother like she was his mommy. My heart stopped beating. My mother-in-law told me that he really hadn't died, that he was revived but wasn't the same. She continued, somewhat choked up, saying that he had recovered the ability to move his body and was recovering his memories, but it was hard to tell what he knew and what he didn't, since he wasn't able to speak.

I was so confused. I wanted to rush toward him and wrap my arms around him and kiss him all over. I also wanted to smack him, punch him, and beat him to a pulp for all the pain and suffering that I had been through. But I knew doing that would be pointless. How could this be? It didn't make any sense. It had been two and a half years since his death.

I woke up abruptly, completely rattled.

I loved school. I thought the classes gave me a sense of purpose—and I excelled. In Calculus class I made one really good friend from northern Virginia who had transferred to UVA from George Mason. His name was Robert. He was eight years younger than I but wise beyond his years, easy to be with, and a real gentleman. I loved to tease him about his looks. Though he was Virginia born and bred, with his jet-black hair, dark eyes, and dark, olive skin he looked to be from the Middle East. Besides that, his middle name, Tulloss, was hardly southern. What was up with that?

After I met his parents I teased him about being adopted. His mother looked like Aunt Pittypat from *Gone with the Wind* and was an active member of the DAR. His father, a collector of Civil War memorabilia among other things, could easily have been a member of the KKK. We hung out together at school, did homework together, laughed, went to the movies, and brought Kim with us everywhere. He came over for dinner and played games with Kim while I did the dishes.

He was like a brother. Together we went to the home football games of the Virginia Cavaliers singing the "Good Ole Song" arm in arm after every touchdown. He didn't wear the typical Cavalier uniform of khaki pants, an oxford shirt, tie, and blazer. He wore jeans and a T-shirt. His friendship saw me through Kim's chickenpox outbreak during finals and later the infamous Norwalk winter vomiting virus attack, which occurred during a crushing COBOL programming project. The virus saw each of us at the student health center requiring intravenous fluids for severe dehydration.

When the computer center was swamped, he came over and borrowed my Compaq portable computer with the two 5¼-inch floppy drives. I could dial into the school's mainframe telephone number by detaching the phone from the wall and plugging the computer into the jack using a telephone cord and a 300-baud modem. Then each of us slogged through and corrected the "trivial" and "fatal" errors in the semester-long projects for our system programming class. We were usually doubled over laughing—the irony being that the program didn't execute regardless of how "trivial" an error in the program was.

Together as a kind of family, we watched movies on HBO on cable and rocked out to some of the tamer displays on MTV. When I bought my first CD player, Robert said I had to get the disc by the new artist

Whitney Houston, whom he, like all the other guys at school, thought was hot. Unlike me, he could sit and watch cartoons with Kim for hours. He helped me buy and put together Kim's first bicycle, with training wheels, and took her around the block in circles weekend after weekend until she got tired or it got dark.

I didn't really feel like I had much in common with other students besides school, but welcomed groups of them over to my house for group work and fed them home-cooked meals in the dining room. Kim enjoyed all the attention, but I was still lonely, longing for the intimacy of my partner.

I went with Kim to the local church, a southern charismatic Catholic parish. At the time it didn't really register that there could be other options. I knew that I needed to have a spiritual connection to something greater, mystical, more magnificent, more holy, more transcendent, more something beyond the ticking of the clock and the flipping of pages on the calendar. I wanted to understand the church and its sense of history. I wanted to understand how the rituals and traditions came to be and what they meant. I needed to belong to something. I needed community, a community of adults with grownup lives, children, babies, real death.

I met with the pastor of the Incarnation Church and told him about how lost I felt. He asked many questions. He told me I could read about the faith. I told him I didn't have time to read anything else. I asked, wasn't there a program for Catholics that fell off the wagon? He told me that they had a program for people wanting to become Catholics but I was already one. He kept looking at his watch.

He told me, "You know, you are a very angry person. You exude anger."

Rather than storming out of his office citing his poor real-time example of the story of the prodigal son, my reaction to his comments was to set out to prove that I was good—a good sheep ready to join the flock in following the Shepherd up the hill to salvation. I signed up for the program to become an initiate in the Roman Catholic faith for adults. And yes, I was angry. I was angry that my husband died. I was angry that I felt lost and alone. I was trying to feel something else, and the pastor couldn't see that. For that, I was frustrated.

I was assigned a sponsor, a highly educated black woman who was "born again." We met once or twice a week to address my inquiries. We attended church together. She walked by my side with the other initiates, the real initiates, as they were all baptized in the faith (I was already baptized), and we were all welcomed by the church at the Easter Vigil, surrounded by the large congregation and the mystical light of candles, each of us wearing a white robe.

So I became a practicing Catholic, "practicing" for what I didn't know. The Church gave me a sense of home, some continuity with the life I knew before, as a child. But, though the community was there, I still didn't feel like I fit in. I had one foot in the world of being a student, the other in the world of a single mother, still a widow. I never came to feel any closer to Dave through my involvement in the Church, and no one had any answers that resonated with me about *why* we are here. But at least the light of Christ was in my heart—though it was just a tiny, fragile flicker of a candle flame, still a pinprick of light nonetheless.

In the summer of 1986, I woke up one morning drenched in sweat, having spent the last few hours making wild whoop with Dave. Unfortunately, it was another dream—but it felt so real. It spoke to the hunger of a 29-year-old woman with raging hormones, and proved I was still alive even if it was just fantastical. One of my girlfriends had been asking if she could set me up on a date with her brother, an attorney in Washington D.C. I finally said yes. It was my first date since I was a junior in high school. I hated it.

I packed up the car and headed to New Jersey to visit with my girlfriend Nancy. She was Aunt Nancy to Kim, a sympathetic ear for my grief, and a stalwart supporter of my move to Virginia. Everyone else said, "Why do you want to throw away all your nursing experience?" upon hearing that I was switching to major in business. Nancy said, "That's great, a new beginning. You will always have your nursing; it is part of who you are."

She was hosting what she called "Party Aid," an ironic homage to the previous summer's Farm Aid and Live Aid events—a *party* to *aid* in the consumption of large quantities of alcohol. It was there that I met Mark. Mark was charming, a not-so-tall but dark-haired and handsome guy around my age. We drank, laughed, danced, and sang. After the party we got together for dinner before I headed back to Virginia with Kim for her start of kindergarten and my last year of school. We exchanged phone numbers. It was three years after Dave died.

In the late fall, after numerous telephone conversations, Mark flew to Charlottesville for a visit. He was working full time at the corporate headquarters of AT&T. He said he was living at home temporarily. I wasn't looking for the next love of my life and he lived hundreds of miles away, which was perfect. He was easy to be with on a limited basis. He was funny and sang well. We cooked and drank, which then led to sex. The sex was good and I was happy to know that everything still worked. But there were no sparks; my heart was still with Dave.

He visited every couple of months, and in between those visits I went up north and saw him in New Jersey on my trips to see family. I also spent time in New York City for inspiration, job interviews, and firm office visits for positions after graduation. The year went by quickly.

Toward the end of my time at UVA, as I was preparing for finals, studying for the CPA exam, packing up the townhouse, and readying for a move back to New Jersey, I started adding up the things about Mark that didn't add up. Yes, he lived at home with his parents. His job didn't require a college degree. Oh, and why didn't he own a car? My parents met him at Easter and weren't very happy when he announced to all of us that he used to be addicted to cocaine. Then my parents asked me, "Why are you exposing your daughter to someone like this?" How could I say, *Because the sex is very good*?

He attended Robert's and my graduation from the university, displaying overt jealousy of Robert and more possessive pride in me than he should. Later that weekend, after the festivities were over, for some reason I decided to check his coat pocket for something, found his wallet, opened it, looked at his driver's license and saw that the expiration date had been badly forged. I confronted him, only to find out that he lost his driver's license for drunk driving a couple of years before, which indicated to me that he still wasn't driving legally and this was not a first offense. During the past year he had been driving Kim and me around on a suspended license in *my car*. I was furious. What was I thinking? He was very cavalier about the whole thing.

So, a few weeks before moving back to New Jersey, I decided to send him packing. No sex was better than good sex with an addict and a pathological liar. Months later, I learned that he was having other relationships during our long-distance relationship and I added *cheater* to the list.

CHAPTER 7

ON TOP OF THE WORLD AT THE CENTER OF THE UNIVERSE

1987–1992

I squeezed into the PATH train at the Hoboken terminal during the morning rush, which was a Darwinian case of survival of the fittest, the aggressive prelude to a day of work in downtown Manhattan. Some were lucky enough to have seats, the rest hung on to support poles. On view were arms over arms of all ages, grasping, mostly in suits, the occasional sparkle of a cufflink or an initialed cuff popping out. While hanging on for the ride of their lives, most commuters were busy reading origami-like foldings of *The New York Times, The Wall Street Journal, Financial Times,* or *Barron's.* The exceptional few read a paperback book.

As the subway car rickety-ricked its way under the Hudson, started up and stopped, slowed and swerved around curves, our bodies moved in unison, tilting this way or that, riding the wave, feet planted firmly on the tiny piece of turf we'd claimed on the train. Bodies touched, colognes were smelled. There were other smells as well—mothballs, coffee breath, armpits, and halitosis. Breath was held, gum was chewed, the herd of humanity prepared to be propelled into battle. The habit of reading, I later learned, immunized one to the alternative of checking out skin quality and the manner of hairs, and (God forbid) making eye contact.

As the announcement was made and we pulled into the station, the conductor called "World Trade Center," newspapers were tucked under arms and briefcases plucked from between legs. En masse, we all exited into the bowels of the World Trade Center complex. Like a school of salmon dressed in shades of gray, blue, and black, we moved toward the multiple lines of escalators that were our river heading upstream to the concourse level. At the top, some headed left, some right, some straight ahead to the towers, some out the doors to the wilds beyond.

As I entered the lobby of One World Trade Center the crowds thinned out. I waited for the 78th floor Sky Lobby elevator, very excited about the first day of my new job as a fledgling accountant and auditor in New York, New York. The express elevator delivered us to the next set of elevators at the Sky Lobby, and finding the one with my final destination, I rode that until stepping off at the 93rd floor lobby of the Touche Ross Financial Services Center.

It was August of 1987. I had arrived. It was four years after Dave died. The vision of working in New York that motivated me through the stressful years of school was realized. Now at age thirty I was about to begin a new career as an auditor.

While on the new hire tour, I noted that, except for the view, the office could have been anywhere—dark paneling, long halls, cubicles and perimeter offices, computer terminals, printers, the smell of coffee, a gathering of men in an inside glass-walled office all in white shirts with ties chuckling about guy stuff, the secretary sitting at a desk in front of a perimeter office with a premium view applying lipstick with a compact or answering a telephone sounding a *whoop, whoop, whoop.*

The floor plan was massively confusing, a maze for worker ants, a labyrinth. The narrow windows along the outside perimeter of the floor let in the light and at night beamed out to the world. Views spanned the Hudson River to the west, the skyscrapers of midtown to the north, the buildings of downtown and Brooklyn to the east, out past Battery Park and the Statue of Liberty to the Atlantic Ocean to the south. Using the view assisted me in finding my way around the office, since after my initial orientation I visited the office only occasionally. Most of the time I was assigned to one client or another, working out of that company's office space elsewhere in the city.

Now in the first grade in Madison, New Jersey, Kim was being watched and shuttled around by Dave's Aunt Emma both to school and after—to gymnastics or dance class and then fed dinner. After my monthlong orientation, which included a trip to Houston, I was assigned to the audit of a new client for the firm, a "broker dealer," the brokerage subsidiary of a large international bank. The senior auditor arranged to meet Janet, a fellow new hire, and me at the office. His name was Doug, and he was to be our supervisor for the next few months. We followed him like little ducklings as he escorted us through the subways and on the streets to the client's office at 30 Rockefeller Plaza, where we would be doing the field work of the audit.

In the next few months, we learned under Doug's tutelage how to audit and began to learn about the brokerage industry. Doug arranged most of our meetings and understood the scope of what needed to be done and how we needed to do it. We set up our satellite office in a client conference room at 30 Rock, using our IBM personal computers with the big heavy CRT terminals. I was already comfortable with computers, so I was given the task of setting up a mirror of the client's financial information on our company's general ledger financial statement program. Every day, Janet and I scurried back and forth from meetings with client personnel, collecting our paper trails, while in the background the high-pitched whine of the Epson dot matrix tractor-feed printer spit out reams of perforated paper into a neat pile. It was a cause for celebration when our version of the client's preliminary trial balance finally totaled to zero and the whining stopped. We all went to Rosie O'Grady's on Seventh Avenue at 52nd for lunch.

Rockefeller Plaza was beautiful, a landmark complex of multiple buildings, with the enormous sculpture of Atlas carrying the world on his back facing Fifth Avenue, and Radio City Music Hall on the Avenue of the Americas side. NBC's studios and the Rainbow Room were in the building where we worked. The concourse under the plaza was like a small city itself, with shops and restaurants from another time all in black and white and metal in the art deco style. Through the maze of the concourse was the Sixth Avenue line of the subway. To work there, I took New Jersey transit to Hoboken, then the Hoboken PATH to 33rd Street, and then the B, D, or F line to Rockefeller Plaza. At night, I would do it all again in reverse, more than ninety minutes each way. But it was worth it.

In 1987, 30 Rock was also known as the GE Building. The façade of the building and the lobby, like the concourse, were covered in art deco elements, from bronze reliefs to enormous murals on the walls and ceilings. The excitement was electrifying. The trees in the plaza had art deco bronze grates around them. If you entered the building through the plaza you passed under a large sculpted relief of a Zeus-like god with the carved inscription "Wisdom and Knowledge Shall Be the Stability of Thy Times." "Wisdom" was flanked on either side by the goddesses of "Sound" and "Light," symbolizing those attributes of radio and television, since this originally had been the RCA building. I loved the details, the creativity that went into the design of the hardscape, the building's exterior and interior, the decoration, and even the bolts on the doors. It seemed everything had meaning. After taking the gilded art deco elevators to the client floor, however, I stepped into an office space that could have been in Kalamazoo—again except for the views.

Spending day after day mostly in a small room with the same people creates a bond, a team, almost family. You learn each person's strengths and foibles pretty quickly. Janet was 22, a recent graduate of Boston University, struggling to make ends meet in New York on a first year auditor's salary. Every night and sometimes at lunch she would rush out to go to the gym to further tone her tight, young, five-foot-one-inch body. She'd storm into our office on a regular basis, sit down with a harrumph, and go off about being flustered in dealing with the client. She'd mutter under her breath more than a few times how she didn't need four years of college to use the copy machine, and fly into a rage in a proverbial New York second when she couldn't unjam the machine. But then she just as easily really laughed at things Doug said that I didn't even find that funny. She would break into uncontrollable chuckles at her own impersonation of a client. She even laughed at her own frustrations.

Doug was very even-keeled and steady, like an ocean liner. He took everything in stride and was a patient teacher. He was tall, six foot three, from New Jersey, balding with wisps of light brown hair, but pleasant looking with large brown eyes, a nice smile, and straight teeth. He seemed self-confident and was deemed an audit god by Janet and me. One day he brought in homemade oatmeal raisin cookies. He wasn't married. He made them himself. He didn't seem gay. Even though we were all so close at work, at night we all went our separate ways.

As time went by, one of them would notice me picking steel wool out of my fingers with a push pin and learned that on weekends I was refinishing the floors of the little Cape Cod I'd bought in Madison for Kim and myself. Soon they started asking on Monday mornings for status reports on the wallpaper stripping and occasionally pointed out the streaks of oil-based paint that remained in my curls even after repeated washings. I began to pin up Kim's first grade art projects on the walls of our office. Since Janet would usually do her own thing at lunch, Doug and I would get a sandwich, and when the weather was nice enough, sit on the benches placed around the perimeter of Rockefeller Plaza with a view of the skating rink, or go to the café when they took out the ice at the end of the season.

We were about the same age and had both grown up in New Jersey, listening to the same music. We talked about our families. He learned about Dave's death. I learned about his younger brother Joe, who was being treated for recurrent brain tumors after receiving an enormous overdose of radiation at 5 years old. Just about the time I noticed how large his hands were and the golden brown hair growing from his strong-looking wrists, he asked me on a date. The timing also corresponded with our finishing up with the client at 30 Rock and, individually, joining teams at other clients.

After we'd gone on a few dates in the city, one weekend day Doug pulled up in his Volvo sedan in front of my 875-square-foot turquoise mess of a house to pick up Kim and me for an outing to pick apples. Kim was full of energy, a little hyper, babbling on and on, interrupting and asking question after question. When we finally arrived at the apple orchard in Upstate New York, I let Kim run around within eye range to burn off some of her energy. I think she was nervous. I know I was. Doug seemed cool as a cucumber, as usual, although I noted he was very quiet. He seemed to like Kim, and together they collected a bag of delicious high-limb apples left hanging on the trees. He lifted her up over and over, placed her onto sturdy branches, then gently placed her back on the ground.

Overall, I thought the day went great. There were some laughs. I was impressed by how well he got along with Kim. When he dropped us off, Kim ran to hug Doug good-bye. He lifted her up, and—maybe she thought he was going to kiss her—she bit him on the chest, through his shirt, and drew blood. He told me not to worry and said good-bye. I thanked him for the day and Kim, and I went inside.

I didn't know what to make of any of this. I had just started a job, my new career. I had just bought a 1950s fixer-upper with me, myself, and I doing the fixing. Kim was happy being back in New Jersey near her grandmother (Dave's mother) and spending time with Aunt Emma. The fact that she was happy helped me to transition to working sixty hours or more a week. But the stability was fragile. *Do I want to complicate my life at this time?* I asked myself over and over again.

Doug and I continued to date. We met for lunches in the city, sometimes in Chinatown or for sandwiches in the World Trade Center Plaza, at the Sphere fountain. We ate in the Winter Garden atrium of the World Financial Center or at the Greenhouse Restaurant at the Vista Hotel or our usual spot, The Big Kitchen in the WTC mall. We had dinners in the city, some of them very expensive. We saw an occasional Broadway show or performance at Lincoln Center, which usually turned into expensive naps after a long week of work. Sometimes we just met for drinks at the Tall Ships Bar.

In January we returned to the broker-dealer at 30 Rock where we'd met for the year-end audit, and had to pretend that nothing had changed. Janet was amused by our constant bickering. Doug was a teaser, and I was quick with a response or a put-down. Before we finished the job we were all working seven days a week for weeks on end.

In March, when the audit was finally done, Doug started coming over to my house on the weekends. He seemed to like ripping out linoleum, going to the hardware store, picking out wallpaper, scrubbing. We worked well together.

In the spring he started talking about getting married. I told him it was too soon, but two months later I asked Nancy to babysit for the dinner date when I suspected he was going to propose. In the antique railroad car at Rod's Ranch House in Convent Station, Doug—who'd brought a rose, a letter of proposal, *and* a love letter—asked me to marry him. I agreed, but the engagement had to remain secret since we worked together. We planned the wedding for the following fall.

I was 31, he was 30. We had fun spending time together. We worked well together and had enough in common. He cooked well. He was responsible. I was happy not to be so lonely. On his balance sheet I tallied up the debits and credits and concluded that his assets far outweighed his liabilities. Everything happened so fast. The feelings of love were the same as they'd been with Dave—the expectant feeling of joy getting ready to see him, the full, warm feeling in my heart when I thought of him, the care I felt, the desire. At times I had to remind myself that this was Doug and not Dave.

The summer before our wedding, Doug's apartment lease came up for renewal. Since he was working at my house all the time and we would be married in a couple of months anyway, we decided he should move in. We started making a life together. For over a week he carefully cut the wick cord draining the newly lanced abscessed boil on the cheek of my ass every morning before work. We grocery shopped together. I learned he snored, a lot. He bought Kim a Nintendo Entertainment System with Super Mario Brothers, and when they weren't playing it together she was playing it alone. Just thinking of that repeating jingle still makes me want to get a hammer and smash something.

After spending the weekend together living in the same house, at work Doug would question me in front of others. "How are you doing?" "How is your daughter?" "How's the work on the house coming along?"

I didn't think it was funny. It made me anxious.

"You are no fun!" he said.

We planned the wedding. I didn't want a big affair, since I'd been there, done that, but Doug did. We were to be the hosts and would foot the bill. Together we compromised on a guest list of about eighty-five people. One weekend we went to Massachusetts for Kim and me to meet Doug's family. I didn't understand why they didn't seem very welcoming. In the weeks that followed, Nancy and my sisters planned a wedding shower—a small lingerie party at a Japanese steakhouse, since this was my second time around. Not one member of his family came. Just like a Romeo, he wrote his family a scathing letter in defense of me. I told him I didn't think he should send it, so out of deference to me, he didn't. The apparent lack of closeness in his family was strange to me. I was glad they lived far away.

After planning our wedding with the priest, who questioned why we were still keeping our impending marriage a secret, we met with the human resources partner at work to tell him our upcoming plans. Doug volunteered to leave the firm since he was a manager now and the company had an antinepotism policy. The partner laughed with delight at the news and insisted that neither of us would be leaving.

As the news of our engagement spread through the office, we heard the usual jokes about supply closets and conference room tables. When we told Janet we were engaged at the "end of busy season" party at the Copacabana, she practically fainted.

"I thought you two hated each other."

On the day of the wedding, a peak weekend for fall colors, the storm clouds rolled in. My parents came to my house. Nancy helped me dress in my blush pink ball-gown. Kim, our designated flower girl, was dressed as a pink princess and missing her two front teeth. The limousine pulled up to the house. The photographer finished and left for the church. We got into the limo but, to my horror, it wouldn't start. My father ran to the neighbor's house in his tuxedo to try to get the limo jump-started. I began perspiring. Doug had been threatening to abandon me at the altar if I didn't turn up on time. But it was Doug who'd booked the limousine at the lowest possible cost.

We made it to the church thirty minutes late. Doug was still there, and the ceremony was very nice. It was magical for Kim. We were too cheap to hire someone to videotape it, but Doug's father had just bought a new video camera, and our copy of his tape includes snippets of the ceremony between his test shots playing with the zoom feature and panning head to ankles while we took our vows.

The reception was at an elegant night club, The Black Orchid, in a hotel in Morristown. Everything was beautiful. Doug's brother toasted Doug and forgot about the wife. Doug's mother drank too much, and there was an incident with a couple of my aunts in the ladies' room. An eyewitness said Doug's mother was complaining to her oldest daughter that I wasn't good enough for her son when one of my aunts flew out of the bathroom stall pointing a finger in her face and saying that she and her family weren't "fit to shine her niece's shoes." My sister ran out of the bathroom and grabbed my Aunt Marion, fearing that the fight would become physical, and dragged both her and my other aunt away.

I did get general wind of the scuffle but was quickly distracted by the many other guests and general merrymaking. Doug had warned me that his mother drank too much. Then I noticed out of the corner of my eye Doug's father physically removing her after she stumbled repeatedly into my father on the dance floor. Before the main course had even been served, she had been removed to her room for the rest of the night.

At the end of the evening Doug and I went to his parents' hotel room to say goodnight and good-bye. Their door was open, but when his mother saw us coming down the hall she slammed it in our faces. I thought she was mourning the loss of her son. I didn't know at the time that, since I had been married before, even though I was widowed, I was tainted for her—dressed not in blush pink but in scarlet red.

For our honeymoon, we went to Acapulco. It was wonderful even though I cried the whole time. I was a mess of emotions, sad because I thought my wedding was ruined by Doug's family, depressed from quitting smoking, overjoyed and hysterical. I had not had a single break in five solid years. I felt relief, love, and then guilt. I had for all intents and purposes closed the chapter on Dave and started a new chapter with Doug, five years and two months later.

We hung out at the pools by day, reading and playing spades, and ate ourselves into a food coma every night. We flew home at Halloween to be with Kim for trick-or-treating and then left for Kennebunk, Maine, where we stayed at a bed-and-breakfast for another week. The place was so simple, so quaint, I wanted to move there. I think Doug would have too. Even though I loved my job, my life, I was feeling the effects of the rat race and all the stress from all the life changes—college graduation, career change, new job, buying a house, taking and passing the CPA exam, getting married, all in eighteen months.

I came home, still depressed. Kim and I had become three—Doug, Kim, and me. I remember thinking, *Oh my God, what did I do? Great, now I have another person to take care of, with all the associated expectations and disappointments.* At that time, I really focused on the negatives, but in the years that followed we became a family—for better or for worse. We remodeled the little Cape Cod, went to Kim's softball games and dance recitals.

I also gained ten pounds. I decided my depression must have been nicotine withdrawal. During the busy season at work, while spending three months of my life in a conference room auditing a precious metals dealer in the company of two chain smokers, I started clipping their cigarettes and smoking them in the ladies room. Within a week I was buying again. Doug and Kim were very disappointed. I'd failed.

Doug and I weren't getting any younger, so before our second anniversary the three of us became four. Blue was the color of my newborn son at his one-minute Apgar score in August of 1990. What the doctors didn't tell us—between delivering the head and then the shoulder and saying, "This kid is a football player"—was that the cord was wrapped around his neck. I heard "It's a boy," saw the blue, didn't hear the cry, inhaled and exhaled the relief that comes with the delivery, and then held my breath, waiting for him to breathe. Hearing my own heartbeat in my ears, I watched the neonatologist suction my baby boy, wiping meconium stool from his face under the neon light of the hood of the open-air incubator.

And then I heard it, the cry, the repeated air-gasping cry that announced, *Mommy, I'm here! Daddy, I'm not going anywhere!* I cried with relief, tears rolling down my cheeks as the placenta slid out. Then Bradford, our baby, was brought over to Doug and me, wrapped up snuggly, red from all the crying. We cried tears of joy, tears of relief, awestruck by the act of witnessing a miracle, assisted by the obstetrician and the neonatologist. I was worshipped like the Madonna by my husband for two weeks and one day. Then, I was just me.

It was quite a change from just having a 9-year-old daughter in the house. We were showered with blue—baby blue onesies, blue sweater sets, mini blue jeans with snaps, blue rattles, blue cards, and blue baby wrappings infiltrated our home like the cloudless blue sky on those hot August days. I loved every minute of it. I knew he was to be my last child so I savored every second of his tiny new life. Many a day I would just sit and hold him on my chest while he slept between feedings.

Shortly after Brad was born, my Aunt Marion was diagnosed with metastasized bladder cancer and given less than six months to live. I was beside myself. I decided to stop smoking (again), giving up each cigarette as a prayer offering for her healing. I stopped smoking for good. Besides, since I spent most of my time in the house, I didn't want Brad to breathe in secondhand smoke. It didn't occur to me that I could have smoked outside, nor had it occurred to me to stop smoking when I was pregnant, even though people smarter than me freely commented that smoking wasn't good for my baby. It took my aunt's illness to motivate me to stop.

Miraculously, I later learned that the scans were erroneous, and chemotherapy flushes of her bladder healed her completely. I was so happy.

But after a few weeks, I started crying. I couldn't understand why I felt so blue. Was it hormonal, or nicotine withdrawal, or was it that I knew that I had only four months of maternity leave and then would need to hire a nanny to take care of the children? The idea of leaving my new baby with a stranger made me sad. I wondered why I didn't feel bad about working or school when I didn't think I had a choice, but now felt bad because I thought I *did* have a choice. Guilt, depression, confusion, hormonal upheaval, lack of nicotine, and dilemmas of career versus baby track and dependency versus independence were the ingredients in the soup of my emotional turbulence.

Doug would come home every day from work, shut down and exhausted. He didn't want to talk about anything. I was left to figure this out on my own. He wouldn't weigh in one way or the other. So then I added anger, bitterness, and disappointment to the mix. Tapes of my mother's voice ran through my head. *Snap out of it!* and *What do you have to complain about?*

When the four months were up, a nanny was hired, and back to work I went, complete with the commute and the long hours, smack in the middle of busy season. I started smoking again. But now I had it all, the marriage, the children, the career, the house, working in New York. I was living the dream. Wasn't I?

PART 2

CHAPTER 8

GO WEST

APRIL–DECEMBER 1993

B y 1993, Nancy and I had been best friends for more than twenty years. It was only natural to consult with her regarding the dilemma I was facing. Should I move to California?

As we sat over lunch, I reiterated the main reasons why I was reluctant. She knew one of my aspirations since Dave's death was to be financially independent, have a successful career, and to work in Manhattan. During the past year Doug had been commuting from the firm's New York office to its San Francisco office to assist the team out there in winning a new client. In the proposal, the client had been promised that Doug would be part of the ongoing audit team. We knew that if he agreed to move, it would demonstrate his commitment to the firm and be positive for his career. I didn't really plan on the firm's winning the engagement, but Doug did. The firm won and asked Doug to move.

Second, I was disillusioned about our marriage. I hadn't felt supported when I took some time to stay at home after Brad was born, first during maternity leave but then for a full two years. We started fighting all the time, probably for sport, but also I think because we were both by nature professionally competitive and probably envious of what we perceived as each other's greener grass. I suppose on some level I envied his opportunity to advance, to receive recognition, and to be paid for his efforts even though I wanted to stay home with the children. I believe he envied my freedom.

He would comment, "What do you have to complain about when you have the whole day 'free'?"

He further suggested, "You should go back to work, then I can take the baby golfing all day. What's the big deal?"

These types of comments basically summed up the extent of valida-tion and support I received for staying at home. Therefore, I returned to work. I was back to commuting to my fifty- to an occasional eighty-hour-per-week, stressful but rewarding job—while also caring for our two children, managing the nanny, homework, the house, the bills, shopping, and the rest. By this time, my daughter Kim was 12, a sixth grader, and Brad was 3. It was clear to me that Doug and I weren't con-necting at a satisfying level quite a bit of the time.

The other reason I was hesitant about committing to the move was a concern about uprooting Kim. We had always lived on the East Coast. All of our family and friends were there. Two thousand, six hundred plus air miles was logistically too far away to attend a family picnic. Besides that, the three-hour time difference was a big deal in the days before cell phones. And when Doug was home, his fatigue and disengagement were irritating. Because of all of these circumstances, I thought that perhaps now would be a good time to call it quits and go our separate ways. I had to wonder, did I want to give up all my dreams for him?

Nancy and I weighed all the pros and cons, and as would be expected of any great friend, she couldn't and wouldn't tell me what to do. Talking all of this over with her helped, though.

I decided we should all go. I thought of it as a chance to start anew. I also believed in the personal values around family, commitment, and perseverance, and I was always hopeful. I got on board with the plan, even if I did have reservations—which of course I kept to myself. I did love Doug enough that I wanted him to be happy. I wanted *us* to be happy.

Instead of looking for the gold of the forty-niners, I was hoping to find love, peace, and contentment. I thought, *What better place than the Golden State?* So, we were going to California, and by golly, we were going to make the best of it! I did strike a deal with Doug, asking him to take some areas of responsibility off my plate once we arrived. He agreed to pay the bills and do complete kitchen management, which included shopping, meal planning, cooking, and cleaning up. Maybe now I would have some time to relax, to take care of myself.

The next few months were a flurry of activity in preparation for our move. For the sale of our house, the relocation company required that we have all sorts of inspections, one of which was a test for radon. Radon, a radioactive gas, was detected in the basement of the house. This problem had to be remedied before we could put the house on the market and before the relocation company would sign the papers agreeing to buy it if it didn't sell. At the cost of several thousand dollars, a large contraption was erected in the corner of the basement that looked like the robotic invader from a war with another world, complete with its large radioactivity sticker placed like a medal in the center of its chest. The radon was vented to the outside of the house, invisible, odorless, and undetectable by us either before or after the remediation.

Surprisingly, the house sold quickly. In fact we had two buyers. I came home from work early to find the first buyer at the house with the realtor and a home inspector, and was there when they received the call that we had rescinded the contract and sold to a higher bidder. Of course Doug had not informed me of this development. I was blindsided and had to endure the wrath, tears, and name calling by the people in my house until they stormed out, slamming the door.

Doug's response was the usual, "What's the big deal. It's over. We made more money." What, as usual, was I complaining about?

It was a time of high stress to say the least, the highlight of which was dealing with the horrifying real estate costs in the San Francisco Bay Area. It would be essential for me to return to work immediately so we could buy a house that we felt we could live in without going backwards in our accommodations and lifestyle. Unfortunately, I didn't have a job since my company had no positions to offer me in California. Fortunately, however, Doug's relocation package guaranteed mortgage financing, factoring in 100 percent of the trailing spouse's income. After four or five discouraging trips back and forth across the country, we finally bought a cosmetically challenged typical California ranch house in a great neighborhood in Danville. For me, this move was incredibly scary and a huge commitment financially, emotionally, and most important, for our relationship. Now, I was not only reluctantly committed and perpetually depressed, but also a trailing spouse. This in and of itself was problematic for me, since I was used to having my own identity. I despised the idea of being someone's luggage.

Then, just before leaving my job in New York, a recruiter in Chicago contacted me about a job in San Francisco. Bank of America headquarters was very interested in my credentials and I would have an interview once we arrived. So we hugged and kissed our family and friends, and temporarily said good-bye to our household belongings. On the way to Newark Airport, we made a detour into Manhattan, where we picked up a beautiful, luminous, eighteen-inch cultured pearl necklace Doug had had made for me. Then we all boarded the westbound one-way flight to San Francisco on July 13, the day before my thirty-sixth birthday.

We were homeless for about a week, roughing it in a posh suite of rooms on Nob Hill in the city by the bay, all on Doug's company's dime while we awaited close of escrow on our new house and the subsequent arrival of our belongings. The day of my birthday was spent interviewing at what was to be my next job, at BofA. After returning to the hotel and trying to change my clothes while Kim and Brad waited impatiently to go for ice cream, Doug informed me that we were not getting our mortgage since I didn't have a job. So much for guarantees, I thought. I told Doug I expected him to handle this latest problem and left the room with the kids, exhausted, thinking, *What the hell am I doing?* After some phone calls and his company's involvement, it did all work out. We got financing, moved in, I had second and third interviews, and got the job offer. Things so far were working out in the Golden State.

It was summertime in Northern California. In Danville, nestled in the San Ramon Valley, the nights were cool and clear, without humidity, completely star-filled. There were no mosquitoes. The days were always sunny, so bright and clear. Every day while driving the kids around, doing our errands, setting up house, going to swim lessons, I would say, "Hey, kids, it's another beautiful day in California!"

Kim was miserable. She asked, "How could you have done this to me? Because of you, now I have no friends!" It quickly got to the point that she would tell me "*Shut up!*" as soon as I said, "Hey, kids, it's …." I enjoyed the weather anyway and tried to stay positive.

While Doug hit the ground running, totally consumed in his new office and job responsibilities, I had a few weeks to hire a live-in nanny, set up nursery school arrangements, and finalize everything before I started my job. I knew that Kim would make new friends as soon as school started, and I understood her anger. I had to believe that things would be all right. Meanwhile, Brad was happy riding his tricycle all over the house, helping deliver unpacked items using the attached wagon, when he wasn't heading out the back door to try to drown in the pool if I didn't watch him like a hawk.

I started working again, which I enjoyed, even if it was mostly a way to escape everything else. At home, I met and really liked my new neighbor Lyn, who invited me to join the neighborhood book group. She and her husband hosted a get-to-know-you barbeque and invited some other couples from the neighborhood. I became a little concerned when the barbeque was served with complete china and silver service in the dining room. Our entertaining was done more spontaneously on a wing and a prayer and paper plates.

One unusually warm summer evening Lyn and I were sitting in my yard talking and we heard an owl hooting. I wasn't used to owls hooting in New Jersey. "When you hear an owl hooting, it means someone is going to die," Lyn said.

Interesting, I thought. Her comment reminded me of Girl Scout campfire stories.

Unfortunately, Kim's misery escalated after school started, and she thought everyone was stupid. I came home after twelve hours out of the house commuting and working in a state of physical, mental, and emotional exhaustion. But at home, my refuge, I had to face an angry, hormonal preteen, a middle-aged Swedish nanny making eyes at my husband while glaring at me judgmentally, and a husband who complained about everything. The complaining was the worst. No topic was safe—the abysmal commute, the cost of everything, how long it took to get to a grocery store, the traffic lights, the illogical planning of one-way traffic. It never ended. By this time, I had to respond with the question, again, "Why did we move here?"

Thank God, being with Brad gave me such joy. He was the sunshine of my life. In the evenings, I couldn't call and talk to anyone on the East Coast for support, comfort, or just plain commiseration, because they were all already in bed. So I escaped into the world of children's fantasy, dinosaurs, and Dr. Seuss, reading Brad bedtime stories until I nodded off and he had to wake me to finish. Of necessity, he also learned to read to himself at a very young age.

By the end of September, during the best of the Northern California weather, clouds were appearing over just our house. I was worried that

Brad hadn't warmed up to the nanny. I didn't know if he was just missing me or the old house or if there was something weird about the nanny. Kim was having problems in her new school, and I was meeting regularly with the principal to get her schedule changed to ensure that she was in the proper classes for her abilities. She had been a straight A student in New Jersey, but within one month in California she needed a tutor. She went from a class size of nineteen in New Jersey to thirty-five plus at her new school. All the classes were lecture-based, and questions were discouraged. The school culture seemed militaristic. All these things contributed to a huge adjustment for her.

In October, not knowing what else to do, I started looking into private schools. It did not help that she hated us, hated school, and hated her classmates. I thought, oh my God, we have ruined her life. By then I began to realize that maybe the name Golden State had nothing to do with the gold that was discovered in the foothills—maybe it was named for all the grass that turns a golden color and then dies completely from the lack of rain.

When the going got tough, the tough headed for Yosemite. In October, Nancy came out for a visit and joined us for the trip. Some highlights of the trip, which was supposed to allow us to relax and connect with nature, included making a clothing rope to rescue Kim from sliding off a cliff after she ventured out onto mossy slime from a waterfall's overspray, to watching Doug hiking up the steep rail-less stone stairs to Vernal Falls carrying Brad on his shoulders while he slipped repeatedly and laughed at me for screaming in desperate anxiety. Still, despite the near-fatal mishaps, I did enjoy the beauty of it all.

Doug began making legal arrangements to adopt Kim. I thought this showed a real commitment to us as a family and hoped it would be good for Kim. She was now 12, with long brown hair, and was slightly taller than I, tipping into full-blown adolescence and the illusion of independence faster than a high-category typhoon.

When I wasn't working at my job, there were Kim's orthodontist appointments, dermatology appointments, tutors, religion classes, school activities, and private school open houses to attend. Brad was still young enough not to be overscheduled; he was going to nursery school only three times a week. Doug spent a lot of his free time with him. I spent what spare time I had painting walls, unpacking and decorating. I was always totally exhausted and got two speeding tickets in one week. The message I took away from this was *slow down*.

By November it had been three months since I joined the bank. A position called Technical Accounting Manager had been created for me. I interpreted accounting pronouncements and wrote about how they would impact the capital markets area of the bank. Most of my time was spent on special projects and getting to know my boss, Jacqui. Jacqui was a self-made woman almost a decade my senior, originally French Canadian, but she had spent most of her time in California. She had one son and was in the process of getting a divorce. She and I seemed to get along well from the beginning. She seemed to take me under her wing from day one, which helped me to transition from the fast and furious energy of working in New York.

In November Jacqui informed me that she wanted me to replace the current controller of the bank's retail broker-dealer. She asked me to accompany her to a business conference in New York City at the end of the month for a few days. I jumped at the chance to escape bedlam. I fantasized about the ability to sleep or just to be able to read on the plane. Four days of no whining, complaining, or driving was very appealing. We were going to stay at the Marriott Marquis in Midtown. On the night we arrived, I was elated to be back on my own turf. The real-time experience of the noise, the people, the garbage—all were exhilarating.

At bedtime I noticed that my right arm and armpit were tingling and really bothering me. I thought that maybe the cause of this discomfort was the fact that I had just schlepped through the airport carrying my heavy garment bag packed for every uncertainty. Naturally, Jacqui had a small two-wheeled suitcase. I started massaging my arm, feeling around my armpit and landed on my right breast, where right below my nipple was a big lump.

The date was December 2. I thought to myself, you have got to be kidding. I waited a bit but the lump was still there after rechecking several times. I had a horrible sinking feeling, and then a sense of dread. Then panic crept into my mind. I knew something bad was going on. I called Doug. He told me it was probably nothing and to stop worrying. He told me that if it was still there and I was still worried, I could see a doctor when I returned to California. I didn't know if he wasn't concerned or if this was his way of comforting me. What I did know was that he really didn't help at all. I could never tell what he was thinking. It had truly never entered my mind that I might be a hypochondriac.

The next day Nancy came to the city, and I met her for cocktails in the hotel lobby and shared my discovery. We were both worried. We even cried in between sips of wine. A few more glasses was all it took to assure each other that since I was only thirty-six, maybe it was only a cyst. Besides which, we rationalized, hadn't I just had a perfectly normal mammogram one year before? I remembered reading somewhere that approximately 80 percent of all lumps found in the breast are benign. After seeing Nancy, I felt a little better, and I was off to see *Kiss of the Spider Woman* on Broadway.

That night, while I tossed and turned, I recalled that I had felt this lump about six months earlier, before we had moved, but I could not remember if that was real or if I'd dreamt it. *After all,* I thought, *it had been such a crazy time. How scary to think about the implications of whether you can't remember what is real and what's not. Aren't most working mothers this busy?* As it turned out, in New York, I escaped bedlam only to be volleying between feelings of horror and trying to assure myself that everything was fine. It's funny how ordinary bedlam can suddenly become appealing, even preferable.

CHAPTER 9

REALITY CHECK

DECEMBER 1993–MARCH 1994

When I wasn't working, all I could think about was the lump. I felt like I was becoming the lump. Within a few days of returning home I saw a doctor, and he immediately scheduled me for a mammography appointment. On December 8 I went by myself to radiology. They put a metal bead on the lump with adhesive, did the mammogram, and told me to wait in the dressing room. I waited for what seemed like forever in that little curtained cubicle. When the technician returned, she said that the radiologist wanted to take magnified views, which she explained were more detailed.

I knew deep inside that the inevitable was just around the corner. I wasn't a negative person—I just knew. After they were done with the magnified view, they wanted to do an ultrasound. I am sure I appeared calm and reasonable on the outside. Inside, I was terrified and started praying harder for this to be OK, a fluke, and for strength no matter what.

I was brought into the doctor's office/reading room where the radiologist, the MD, met with me and told me it was not a cyst. He pointed out on the films where it showed microcalcifications (translated to little points of light, like stars in the night sky) in the area of the lump, a galaxy contained within my breast, the Milky Way without the milk. He suggested that I should follow up immediately with my doctor to schedule a biopsy. I called Doug from the radiologist's office. He sounded very upset. I could tell this time.

Doug and I met with the surgeon, and two days later I was scheduled for a breast biopsy. I hoped that I would have enough time to recover and be back at work by Monday. The surgeon explained that she would do a peri-alveolar incision for the biopsy and possible lumpectomy so that there would be no visible scar. The whole process seemed like driving fast in a well-cushioned bus around hairpin turns with no idea where you were going to end up or if you would just crash. I just had to believe I was going to be all right.

By this point, I had told my boss, a few of my friends, and my two sisters. Talking about possibly having cancer wasn't that prevalent in 1993, certainly not at all in my mid-30s age group. I was afraid to tell my parents. I knew they'd be upset. And for some strange reason I was embarrassed, thinking on some level that I was letting them down, giving them something to worry about. They were not usually the ones who did the comforting. I was.

I went to bed the night before the biopsy thinking that the next day we would either celebrate or my life would never be the same, and I didn't have any idea what that would mean. I didn't sleep. What allowed me to face the fear of that day was a leap of faith. I just had to trust in God and believe that I'd be all right. Even though I was a control freak, I still had faith.

I woke up in the recovery room still drugged and fading in and out of consciousness. Doug was there, leaning over the bedrails holding my hand, the look of helpless love in his eyes. I smiled inside, thinking that at last we were a team. Then the surgeon came in wearing her scrubs and hair-covering cap. I was still a little groggy. After asking how I was doing, she told us that the final pathology was not back yet but she was certain that it was cancer, possibly ductal carcinoma in situ, or DCIS, a noninvasive cancer. She'd done the lumpectomy but doubted she'd removed it all because all the tissue of my right breast felt "gritty." She said the tissue she removed was gray and had tentacles.

It sounded ugly.

She said I would probably need a mastectomy but we would know more later in the week when the final pathology came back. I thought, then hoped, and then prayed that I was having a horrible nightmare from the anesthesia. I wasn't. I was crying, sobbing even. But then, I noticed, so was Doug. I had never seen him this upset. This scared me as well.

I stopped crying. In fact, after that I wouldn't let myself cry again for a long time. I figured both of us couldn't lose it; I needed to be strong.

What were we going to do? Months later, the surgeon told us that the anesthesiologist had said putting me under for this procedure was like trying to put down a racehorse. I even talked while I was knocked out. I couldn't let go of control even during anesthesia.

That night I was emotionally numb. I had a tight, white elastic dressing on my right breast and was having horrible pain—so much so that I called the doctor (she had given me her home number). She said to make sure to take more painkillers; she would be away on vacation and Dr. So-and-So could follow up.

We didn't tell Kim anything at that time, although I think she knew something was going on. She was very self-absorbed during this period and quite nasty. Brad was too young to understand. I was scared and sad but well-practiced in putting up the "I'm just fine" front. I told my parents and siblings what was going on, but at that point, I still didn't know what any of it meant going forward.

The next week I went with Doug to the on-call surgeon and she removed the dressing. Not only did we find out that I was allergic to the adhesive of the bandage so my skin was all blistered, but also that my incision was split open from the pressure of a large "liver" clot that had formed under the incision. It was visible in the hole like a purple alien eye and was bleeding, slowly weeping clear, deep red tears. A new dressing was applied with different tape and I was given wound care instructions and a box of supplies. We went home to await the pathology results that would start the ball rolling on how to deal with the liver clot and the rest of the breast.

In the meantime, I returned to work at my new location, in my new position, though I wasn't that excited about it anymore. I couldn't focus and didn't feel on top of my game. My boss knew what was going on in my personal life, but work was still work. I didn't want this setback to affect my career. So I became an actor, going to work and putting on my game face. I was still glad to be working since it gave me a break from obsessing about everything else.

Doug was also back at work at his demanding job and somewhat emotionally absent, as usual. The stress with Anki, the Swedish nanny, was escalating. She didn't understand or agree with my firmness with my daughter, which she demonstrated with eye rolling and tsking sounds. Then we found out that she was locking Brad in his room. There were dried puddles of urine on the carpet just inside his bedroom door. I kept praying to God for the strength to deal with all of this. Meanwhile, I just wanted to run away, scream until I had no voice, hide just to be let alone.

I soon learned that the final pathology report indicated that the tissue they removed was the noninvasive form of breast cancer, DCIS. Unfortunately, there weren't clear margins on the specimen. This meant that they would have to go back in and surgically remove more tissue. It was now the time to meet with all the specialists to determine how to treat the remaining breast.

Doug accompanied me to meet with the radiation oncologist. When an older man in a lab coat entered the examination room, we rose. He extended his hand and introduced himself to my husband but not to me, the patient. He said the bottom line was that I could have "breast-sparing" surgery to remove the rest of the affected tissue and then radiation therapy. But since I would have what was referred to in medical parlance as an "acquired breast defect" from the missing tissue and the blood clot, he suggested that I might want to consider a mastectomy, with or without reconstruction. Then he continued on with a spate of scenarios and statistics that seemed to me like a canned presentation. He lost me at hello. I was depressed. I felt like I became the woman with the acquired breast defect, or was now just plain defective.

Doug and I next met with the recommended oncologist. He told us that breast cancer was a relatively slow-growing cancer and that this tumor had probably started ten years earlier. I remember thinking that ten years ago was exactly how long it had been since Dave died. *Interesting,* I thought, vacillating between horror and detached objectivity. He recommended a mastectomy but said I would not require chemotherapy.

I didn't have large breasts to begin with. What would be left if I had breast-sparing surgery? According to him, I also had the most virulent form of DCIS, which meant that it had the greatest chance of becoming invasive. I spent countless hours at home using Prodigy and a dial-up modem to do research on the "Worldwide Web," which was then a relatively new thing. I learned that DCIS is a type of breast cancer that is confined to the milk ducts. It had not yet invaded the wall of the duct, so it was not invasive, a criterion for cancer. Did I have cancer or not? This question really bothered me for a while. I wondered what I should tell people. How many times would I have to explain what all this meant? Should I say I have precancer, cancer but not invasive, early cancer?

I arranged to have my case presented at the hospital's tumor board. Taking these steps and doing my due diligence helped me to think that I was in control. Unfortunately, I found the entire experience to be dehumanizing. I was a case, a specimen to be examined and prodded, as well as a statistical oddity, since there was no known history of breast cancer in my family. That's not to say that a relative couldn't have died an early death before it manifested itself. But I was only 36! Now I had entered this population of mostly unfortunate old people and the occasional young ones for whom you feel great empathy. They recommended a mastectomy.

I determined from my research that since so much of what should happen was based on the pathology, I should get another opinion from a pathology expert, and I arranged to send my tissue slides. I made an appointment with another surgeon outside of my HMO provider group to get his opinion on whether to have a mastectomy. I already felt that my medical team in the HMO was incestuous—none of them would ever disagree with a colleague. But the second surgical opinion was the same. All roads were leading to having a mastectomy.

How did this happen to me? Why me? I didn't want to be one of them. According to the medical specialist's consultation reports, I was the "lovely 36-year-old accountant and former nurse, mother of two, recently moved from New Jersey, with the bleeding breast defect."

I wasn't really sleeping anymore. My mind wouldn't stop. If there was any good news in all of this, I learned that since the cancer was not invasive, after a mastectomy I would have a 98 percent chance of survival. I wasn't sure how this was meaningful information. Everything was happening too fast. All I could think about was that I was going to lose my breast. Part of me would be gone forever. Fear turned into grieving.

There was such an enormous learning curve to climb. Decisions needed to be made about reconstruction—yes or no, and if yes, then what type and who should do it? When I tried to discuss this with Doug at the end of the day, he would glaze over. He couldn't handle it. I felt very alone.

Christmas was coming. I told the surgeon who did the original biopsy that I'd be able to schedule the mastectomy in March when financial reporting at the broker-dealer was finished. She looked at me like I was crazy.

"This is something you don't want to mess around with. The sooner you have the surgery, the better."

We told Kim. She was scared and noticeably upset. The only answer we had to most of her questions was "We don't know." We tried to be as comforting as we could be under the circumstances. It was hard to give assurances when you had no idea yourself.

Christmas came and went complete with a hovering black cloud and homemade traditional Swedish glug prepared by Anki. She also came into our bedroom in the middle of the night, singing and dressed up as Santa Lucia with her head lit up by a crown of burning candles. This too was a Swedish tradition, apparently. I knew she wasn't the angel of death—or any other angel for that matter. I wasn't asleep, of course, but Doug was. I didn't like her, and I still had to deal with her. *One thing at a time,* I thought.

The rest of 1993 and early January was spent meeting with plastic surgeons, having more tests, and working. I was overwhelmed and depressed. I wanted to quit my job, but then how could we afford our mortgage?

I finally selected a plastic surgeon and opted for the type of breast reconstruction known as a transverse abdominal flap to be done immediately after the mastectomy. It sounded pretty radical and had a long recovery time, but I was assured it would be the most natural feeling. *For whom?* I thought. The bonus in this surgery was that in addition to using part of the abdominus rectus muscle, they would use most of my abdominal fat. I really didn't have all that much, even though Doug was fond of what he called my "Buddha belly." I decided to add another positive to this scenario—why not have my other breast enlarged at the same time? Since I had ruthlessly been teased growing up about being flat-chested, I thought, *Why not have a C cup?*

Surgery was scheduled for January 14. I discussed it with Jacqui, and she agreed to let me work from home on a project during my recovery so that I wouldn't lose pay. I was worried about money, the surgery, Kim, my life, my career. I was also worried that Doug was not going to be able to be supportive, so I found for both of us a psychologist that dealt with cancer.

Doug was acting like Dr. Jekyll and Mr. Hyde. He was astrologically and not coincidentally a Gemini, the twins, or more simplistically, a split personality. When Doug was Dr. Jekyll, he agreed to come with me to an appointment with a psychologist where we (I) could discuss our (my) concerns, since I thought what we were facing was enormous. When Doug was Mr. Hyde, he seemed to feel that, since I wasn't dying anymore, what was the big deal—it was only a breast. I interpreted this as the usual response to my expressing a need—*Get over it* and *Don't bother me*. And as usual, I felt hurt and angry.

The psychologist was very macho, short and snappy. After hearing my list of concerns and hearing from Doug that he was "just fine," he immediately determined that things had escalated to the point where the nanny had to go.

"Doug, you are the person that has to fire the nanny. Your wife does not need to be more taxed or stressed at this time," he said. "Rest and a peaceful environment is what are necessary before the surgery and the recovery afterwards."

He convinced Doug to come on his own for a few more visits after the surgery. I liked macho man. Meanwhile, I arranged for my parents to come to California during my surgery to take care of the children, and Doug fired the nanny, just like that. We would search for another nanny while I was recovering. I assumed Doug would take care of me.

The six-plus-hour surgery went as expected. What I was not prepared for is what I woke up to. Oh my God—the pain, the multiple drains, the air stockings, the cycle of the pump, the tubes and oxygen. I had never experienced an extensive surgery. Cut in so many places, covered from neck to pubis in dressings, burning with pain. My bed was fully upright since my abdomen was so tight. I couldn't figure out in the morphine haze how they'd flapped this muscle from my abdomen into my breast. Later I realized that they must have tunneled their arm up my abdomen under the skin.

Doug stayed with me at the hospital for the most part, and was very loving and caring, even pressing the button for the morphine pump when I couldn't. I remember many bouquets of flowers, cards, and well wishes from the friends and family who knew what I was going through. I felt really loved and really lousy. I also remember Jacqui calling the hospital room all the time, at any hour, with questions about work. For many days my stomach muscles were so tight from the reconstruction that I was stuck in a cashew shape—I couldn't straighten out.

When I could tolerate oral painkillers, I was discharged, though hardly ready to return to my world. And, since I was well enough to go home, naturally that meant Doug could go back to work. My mother would help me. I was instructed not to drive for six weeks, which didn't matter since I could barely stand. The bandages and all the drains would be removed in a week. I could take a shower if I covered everything with plastic. I wouldn't need any further treatments other than a follow-up mammogram of the left breast every six months. Case closed, and that's that.

My parents did their best. My mother was very attentive. She would help me safety pin the drains onto a clothes hanger and cover me in plastic wrap so I could shower. With me in my wounded nakedness, she finally seemed maternally bonded. My parents were not only caring for me but doing the nanny's job as well, for which I was as grateful as I could be. Between the pain and the blur of Vicodin, I didn't care about anything very much.

In a few days, my drains were removed, and so were my dressings. Things looked pretty ugly at first. The muscle that was flapped over into my reconstructed breast created a large lemon-sized lump where I used to have cleavage. Everything was still swollen. They had created a new nipple on my reconstructed breast using skin from my belly. *Did they have to use the hairy part?* I thought. They said I could have electrolysis and have the whole thing tattooed to look more natural. *For whom?* I wondered again. By the way, they'd also needed to use a small implant for the reconstructed breast since I didn't have enough abdominal fat. I felt slightly vindicated—imagine that! Doug seemed positive about how I looked and did nothing to make me feel bad or worse in any way.

After my parents left, my sister Alane, who was a business owner and recently divorced, left her son in the care of friends and came to help me. With her visiting, I would finally have someone to really talk with. Being with Alane was wonderful, as usual. When she wasn't doing everything to care for my family and me—we spent the time trying to understand how I could have gotten cancer. We even laughed, while splinting my abdomen of course. Then, unfortunately, she had to go home.

After a month, I still wasn't able to stand up straight and was disheartened when my friend and neighbor Lyn told me of a friend of hers who'd had the same surgery and was shopping at the mall two weeks later. Meanwhile, Jacqui was always calling for her daily pound of flesh. And by the way, when was I coming back?

Then Lyn was diagnosed with breast cancer. I was horrified for her. I tried to forget about myself for a while to be there for her. We could walk this journey together, I thought.

There were some differences in our walk, however. She needed chemotherapy and radiation. She didn't work. She told everyone about her condition and as a result was showered with care. In contrast, I, true to form, didn't "need" help. Most people still didn't know about my cancer or surgery—or at least they didn't admit to me they knew.

I returned to work in March. I'd lost the opportunity at the broker-dealer; my boss gave it to someone else. But she had another opportunity for me. I got the job of the person who was given my broker-dealer post. *Well,* I thought, *what are you going to do?* As promised when I was hired, I was officially promoted to vice president (not as big a deal in banking as you might think). I went through the motions at work but was still very focused on my health crisis, or my new lack of health.

At some point Doug expressed that moving to California wasn't turning out to be what he expected. I understood. He had left behind his family, friends, the familiarity of his New York associates. He had all he could do to manage adjusting to the new environment, the people, the new office, proving himself to a new client. In addition, the months of November through March being the busiest time of year for his profession, let's heap on a mega-mortgage, a wife of five years with cancer who is grieving and juggling a career, and a family that includes an angry teenager and a preschooler. He tried so hard to be positive.

"We'll get through this," he would say.

CHAPTER 10

LOOKING FOR NORMAL

APRIL–DECEMBER 1994

Doug was so busy at work, he was even working some weekends. We hired a new nanny named Suzanne, who soon became a hit with everyone. She was cheerful and full of energy. She was also young, blonde, and athletic. She was just what we needed, a real Mary Poppins who blew in with an umbrella on the wind of a rainy day. Yes, it was still raining. The winter in California was not that cold compared to the East Coast but was bone-chillingly damp nonetheless. Our plywood ranch was drafty and I always felt cold.

Doug was continuing to sporadically see the macho psychologist. I also contacted a therapist, whom I saw for maybe three visits. It was a waste of time. I wanted and needed specific skills and constructive techniques to live and think differently, and I got nothing. So I began reading voraciously about physical and mental health, living in the moment, about meditation and doing anything that I thought might be relevant. I started going to the spa for massages. I joined a gym.

Meanwhile, things were busier than ever at work. I was selected for a team that was involved in the merger and integration of a newly acquired bank in Chicago. It was exciting work, but now I was also traveling back and forth to the Midwest on a regular basis.

Suzanne was creative and planned loads of great activities for Brad. Kim also seemed to bond with her and was finally making friends. For her thirteenth birthday, she had a group of girls over for a mystery party and a sleepover. Many of her new friends shared choir and dance as a passion both in and outside of school.

Kim had also discovered boys. She had a series of boyfriends and typically spent excessive amounts of time on the telephone. She was just holding her own at school as a C student but was not interested in changing to a private school. We'd have to revisit that again the next year.

Having a great nanny eased my sense of guilt about working and traveling. But something huge had just happened to me and I didn't think I should just forget about it. My friend Lyn was progressing with her chemotherapy and radiation. She had become a vegetarian and was tapping into all sorts of avenues to assist with her healing. And then it struck me. All of this had happened to my body, but I hadn't really healed.

I had no feeling in my reconstructed breast, my abdomen, or my newly enhanced remaining breast. I did not even get goose bumps in these areas. No one had told me to expect this. I remembered that the plastic surgeon, though skilled and knowledgeable, was male, and with him everything had been about the aesthetics. He was an artist. He'd created a new breast that would look and feel as close to a real one as possible—but only to others, not to me. The implant on the left side certainly did look good, but I had no feeling anymore in the unaffected breast. I'd completely lost sensation on both sides. I felt betrayed and very angry. No one said there'd be a loss of feeling when we were discussing the left breast augmentation. If they had, I would have evaluated the pros and cons quickly and opted not to do it.

I beat myself up for my vanity and realized I had no one to blame but myself for this irreparable mistake. Since my breasts played an important role for Doug and me when making love, I had another loss to mourn.

Years before, when I was in nursing school, we had learned about the stages of grief as promulgated by Dr. Elisabeth Kübler-Ross in her book *On Death and Dying*. Her theory was that with any significant loss, a fatal diagnosis, or the death of a loved one, most people go through five stages of grief. The first stage is shock, denial, and isolation; the second stage is anger; the third and fourth are depression and bargaining, respectively; followed finally by the fifth stage, acceptance. But it's not a simple progression. People who are grieving can go back and forth between the stages until they finally reach acceptance—and even then, they can backslide.

I realized that of course I had experienced shock when I first found out about the cancer. Then, when I wanted to delay the surgery until

I had finished the financial reporting quarter at work, I was in denial. Denial also played a part in not wanting to tell anyone. Now that I was back to work and acting as if nothing happened, I was still in denial. But something had happened, and every time I saw my scarred body or was reminded that I had no sensation, I was angry—stage three.

I was also at the beginning of the bargaining stage of my grief, since I was trying to ensure that this wouldn't happen to me again. So I started to mobilize. I went to a talk given by Dr. Susan Love, who had written the quintessential bible of breast cancer at the time, *Dr. Susan Love's Breast Book*, to learn more about the latest news on the disease. I wanted to know as much as possible.

I ordered the videotapes of Bill Moyers's series *Healing and the Mind* to find out more about new theories of the mind-body connection (America's version anyway). There was a segment of the program that discussed how your thoughts and emotions create chemicals that affect every cell of your body. There was also a segment about Chinese medicine and one on living in the moment. The program also discussed scientific studies that showed that breast cancer patients survived longer if they were involved in a support group. It included a segment of a live support group. Because of their common diagnosis, they could be real with one another. They didn't need to wear a mask for the world and could discuss their fears and grief in a safe environment. The last segment introduced a place called Commonweal in Bolinas, California, which was a retreat for healing when dealing with cancer. I sent away for the paperwork and applied.

A few years before this, I had read Gilda Radner's book *It's Always Something*, a candid account of her struggle with ovarian cancer and her remarkable ability to stay upbeat, which she finished writing only a month before her death. I had always been a big fan of hers, having watched her often on *Saturday Night Live*. The book also recounted her and her husband Gene Wilder's journey of being diagnosed and then joining an organization started by Dr. Harold Benjamin called the Wellness Community. This organization provided support to people dealing with cancer and the significant person providing care and support to the cancer patient.

As luck would have it, there was a branch of the Wellness Community not far from our home. Soon after watching the Moyers program, Doug and I joined the Wellness Community for a weekly immersion into the world of cancer. I was assigned to a participants' group and he to a support persons' group. We became members of the village called Cancer.

At the Wellness Community I was attending guided-imagery workshops and taking classes in tai chi and qigong. While listening to the stories and trials of people in the group on a weekly basis, I realized that most of them weren't as lucky as I was from the prognosis standpoint. Once again, I fell back on my old mantra—*What do I have to complain about?*

The group's demographics ran the gamut—all types of cancer were represented and the average age was probably late sixties. I learned so much from these people. I was so impressed with their humor, their courageous spirits, and knowledge of alternative treatments, but most important, I was inspired by their hope. I became attached to many of them and was sad and frightened when any of them died, which a couple of people did during my tenure. And it was in the group that I finally cried—the first time since the surgery—when I had to tell them my story. I was usually just a bystander and a listener, certainly not a veteran of this war. What made my story unique in my support group was that I was so young, with a toddler and a teenager.

One man in the group believed he'd cured his colon cancer by doing coffee enemas and following a special diet. Some people swore by the Gerson diet or the macrobiotic diet, or they became strict vegetarians or drank essiac tea. One person was going to an alternative medical treatment center in Mexico, against her doctor's advice. Their myriad journeys and different approaches to dealing with cancer and healing were an eye-opening education for me. I had always been tuned out to such basic lifestyle issues as healthy eating, getting plenty of sleep and rest, centering myself spiritually, and other basic survival techniques. But now my needs were reduced to exactly these, the simplest of needs.

The commonality of the group was that the individuals were just regular people from all walks of life sharing the experience of living with cancer. Some people in the group had very advanced cancer; others, like me, were supposedly cured. The group forced me to look at my prognosis, which was excellent. I still felt, however, as though I had been hit in the head with a two-by-four. It was a huge wake-up call.

In Doug's support persons' group, they had their own issues to deal with. I remember thinking that he seemed to have sympathy for some of his group's loved ones but was in his own denial about cancer hitting so close to home. I felt like he was going through the motions but still denying and keeping a distance from his deepest feelings of fear and potential loss.

After reading about the gasoline additive MTBE leaching into the water supply, I signed up for purified water delivery. Seeing the five-gallon jug in its porcelain and wooden stand gave me some comfort, even if Doug insisted that the water wasn't any better. I didn't care.

I can't imagine I was much fun to live with at this time. I was tired, stressed, depressed, mourning, and mostly sad. Family life, though, goes on. The kids would ask Doug, "What's the matter with Mom?" His regular reply was, "She's in a bad mood."

How do you get from what I had just been through and how I was feeling to being in a bad mood? Is that like a bad hair day? I felt like Doug minimized everything. Perhaps that's how he survived. I would share my heart, my soul, and deepest fears with him to either see him tuning in to the television or actually falling asleep as I was talking. I'd become just another talking head like the ones on TV.

One night, in a flaming rage of utter frustration and bleakest despair, I wanted to murder him—I actually had a chef's knife in my hand. Fortunately I took my fury out on the knife block instead of him. But I could understand the passion of murder now. After that episode I still didn't feel any better. In fact, I found I didn't like myself anymore at all.

Things hit an all-time low when he proclaimed, "I never would have married you if I thought you would be so needy."

Thanks a lot, pal! Now my anger found an object. I was furious at myself for deciding to marry him and, more important, I was furious with my husband, just because.

Winter became spring, and the grass turned green. California looked like Oz. That spring Doug and I went to Hawaii for the first time. We actually had a wonderful time—except for the suitcase-throwing fight. I loved everything about Hawaii—the warmth, the smells, the flowers, the trade winds, the language, and the music. It felt like you could see heaven watching the sunrise from the top of the volcano on Maui called Haleakala.

I fantasized about moving there and becoming a beach bum. I thought, *Why do I seem to want to be everywhere except where I am?* Nonetheless, I realized finally that life could still be good, even after breast cancer. What was amazing to me was that all this could be had with only a five-hour plane trip and a few thousand dollars. I felt so fortunate to be there. I was starting to heal.

The school year ended with a myriad of dance recitals, concerts, nursery school open houses, and whatnot. Spring turned into summer. The summer was relatively uneventful, except for the boy I caught trying to fondle Kim in the backyard pool—he was immediately picked up after a call to his father and then never seen again. Doug was traveling all over the country and never home. The nanny took the kids to the zoo, water parks, the beach, swimming lessons…. It was a full schedule.

For me there were too many follow-up doctor appointments and tests along with the associated anxiety, then relief. Except for another week off with the kids at home, I worked. I got a bonus and a raise. We skipped our weekly meetings at the Wellness Community, mostly due to exhaustion. In the fall, Kim started eighth grade and Brad another year in preschool. In October, Doug and I went to Palm Springs to rekindle our relationship yet again. That trip was a disaster. We fought all the time. We could still be so angry and needy.

When we returned home, I noticed our Mary Poppins nanny was starting to act a little strange. Some of her stories about where she and the children had been and what had happened didn't make sense. I began to have the feeling that she was lying. Things escalated until Thanksgiving weekend, when she told us in tears that the reason she hadn't returned our car was that her brother was in a horrible accident and was admitted to the trauma unit of the local hospital. When we tried to check out her story the following Monday, unsuccessfully, we confirmed that it was all lies. I confronted her, and she told lie upon lie in response. I fired her.

Subsequently, I found out she had used one of my credit cards. We reported it to the police, and the officers that were sent to the house told us that she also had two bench warrants for her arrest stemming from having previously jumped bail and failed to appear in court after a drunk-driving incident. Shortly after that, I discovered that she had been refilling my prescriptions for sedatives and sleeping pills and had forged my name repeatedly at the pharmacy. She had used all my left-over pain pills from when I had the surgery, which I thought I'd hidden pretty well. We found empty bottles of our wine and liquor under her bed. I remember thinking, *No wonder she was never frazzled!* I was especially creeped out when I found my clothes in her closet.

It's funny what you can find so easily if only you spend the time to look. I felt like such a fool. Doug and I had checked all her references before we hired her. In hindsight, we realized that her references were probably her friends. We trusted her with our children. She drove them everywhere. She had infiltrated our lives completely and rifled through our things. I was terrified of what she might still do using my identity to rack up new fraudulent bills, but we never heard from her again. Of course, Kim and Brad were actually mad at us for firing her. They really loved her.

Once again, Doug and I took turns working from home until we left for North Carolina, where my parents, brother, and Alane now lived, for a family reunion and Christmas. At the family reunion, we had professional photographs taken. We all looked so happy, young, and healthy. It was almost a year since the breast cancer, but I still wasn't myself, whatever that was.

Everyone said, "Oh, you look great!" *Great,* I thought. Doug was looking for normal. Where was Linda? Inside, I was in shock and denial, angry and sad—all at the same time. Why did no one seem to understand this? Well, I thought, at least this Christmas would be better than the last one.

Doug, not one to dwell on the past, just wanted our old life back. "Thinking and talking about all that has just happened," he would say, "only makes me feel bad—and who wants to choose to feel bad? Let's just focus on moving forward and planning the future. All I want is a normal wife, a normal family, a rewarding career, and a normal sex life."

CHAPTER 11

STILL LOOKING

JANUARY–OCTOBER 1995

W̲e started the year of 1995 as usual and hired a new nanny. She was a local college student. I was getting so sick of this. Why did we have all these problems finding good childcare? Besides, it was costing a fortune.

In any case, I tried to take it in stride. My department at work moved to a new location so I had to drive to work every day instead of using mass transit. If I didn't leave the house by 6 a.m., it took an extra hour to get there because of the traffic. Since the new nanny lived out and didn't arrive at our home until 7 a.m. Doug and I had to negotiate daily to determine who would be able to leave for work first. I usually lost the race out of the house since I didn't easily wake up after lying awake most of the night.

At the beginning of the year, I got a bonus and restricted shares of stock. Work, at least, was something in my life that was going well.

That winter, in the mornings on my drive to work I began to notice that my fingers would turn white with straight horizontal lines, then blue, and then eventually become hot and red. I thought it had something to do with holding the steering wheel. Then the pattern began happening at random times throughout the day. I went to my see my primary care doctor and found out this was symptomatic of an auto-immune disease called Raynaud's syndrome and that stress didn't help, since it contributed to the vasoconstriction, or tightening, of the smaller arteries called arterioles, the blood vessels just before the capillaries. The Raynaud's hallmark for me was the arteriole spasms and constriction of blood flow to my fingers and toes. My doctor ordered some blood tests and told me I needed to reduce stress.

Ha, ha, I thought, *How does any person live without stress?* I thought that my body was trying to tell me once again that I had better start to figure out how to do things differently. What was I supposed to change? I couldn't stop working, being a mother, being mad at the world. I was so ineffective at dealing with stress that I was causing this Raynaud's myself. I started taking cayenne pepper supplements in the morning, since I read that it would help dilate the blood vessels.

Around this same time, I read an article about stress in a magazine at work. It described the Holmes and Rahe Stress Scale. The scale had a long list of life events with associated points ranging between 10 and 100 for each event. If your score totaled 150 to 299 "life change units" per year, Holmes and Rahe predicted a 50 percent chance of illness. If your score was greater than 300 units, then you had an 80 percent chance of illness. My points were well over 150. In fact, they had been that high or higher for each of the previous twelve years. I thought, *OK, now what do you do with this information?* Well, what would an idiot do? I decided that maybe I should study for the GMAT exam and go back to school for my MBA. I was a spinning top, out of control, running from my life. Fortunately, I needed a root canal and a crown, which temporarily derailed that plan.

Up to this point, Doug and I were still going sporadically to the Wellness Community, but that was about to end. How much time can you spend on counseling? Months before, at my urging, Doug had started participating in a weekly men's therapy group that I referred to as "Executive Men with Hearts of Stone." It was facilitated by a PhD and recommended by his first therapist. I was hoping, praying, that he would learn empathy as defined by me—be a soul mate (the term du jour) and learn to really roll around in my sadness with me.

In March, I began having some problems with my reconstructed breast. A hard spot had formed on the side and it was painful, pulling. I went back to the plastic surgeon and he told me that it was not a big deal to fix. I had corrective surgery as an outpatient and bounced back to normal pretty quickly. Anesthesia was becoming the only time I was able to really rest—imagine having to be knocked out just to relax.

I thought I must be mentally ill. I decided to see the therapist who was in charge of my group at the Wellness Community. The fact that she was always asking "So tell me, how is this helping in your recovery?" really appealed to me. She had plenty of great suggestions and was helping me to deal with difficult people—just about everyone in my life, I told her. She urged me to start keeping a journal. She asked me where was a place I could go that would be healing. I knew it had to be somewhere warm and near the ocean.

The beaches in Northern California are not warm, ever. I wanted to go to Hawaii again or some other tropical island. Instead, Doug planned a family RV vacation to Yellowstone and the Grand Tetons for the following summer. That was what Doug wanted to do, and he asked, "When is it ever about what I want anymore?" I felt guilty about being so self-absorbed, and he was right, I was being selfish. He thought maybe now we could start to live again. Things were looking up. We were getting along so much better. I had hope.

I received a letter from Commonweal, the cancer retreat I had applied for, notifying me that I had been wait-listed. Our nanny gave notice at the end of her school term. She was ready to move on. We interviewed several nannies again and hired another. She was the mother of two teens. She told us that she was on a diet and ate only raw carrots and boneless, skinless chicken breast. She insisted that she was never late.

On her first day she arrived at our house thirty minutes late, carrying bags of potato chips and a box of white powdered donuts. On her third day, Kim came home from school and found Brad watching *Barney* on the television in the family room in wet underwear while the nanny snored loudly, lying on the floor behind the living room sofa. In hysterics, Kim called Doug at the office, and he immediately left work, came home, and fired the nanny. We spent the next couple of weeks alternating working from home again until we found a new nanny. I wondered when the screaming roller coaster would end. We needed a break.

We found and hired yet another nanny. Her name was Jill. She was in her early twenties, from Colorado, and was to live in our home, complete with her two cats. We had the now-standard criminal background check performed on her as well, and she did fine. The children really liked her and she came highly recommended. She was looking for a family she could work with for one or two years. And we were looking for continuity, especially since Brad was going to start kindergarten and Kim, high school in the fall. Jill was responsible, and she truly tried her hardest every day.

Early that summer I finally had a Pap test, the first one I had time for since moving to California, even though it had been on my calendar as a to-do for months. The doctor called me and told me that it was abnormal, but not alarmingly so. He wanted to take some samples of my cervix. It could be done in his office. Lyn went with me. I was not particularly concerned, but it was just one more thing. It was hardly a pleasant experience, but considering what I had been through, it also wasn't that bad. While I was waiting for the results, we celebrated my thirty-eighth birthday.

For my birthday, Doug bought me a Victorian dollhouse kit. Our own house was dark inside, dated by almost two decades, and needed a lot of work. We had already been living in it for two years but we never seemed to have any time to focus on fixing it up. I was excited about the dollhouse. I could build and create a fantasy house. It was 1:12-inch scale, something I could manage. I always loved having projects. I thought this would be something the kids and I could do together. It was a perfect gift.

That night while I was taking a shower before bed, without even trying, I found a new lump near my armpit in my other breast, the left one. I knew it was not there the day before and I would know, since I was now checking obsessively. The doctor had just done a breast exam earlier that month. I had just had a mammogram, even magnified views. I don't know how I found it. Maybe my unconscious was guiding me to find this lump. I told Doug. He felt it. We went to bed in tears. I think we both knew—*Here we go again.*

That weekend Lyn came over and I asked her to feel the lump. She did and was upset as well. I think she knew it wasn't good news. Four days after finding the lump, I had another mammogram, which of course now showed a questionable area later documented as "highly suggestive of malignancy." No surprise there. Once you put a metallic bead on a palpable lump, well what do you know? There it is on the film for all to see! Did they even look to see if they missed it when reading the last set of films?

The next day I was on a plane for a business trip to New York. I thought, *Is New York now to become a place to feel dread rather than energized?* I realized at this point that I had a new habit—holding my breath.

When I saw the surgeon the following week, I told her that if this breast also proved to have cancer that I wanted both this breast and the reconstructed breast removed. I was sick and tired of dealing with these breasts. Who would have thought that my little titties would be the cause of so many problems? While she understood my reaction to the news of my other breast possibly having cancer, she strongly urged me not to have such a radical surgery. The next day I took a scheduled stress management class at work. *Do you want to hear about stress?* I thought. *What a riot!*

Three days later, just two weeks after my birthday, one and a half years after the first mastectomy, I had a left breast lumpectomy. The pathology confirmed that I had invasive cancer this time. This was a new primary cancer, not related to the other breast. But according to the surgeon, when we met three days later, they got it all out. *Thank God.*

She told me I did not need to have another mastectomy. However, I would need chemotherapy, radiation, a lymph node dissection and biopsies, a metastatic workup, and assorted other assaults. Also, since they had such a hard time starting an IV for the lumpectomy, she recommended putting a Port-A-Cath into my arm to facilitate the chemo treatments. The good news really wasn't that good.

I spent the next few weeks trying to work while at the same time making a flood of medical appointments with specialists, each recommending their particular brand of roadside remedy. I found out that the treatment was relatively standardized, based on tumor size, grade, and the degree of metastasis. The doctors told me that after the treatments, I had somewhere around an 80 percent chance of being cancer-free for five years. This news certainly was not as optimistic as the first time around, but I still felt hopeful.

The only way to deal with the barrage of good and bad news was to take one day at a time, literally. I already knew that I was a strong—whatever it is, I can take it—type of person. I couldn't help but remember the expression "God never gives you more than you can bear." I think I first heard that from my maternal grandmother at my first husband's funeral. I remembered thinking at the time, *Why would God give you these unhappy and sad times and then give you more than you can bear?* I thought the whole expression was absolutely ridiculous. I knew I would get through this and was not yet ready to fold up my tent, but I was sad that another year of my life would be gone when this episode was over with.

I decided to heed my therapist's advice and keep a journal as best I could. I found the perfect journal. The cover art was by Mary Engelbreit, and it was aptly titled "Snap Out Of It."

AUGUST 3, 1995

I don't think I can be superwoman anymore. I'm starting to tremble. I can't think. I can't finish sentences. I feel like I'm going to throw up most of the day. Tomorrow I am not working a full day. I'm leaving at lunch.

I'm starting to feel scared. I'm tired of all this waiting. I want to know what I'm dealing with. One thing I do know, I don't have time for anything. Not enough sleep, not enough time for the children, no time for me.

My therapist told me today that my life is killing me. I've known this and have told Doug this exact same thing for the last year. What do I change? I don't know what I am doing wrong.

AUGUST 7

We celebrated Brad's 5th birthday a couple of days ago. His party was at the Jungle, which is an indoor play gym. He had a wonderful time. He's all boy—rough, tough, and tumble. Kim has her best friend from NJ here. Kim has been testy and has been getting in a lot of trouble. We haven't decided if she is showing off or acting out. In any case, we don't like it.

Tomorrow is a day at the hospital. It starts off with a visit with the radiation oncologist, followed shortly after with blood work, a radioisotope injection for the bone scan, chest X-ray, a break for lunch, and then for the signature treatment, the bone scan. What fun!

I'm really starting to get cranky. I keep dreaming about a crown on my tooth that keeps coming off and I bite it back down. (Interpretation—I'm either about to lose it like a volcanic eruption or there is an unplugging of the dike or, put simply, I'm just falling apart.)

We went to the ocean yesterday at Santa Cruz. I love the ocean. It is so peaceful and healing there for me. I love the smell, the sound of the waves, the seagulls. I have a CD of the waves. My family tells me I'm crazy.

AUGUST 8

Well, today wasn't too awful when it is put into perspective. The good news is that the bone scan was negative. The bad news was that the 2.0 cm tumor was as virulently aggressive as one could get. An SBR grade III, estrogen receptor negative, therefore, no tamoxifen. It even had hair in it.

I didn't think about work all day. It was wonderful. Doug and I went out after lunch and bought paint for the dollhouse kit he gave me for my birthday. I'm so excited. I really think this is going to be so much fun for Kim and me to do. I identified all of the parts today. Now I'm ready to sand.

What we do know from today? Radiation for 5½ weeks, daily. Supposedly that would kill any residual DCIS in the breast, which I just learned they found as well. I hate this.

AUGUST 11

My youngest sister Diane sent me a letter apologizing for her behavior when I was in NJ a month ago. She is so unhappy. She is an at-home mother of four children with maybe seven or eight years between the oldest and youngest. While I was visiting her, she was always yelling at her kids and smacked one. I told her to calm down and she told me that at least she knew what was happening to her children. She said since I had a nanny, what did I know? I feel so lucky when I look at her life. Anyway, she sent me a book *When God Doesn't Make Sense*. I don't think I want to read it. I don't feel like I'm being punished or "why is this happening to me?" like the last time. I feel like the last time prepared me for this time.

I saw the oncologist today. He is saying 6 months of chemo, which is half the treatment time I had imagined. I don't understand how I could feel so good. Do you think I'm deluded or have perhaps become immune? Am I in shock? Are all the prayers for me working?

It is definitely helping that Doug is being more supportive. I actually think we are closer since this has happened. Wow, isn't that the way it is supposed to be!

AUGUST 13

Friday night we went to San Francisco for dinner. Afterwards we went dancing. It's so great to have fun. I laughed a lot.

Yesterday I took Kim and her girlfriend to English tea at the Sheraton Palace Garden Court restaurant. I felt like we were living in *Victoria* magazine.

Overall, it was a nice weekend. Too busy as usual. I didn't get any time to read or work on the dollhouse. I called Simone today—the woman in my jazz dance class at the gym who just found out she has lymphoma. Her situation is much more serious than mine right now. I hope I was a help to her.

This afternoon a friend came over. After she left, I went shopping. That's it for tonight. We see the surgeon tomorrow and get the lowdown.

'Till then … (I'm listening to the Mills Brothers—one of my father's favorite groups.)

AUGUST 25

I really enjoyed spending time with Brad today. He is just such a joy. We went out for ice cream and registered for kindergarten. I worked on my dollhouse while he did a dinosaur connect the dots. I love him so much.

Tonight Kim and I went to the mall. She says her friend Adam makes her feel special and he helps her to feel better about things. I think I'll let them spend more time together. I really want her to be happy.

AUGUST 30

Things are calmer now. I had the lymph node surgery two days ago. The surgery went well. In other words, I woke up in pain with a drain. The news was bad. Of 16 nodes sampled, one was completely breast cancer, the rest were abnormal. I can't believe this is all happening. How did it all change so fast? What it means now is that I'll need to go on Adriamycin for 4 doses and then get CMF (cytoxan, methotrexate and 5-fluorouracil) for 8. This will happen every 3 weeks. I'll lose my hair everywhere, and I guess I'll get pretty sick.

I'm scared. What if I'm not here to see my kids grow up? I hope I can keep my job. It's hard to deal with so much loss all the time.

Lyn came over and started crying uncontrollably about me losing my hair. I didn't cry. I told her it would be all right. Who am I kidding anyway? Doug has been behaving better. When he told me that the therapist who leads the male group (now referred to by me as "the he-man women-haters club") said, "Your wife better start thinking about what she is doing to cause her cancer," I blew a gasket. I threatened that if he didn't leave that group, I was leaving him. Let's talk about the blame-the-victim game. Just what I needed when he was supposed to learn empathy. He promised he is going to get individual counseling again.

I have to go have a heart test, a Mugascan, because of the Adriamycin. It's so toxic it burns your skin. What does it do to your insides? They are going to put the port in my arm in a couple of weeks. I have decided that I am going to cut my hair very short, probably next week, because I don't want to deal with its falling out in chunks. I want to know if I am going to be OK.

When is someone going to wake me up? Am I really in hell now? Maybe I died during my first surgery and all the rest since then is hell.

I am looking and haven't yet found the courage to face this. If I need to go on disability, God only knows what we will be able to afford. I have a feeling we will find out soon enough. I think I am going to get sick pretty fast.

All we can do is pray and have the faith to believe God will see us through all of this.

SEPTEMBER 7

I have gone back to work on day 3. I am trying to limit my hours. There is so much going on there. I haven't been sleeping well. Last night I think I slept with my eye open. Today it is blood red and will not stop tearing. I will have to see how it is in the morning.

The children have started school. It is so busy around here with so much to manage. I worry about everything. I sound just like my mother, and Kim sounds like me. I am going to send her for counseling. Hopefully, it will break the worry cycle. Tomorrow I have some blood work and the heart scan to get a baseline before starting the Adriamycin, since it's so cardiotoxic—Great! My parents are coming, and I see the therapist today. Another action-packed day. I hope I sleep.

SEPTEMBER 19

The Mugascan went fine except that I had an eye infection and my eye was draining into my ear, tickling me, and I couldn't move. I started crying, thanking God when they were able to draw my blood successfully.

I had the Port-A-Cath surgery, experiencing another layer of hell. I woke up during the surgery. I couldn't move. I had an oxygen mask on. They were trying to thread the catheter into my arm and talking about how it wasn't working. I tried to shake my head back and forth to let them know that I was not asleep. Eventually, they realized I was conscious and knocked me out again. I am still having nightmares about being trapped, screaming, and no one hears, nobody cares if they do hear; either way, there is no help.

They tried both arms and wound up putting the port in the side where my lymph nodes were just removed, the side where, I was told, you should not even carry a purse on to avoid lymphedema. It is also my writing side. Both of my forearms are bruised horribly and are so swollen I look like Popeye or Bluto. I was exhausted after that day.

My parents were waiting at my house when I got home. My mother appears so helpless. She doesn't know what to do. This doesn't make me feel any better. Dad is very quiet. He doesn't know what to say. He spends his time with Brad, playing. Well, at least that keeps Brad busy.

Doug and my mother went with me for the first chemo treatment the next day. The nurses put this huge hooked needle into my swollen, bruised arm. I think some of the chemo leaked out. They call Adriamycin the red devil. They give you so many drugs. I felt strung out like a taut cord. The doctor would give me only Compazine for the possible nausea. After I got home, I felt like I was electrified. I didn't feel like eating and tried to relax in my room. Then the vomiting hit. While this was going on, I could hear my mother, who decided to clean all of my brass planters, banging and clanging from the kitchen. I asked to see Doug, who was with my parents and not me.

"Could you please ask my mother to stop all that banging?"

He asked her very nicely, but of course, she reacted, "I'm only trying to help. Nurses make the worst patients."

Thanks, Mom.

I felt a little better in the morning. My mother and I went wig shopping. It was hard, but we tried to make it fun. Should I be daring and blonde, short or long? Who am I kidding? I want my hair. I decided not to deal with this right now.

My parents have left. They said that they expected me to be more incapacitated. Sorry to disappoint you both. I was and still am cranky and nasty. I pray all the time.

Kim has started seeing a therapist. Today, the latest news was that she does not like food anymore. Why is she so unhappy? It didn't help that my mother got right in her face with that pointer finger of hers and told her that she better start being nice to her mother, because her mother was my mother's daughter and none of her problems were as important as her daughter's.

"So knock it off right now!"

Thanks again, Mom.

SEPTEMBER 21

Beginning next week we will be focusing on getting therapy, back to the Wellness Community again, individual counseling for both of us, plus Kim. My God, what have our lives become? We are such a textbook case of a family in crisis. Things just have to get better. I'm glad Doug is going. I pray it helps.

I feel like I'm already being passed over at work. I am starting to think it would actually be nice to take a break. But I know that would still be no guarantee I would slow down. I am feeling a little more energy every day, even without sleep. My left arm, armpit, and breast are still sore, especially where the port is. My next chemo is the first week of October, yeah!

Kim's therapist told me yesterday that Kim wants to know more about her father. I have a trunk full of his things that I've stored for 12 years. I probably haven't opened it in 10. I told Kim we could look in it on Sunday.

I stopped writing in my journal. Some things just had to go. I was starting to feel like a leper, cut off from the living. Time had become suspended for me. I was a real cancer patient, fighting in the trenches in the cancer war. Meanwhile, life was going on for everyone else. I was receiving many "thinking of you" cards, plants, flowers, and books. The telephone never stopped ringing; close friends and everyone in the family wanted to get the daily update. It was exhausting, and I still wasn't sleeping.

I had returned to work full time until the next chemo treatment. I began taking every kind of drug that I could think of to help me sleep at night. Nothing worked. Every time I started to fall asleep, I would startle awake because of the nightmares. I was having a recurrent nightmare where I was trapped in a cage with a raging Bengal tiger. Just when the tiger was about to kill me with its huge claws, I would wake up in terror, dripping with sweat, my heart racing. I think several weeks had passed since I last slept well.

My sister Alane sent me some books on dealing with cancer and also a book called *Embraced by the Light*, by Betty J. Eadie. I had always been an avid reader since high school and I read every night, usually ripping through at least four or five books per month. I loved to learn and understand other people's experiences. I enjoyed my monthly book club. I was a member of a private library in San Francisco and was involved in other organizations where I could go to author readings. I read biographies, fiction, nonfiction, and I was now becoming addicted to self-help books and the cancer recovery genre. I was devouring books on relaxation techniques, nutrition, and total well-being. My focus then shifted to Taoism, Buddhist thinking, Ayurvedic medicine, Chinese medicine, saints, angels, and the Bible. I probably retained 2 percent of what I read, and internalized and implemented even less.

However, I was very affected by *Embraced by the Light*. It was about what the author had learned about life on earth after a temporary death experience. The part of the book that was most intriguing was Eadie's describing how all of us exist as eternal spiritual beings and opt to spend some time on earth as humans. Before we are born, we select the types of experiences we need to have to grow spiritually, with the ultimate goal being that we become more loving. Prior to being born, as spirits, we mutually agree to share the human journey together at the same time in order to help each other achieve our goals.

The author's story was Christian-based and not too far-fetched from what I knew on some deep level already. I found the book very compelling because it helped me remember the transitory nature of my current situation. It reminded me that I was on earth for a reason and that the people in my life were there for a specific purpose as well. I was about to begin my long journey of learning perspective.

I sent my father a copy of the book, since he was extremely anxious about having a recommended second heart bypass operation. He rarely read, but he read this book. In some small way I think reading this book helped him to be less afraid. He took the leap and successfully survived the operation, which bought him several more years with his family without constant chest pains.

None of this is to say that I began sleeping peacefully or stopped feeling trepidation about my future.

I went to see my oncologist and told him that in spite of all of the sleeping medicine I had tried, which included cocktails of different combinations of pills, I was still not sleeping. I told him I wanted him to refer me to a hypnotherapist. He was reluctant to do this, especially since I was in an HMO and everything had to be approved medically. But I was not going to take no for an answer. Finally, with some reservations, he referred me to an internist who also happened to be trained in hypnosis.

I went to see this doctor twice. I felt he was an exceptional person. He had been an emergency room physician earlier in his career and had become a hypnotherapist to help himself deal with his own stress. He explained to me that, simply put, hypnotherapy was deep relaxation with guided imagery, no hocus-pocus involved.

It was surprisingly easy for me, the ultimate control freak, to relax this way. I remember everything that happened. He told me to imagine somewhere safe where I was happy. I immediately became myself as a child in my imagination. I was in a large, warm, dance studio with wood floors and filtered late afternoon sun streaming in from the windows. The studio, naturally, was in New York City. I was dancing with my favorite red Capezio dance shoes on from when I was about 4 or 5.

He told me to imagine the word *Relax*. So I did. He told me to trace each letter. My imagined *Relax* was in a beautiful script style, and I danced my tracing of all the connected letters musically in some uneducated form of ballet. I started to feel calmer and better. He told me to do this whenever I felt stressed out. It was that easy. I was open to trying it.

The second time I saw him I told him that I was doing better but that I still had tremendous anxiety about dying and leaving my family. I no longer dreamt about being trapped in the cage about to be ravaged by the tiger, but I was still frightened about my future. This time during the hypnosis, he explained to me that most people walk around with this "veil of invulnerability" and that since I had been diagnosed with bilateral breast cancer, I now knew that I was vulnerable to forces that were out of my control. He then recited the 23rd Psalm from his Bible.

"Our walk on earth is and has always been in 'the valley of the shadow of death,' but most people don't know this. People who don't realize this are living with an illusion, that veil of invulnerability."

He explained that since no one knows how or when he or she will die, control is an illusion as well. I was so thankful for this message of wisdom. The entire experience was so profound. This was a message from my loving God, and the doctor was here as an angel to tell me this. I was awestruck. I started sleeping again, with medication.

Between the second and third week after the first chemo, my hair fell out in handfuls one morning while I was taking a shower. I was filled with sorrow. All of my curly brown hair was on the floor of the shower. It looked like a dead poodle. I was home by myself when this happened. I called and left a voicemail message for Jacqui that I was not going to be in that day. She called me. I really resented her intrusion and thought that my trials were becoming fodder for interoffice gossip. It never occurred to me until many years later that she really cared about me, plain and simple.

When Doug came home from work, he helped me to shave off what hair was left on my head. We were both terribly sad, but we reminded each other that it would grow back. I didn't realize how cold your head could feel without hair. Even the pillow was cold. Doug had male pattern baldness, so now I knew what his head felt like.

I had purchased some of those stretchy terrycloth cancer caps, which were actually very comfortable. I had always been told as an adult that

I looked like Sigourney Weaver. Now, I just looked like her in *Alien 3*. How appropriate, I thought.

The loss of my hair became the outward manifestation of this disease, symbolizing to my children that Mom was sick. It was around this time that Brad, just barely 5, asked me, "Are you going to die, Mom?" I was surprised that he was thinking in these terms. I told both the children that I was doing everything I could do so that I wouldn't, but that God decides when it is time for each person to die. I told them that they could ask me any question, at any time, and that I would answer their questions as openly and honestly as I could.

I can't imagine what they might have been thinking or how scared they were. But I decided that I'd try to be as normal as possible and not ignore their fears. I explained that the drugs must have been working since they were strong enough for me to lose my hair, even if only temporarily. I think that explanation helped Brad in a concrete way. I was trying to be a good mother, but I was not sure that I was.

In October, I had chemo number two. I had to argue with my oncologist about getting a better antinausea medication—I was not going to repeat the retching of the first time. He told me that he could prescribe Zofran, but that it was very expensive, about $150 per pill at the time. "So what," I said. I was insulted that he had made assumptions and not even offered it to me the first time. As it turned out, our prescription plan paid for most of it. I was starting to realize that I didn't like this doctor. The Zofran really helped. I scheduled the remaining treatments for Fridays to minimize my downtime at work.

Doug came with me to the second treatment. I decided that I needed to have some sort of ritual around the process of chemo. So, Doug started bringing a "picnic" lunch from a great deli near the oncologist's office—my last big meal before the drugs kicked in and my appetite left for a couple of days. I also decided that I wanted some sort of memento to remember the experience, like a trophy for getting through it, no big deal. I started collecting a whimsical Mary Engelbreit teapot ornament after each treatment.

Later that month Paul, a friend from our days working in New York, came to visit us. A few years earlier Paul had been diagnosed and treated for a brain tumor and subsequent metastasis to his spine. He'd had quite a harrowing experience but was doing just fine now. He wanted to come and be with me and accompany me to my chemo. I really loved this guy. We used to have so much fun working together. We laughed all the time. He and his wife married one month before Doug and I had. We were all friends.

Paul and his wife arrived in time to accompany me to my third chemo. It was great being with a good friend who had been through all of this himself. We compared cancer stories. While I was receiving my chemo treatment, I told him how hard it was juggling marriage, the kids, my career, and being sick. He asked me if I ever thought about what I would do if I had one month left to live. What if I had only one week left to live? For the rest of the treatment time we spent coming up with Linda's Life Priorities. We finally came up with the following list (priorities are not necessarily in order):

> **Linda's Life Priorities**
> To live, to have health
> Spend time with children
> Spend time enjoying marriage
> Self-time: Baths, reading, listening to music, doing
>   nothing, time to create, playing piano
> Time with family and friends
> Grow in faith
> Find inner peace
> Have more fun
> Travel
> Independence

Well lo and behold, we immediately noticed that working was nowhere on the list. I knew this was going to be a huge personal struggle for me. I had worked very hard for my career. I was afraid to let it go, since I vowed to myself after Dave had died that I was never again going to be totally dependent on another person for my income and identity. I was also worried about the financial implications of leaving my career, even if it was only temporarily. But I knew that as long as I continued to work there was no time for my real priorities. I decided to discuss this realization with Doug after our guests had left.

When we finally talked about it, Doug was not exactly supportive. He told me that if I stopped working we would immediately have to move to a smaller home, fire the nanny, etc. I thought how all these changes, let alone all the work involved, could possibly be good for my health or my children's welfare. I felt like he valued money more than my life and me. I was starting to sound like my therapist.

Once again, I was hurt and disappointed. I decided to not rock the boat, but I was uncertain about what I should do. I discussed it with Lyn, and she suggested that we should pray that God would make it abundantly clear what it was that I should do. In hindsight I think it is interesting that I gave Doug and the universe the power to make my decisions for me. Was it because I was too beat up?

I had been told that the effects of the chemotherapy were cumulative. Soon after the third treatment, I felt I was becoming exhausted. Doug was managing everything. I went to work, came home, and collapsed. Doug came with me to the doctor and chemo appointments, went to work, came home, fixed dinner, cleaned up, gave Brad a bath, helped with homework, and then had to deal with me. He was trying his best to be supportive and juggle all the balls.

But then he raised the question again. "What about me?" He began to voice his unhappiness with the situation. He told me, knowing what he knew now, if he had it to do over again, he would never have married. In other words, in my words, he wouldn't have married *me*. I felt bad for him. He never signed up for this either. I know I was too self-absorbed to thank him enough for everything he was doing. He felt bad too, and had only me to complain to. This was not a good situation, when my life was the problem. I must have sinned a great deal.

CHAPTER 12

DEEP IN THE VALLEY

NOVEMBER 1995–FEBRUARY 1996

It was November. I was depressed as usual, hairless to the point that I had lost my eyelashes; my eyebrows were soon to follow. I would look in the mirror and could not even recognize myself anymore. I was fading away. I felt unloved by my husband even though he was doing everything he was capable of to help me—albeit like a detached servant. My sister Alane was scheduled to spend Christmas with us, but that was more than a month away. I needed connection.

The good news was that after the next treatment, the most toxic of the chemo treatments would be over. Then I would have only eight more to go. The radiation oncologist didn't want to start treatments until the Adriamycin cleared my system, since it magnifies the effects of radiation. I was scheduled to start those treatments in December.

In the middle of the month, I had the last chemo injection of the "red devil," rested over the weekend, and then flew to New York on Monday with my boss and a co-worker for an industry conference. On the plane I thought, *What more could I possibly have to despair about?* Before one dinner in New York, Jacqui and my co-worker came to my hotel room and were startled to see me without my wig on. They were actually stuttering. What I thought I saw in their eyes was *Who do you think you are kidding?* Suddenly I felt like a fool. What the hell was I doing here? I should be home taking care of myself. When we flew home at the end of the week, I was so sick and feverish that the flight attendant took pity on me, put me in a first class seat, and kept me well supplied with tea. I was delirious the whole trip.

After arriving back at home, I visited the oncologist for the fever and had some blood tests. My regular oncologist, Dr. L., was on vacation so I saw his partner, Dr. S., instead. I liked him better. He sent me for a chest X-ray and I was diagnosed with acute bronchitis/borderline pneumonia. The doctor scheduled four days of IV antibiotics, which I could do as an outpatient. Taking some sick time from work to recover, I soon started to improve.

When I went back to work, I met with my boss, who was surprisingly very receptive and generous about the idea of my spending more time working from home. Maybe it was having seen me bald. Even though I felt conflicted about continuing to work, I thought the worst was over. In the spring I would be on the other side of this. For the time being, I just needed to hang in there.

A new person joined my support group at the Wellness Community. Her name was Terry. She was younger than I was, full of hope and beaming about her recent engagement and marriage plans. Unfortunately, she had been recently diagnosed with metastasized cervical cancer, had had a hysterectomy, and was about to start chemotherapy and radiation. Weekly, we sat rapt as her journey unfolded—a botched surgery, the subsequent diagnosis of a cantaloupe-sized tumor of the pelvis, more surgeries, the side effects of her radiation, the seesaw relationship with her fiancé.

Meanwhile Barbara, who had been in my first group a couple of years before and was now the veteran in this second group, had just been told she had a significant recurrence of ovarian cancer. At this time, everyone in the group was female and no one had hair except Terry. Everyone's stories were so dramatic. I rarely talked, other than to support others. I felt as if I needed to go to this group every week just to remember that I had cancer. I had come to see chemotherapy as just something I did. I never allowed the thought that I was battling for my life to sit for more than a second in my consciousness. After all, my treatment was termed "adjuvant" therapy. Its purpose, I was told, was to "buy insurance" against the risk of recurrence.

Within a couple of months, Terry with the cantaloupe tumor lost her hair, was married, and died.

Terry's death really shook all of us in the group, including me. It felt as if the grim reaper had come for a visit and was still lurking. Most of us started expressing more fear and less optimism. Her death made cancer real, very intimate. I had never felt sick from the *cancer*. I was sore from the surgery, yes; rotten from the chemo, yes. The cancer was a lump, a bump, words on a pathology report or something discussed abstractly. It was not advanced enough in my case to cause any symptoms. The rapid escalation of my new, now dead, friend's disease forced me more than anything up to this point to face the reality of cancer—that cancer is a killer. It could kill you, duh. It could kill me. But even still, I just couldn't believe that it could be true for me. The idea was not something I could embrace. I was not surrendering. I refused to become defined by cancer. I didn't know then how lucky I was to be able to think this way.

Thanksgiving came and went. My illness was taking a toll on Kim. She retreated into the drama of high school and boyfriends, who were still mostly telephone relationships. She was always angry and nasty to us—and therefore was always grounded as punishment. We didn't know whether this was "normal" adolescent behavior or a way of dealing with my illness. One time Doug had to remove the door from her room when she wouldn't stop slamming it in a rage. We had a temporary respite from the hostility when she met with the priest at her religion class and asked if her mother could receive the Sacrament of the Sick. She and the priest made all the arrangements.

We all went to the church. The service was beautiful and we each received the sacraments. The experience felt holy and peaceful. I found out that you didn't need to be dying or taking your last breath to receive this sacrament, formerly called "extreme unction." Apparently, sometime in my life between catechism class and actually getting cancer, the rules had changed.

The service bound our family in a new and healthy way. I began to see my teenager a little differently after that. She was crying out for help and had found her faith. She joined the church choir and, of course, there she met another boyfriend. But at least she was turning to a positive place for solace. I felt hope.

On weekends, I began to focus on working on my dollhouse project. Brad spent time helping me with it, though Kim wanted no part of it. Brad and I ran the electricity for the lighting. We carefully painted ceiling reliefs, laid parquet floors, pasted and hung wallpaper. I started needlepointing a rug and began buying the furniture. Within the year the dollhouse was becoming a real haven, a peaceful refuge from my life. To my surprise, I realized that the whole house was decorated in shades of pink. I never really cared for pink; I liked red. This was all done before I was aware of the pink ribbon for breast cancer.

In early December, I met with the radiation oncologist, was tattooed with four little blue dots around my left breast, and began radiation. The radiation treatments were scheduled for 2 p.m. Monday through Friday for the next six weeks. *As horrible as it sounds,* I thought, *at least I won't have any choice but will be forced to leave work early every day.*

The first four days of radiation went off without a hitch. The fifth day I had an appointment with the oncologist, blood work, and was to start the first dose of the other chemo drug cocktail, CMF. When I met with the oncologist—my regular one, this time—even though I felt better after my recent bout of bronchitis, he told me my lungs were still congested and he wanted to schedule another X-ray. While he examined me he made conversation, telling me that he had just returned home from a trip to the Himalayas.

"Did you read or hear about the people that were killed in the avalanche?" he asked.

"I think so."

"That was the day after I was in that same area!" he exclaimed.

He just went on and on about what a pivotal experience this was for him.

He concluded, "I could have been the one that was killed in that avalanche, just one day before."

I could not believe I was hearing this. He was an oncologist, a specialist in cancer and in the sunset of his career. What did he think his patients' ordeals were all about? Didn't he connect that they were dealing with *life-threatening* illness? Was he that detached and cold hearted? I suddenly realized that, as far as I was concerned, he was clueless. I'd never really liked him to begin with, so I decided that I was going to fire him on the spot.

"Dr. L., I'm feeling uncomfortable. I think we have a personality conflict, and I want to switch to one of your partners for the remainder of my therapy."

He seemed stunned. I explained it was not a reflection of his technical skills. Quite frankly, I did not care if I hurt his feelings or what he thought. I finally laid claim to the fact that *I* was what was important, probably for the first time in my life. And *I* was more important than being perceived as being nice. Nonetheless, I was still feeling a little shook up when I went off to my radiation treatment. Within the week I made arrangements to be seen by Dr. S. for my next appointment and the foreseeable future.

The following week my breast felt tingly during the radiation treatment. The morning of the next day my breast was a little swollen, and during that day's radiation treatment I had a new sensation—my breast felt like it was frying, like an egg, burning and sizzling.

Frightened after the treatment, imagining water boiling in a microwave, I asked the radiation oncologist, "Could this have anything to do with the saline implant?" (This was my enhanced breast with the implant, still intact after the breast-sparing surgery of the lumpectomy.)

He tried to reassure me. "We have radiated hundreds of breasts with implants, and other than the possibility of an increased risk of capsular contraction, there is nothing to worry about."

By the next day, the swelling of my breast had increased dramatically. It was hot and extremely tender.

After I changed into the gown before the treatment I told the radiation oncologist, "I am very concerned that the radiation is causing this swelling and pain. *I* want to defer any more treatments until this feels better. Besides," I continued, "I have a fever of 102°."

After examining me he agreed—as if it were his idea—and told me I should see my oncologist and be evaluated for antibiotics, then reevaluate continuing radiation at the end of the week. That day I was started on another four-day course of 1 gram of IV Rocephin, an antibiotic. Since I still had a bad cough, they threw in another chest X-ray as a bonus.

By the end of the week, my breast had swelled up to what seemed like football size. I did not think the pain could get any worse, but it did. It felt like it was being torn apart by a knife. I didn't know what to do to escape it. The antibiotics didn't seem to have any effect. That Friday night, the second day of antibiotics, I couldn't stand it anymore. I was writhing. Nothing could distract me. Taking two Vicodin pills every four hours didn't help. At my insistence, Doug called the plastic surgeon that night and got his service on the phone.

When the plastic surgeon called back, Doug asked him, "Do you think this pain could possibly be caused by the implant?"

"I doubt it, but come in and see me early next week," he replied.

That night I passed out from the pain.

I awoke the next morning, Saturday, in so much pain I could have jumped out of a skyscraper just to escape it. I called my surgeon at her home. She came over to our house right away, examined me, and told me to meet her at the hospital for a needle aspiration of the breast to figure out what was going on.

When we got there, Doug and the surgeon stayed with me, each holding one of my hands, while the hospital radiologist used an ultrasound to examine my flaming breast. This was torture, hell, up close and personal. I said the Rosary silently while this was going on. They told me they saw a collection of fluid behind the implant and wanted to do a guided needle aspiration of the fluid. There was a risk that the implant could be hit, causing leakage or deflation, in which case another surgery would be needed to replace it. At this point, I didn't care. Under the guidance of ultrasound, with a steady hand and a very long needle, the radiologist collected 80 cc of cloudy yellowish fluid which was then hand delivered to the lab. They were going to test it for bacteria and do cytology tests to determine if I had a cancer recurrence.

I was deeply grateful for the personal attention of my surgeon that day. Unfortunately, she was leaving the next day for a two-week vacation for the Christmas holiday. The radiation oncologist left me to the medical oncologist. The plastic surgeon didn't think it was the implant. I didn't know how I would get through the day with no answers and no relief. I guessed *I* was in charge of my medical care. And since no one else was, I felt adrift without a paddle.

Sunday I had the fourth and final infusion of the IV antibiotic. I still had a fever of 101°, and my breast was still extremely painful, but maybe less so, and still hot, but maybe less so. The swelling was unchanged. Maybe I was just getting used to the pain, but since I didn't want to jump out of the skyscraper anymore, I thought maybe that it was getting better.

That night we were supposed to go to a holiday party near our home that was hosted by Beth, another woman I really liked from my

Wellness Community support group, who just happened to have recurrent multiple myeloma. I wanted to go for just a little while—to see my fellow group members would give me inspiration and strength. Wearing clothes hurt though, and we didn't stay long.

The next day, Monday, the pain was coming in waves, like labor pains. My chest wall and sternum hurt. I called in sick for the next few days, in advance. I was due to start two-plus weeks of vacation on Thursday, anyway, and besides that, I could barely manage to talk. That same day, I had appointments with the oncologist, radiation oncologist, and the plastic surgeon. With daily multiple doctor visits, it seemed as though my new career was being a cancer patient.

I was switched to IV vancomycin (the superantibiotic at the time) 1 gram IV for the next four days, since I was still running a fever. The radiation oncologist wanted to continue to "hold" the radiation treatments. He thought that I had radiation mastitis, an inflammation of the breast caused by radiation. The plastic surgeon, who for business reasons was now doing cash-only vanity surgeries, examined me and repeated that he didn't think it was the implant causing the problem. He thought it was possibly radiation mastitis as well, and was going to confer with an expert colleague of his at Emory University.

Tuesday I went for my antibiotic infusion at the hospital. In the hall I ran into my just-fired oncologist, who told me that the culture report had just come back. I thought he must be still following my case.

"The culture was negative except for a single colony of staph aureus, a bacteria, which I think is just a fluke," he said with a sense of satisfaction.

I was upset that it was negative for infection, which meant that it was not treatable with antibiotics. Even though he was no longer my doctor, I asked him, "What do you think could be causing this?"

He stated, "It is probably a mild case of radiation mastitis, and eventually it will go away."

I thought, *Why don't you walk around with an ice pick in your testicle until it eventually goes away, asshole!*

That night we went to see Kim in a Christmas concert at her school. I left early. I couldn't stand the pain anymore. It hurt to breathe.

The next morning, after forcing myself to go to Brad's kindergarten Christmas party, I went to my follow-up appointment with the radiation oncologist. With the new information from the culture, he started me on a twelve-day course of prednisone to reduce the inflammation. On my insistence, he ordered an MRI of the breast that day as well. The MRI showed no masses but did show fluid around the implant and swelling in all the tissue. The implant showed multiple folds, probably caused by the fluid collecting around it.

My sister Alane and my nephew Cameron were soon to arrive for Christmas. I don't know how I shopped, wrapped presents, or did anything else for Christmas. I just kept going so I would not think about the pain. Surprisingly, by Christmas day, the pain, swelling, and fever were subsiding a bit. I was a hairless animal in moderate pain on a steroid high for the holiday. This was now our second hellacious Christmas in California, since we had been in North Carolina the year before.

My sister's presence helped me to endure. She and Cameron brought some fresh air into our home. We played piano music for four hands every day, just like when we were children. Kim sang. Doug, Cameron, and Brad played with the trains under the tree. Except for the chemo cap on my head and my wincing pickle puss, the Ghost of Christmas Present would have thought it was a regular Norman Rockwell family holiday.

The year 1996 began with the end of the prednisone and the return with a vengeance of the pain and swelling in my breast, accompanied by the fever. I returned to work, sick, on January 8. That same day I was started on a tapering dose of Decadron, another corticosteroid, for the next fifteen days. Radiation mastitis, I was told, takes time to heal. All I knew was that I'd had six radiation treatments for a total of about five minutes, and one month after discontinuing the treatments, there had been no healing. This time the relief of the symptoms was not as miraculous as with the prednisone (I deemed even slight improvement miraculous). I gradually was tapered off the Decadron and while watching episodes of *Seinfeld*, would sometimes erupt into tears and sobs. The steroid high was obviously followed by a crash—like falling off a cliff.

By the Martin Luther King weekend I didn't know what to do anymore. I was getting weaker by the day. I asked Doug if he could take me to Stanford University's Medical Library, where I thought perhaps if we did some research, we could come up with some answers about what was going on. At this point, I was beginning to lose hope.

We found an article entitled "Breast Cellulitis after Conservative Surgery and Radiotherapy" in the *International Journal of Radiation Oncology*. The article discussed cellulitis (my symptoms) as a previously unreported complication of lumpectomy and radiation. The treatment was antibiotics. We thought we had discovered gold.

On the way home, I told Doug that I couldn't take this stress and suffering anymore and I needed to be by myself to sort some things out in my head. I wanted to get away from the kids, the house, and the doctors for a day or two to get some perspective. He thought I should go ahead and do what I needed to do. So, I arranged to spend two nights at the Claremont Hotel in Berkeley, beginning the next day after my appointment with my oncologist.

In the morning, while driving to the appointment, luggage and my research in tow, the oil light came on in my car. It was the last straw. Already hanging on by a thread, I experienced my first-ever anxiety attack. I felt hollowed out and had heart palpitations. Eventually, I pulled in to the closest gas station, had the attendant add oil to the car, and proceeded to the doctor's office, deep breathing, praying for strength, and trying to calm myself down.

I was at the point of not being able to bear *even one more thing*. "God, are you listening?" I repeated over and over. "No more."

I met with the oncologist, who appeared to be in a hurry, as usual. I told him that I needed a "quarterback" to get to the bottom of my deteriorating situation. I shared my findings from the Stanford library and gave him a copy of the article. He glanced at it, crossed his legs, and told me that the topic of the article wasn't the cause of my problem. He reiterated that the culture was negative. He told me to continue taking my pain pills and wrote a script to refill the prescription.

"See you Friday for chemo, I have to go. Bye-bye." I remember thinking, *I must be going insane*, as I noticed a hole in the sole of his shoe.

I left his office feverish and beaten. I cried during the entire drive to the hotel. When I arrived at my room, I cheered up a little when I saw that Doug had sent a beautiful arrangement of flowers. He knew that I was at the end of my rope. I went for a massage at the hotel's spa, forgetting that I would have to lie on my abdomen, which I couldn't do because of the hard football previously known as a breast. They massaged my feet for part of the hour.

That evening I went to the hotel restaurant by myself and was seated at a window that overlooked the San Francisco Bay. It was a beautiful evening. The jeweled lights of the commuter traffic were streaming over the Bay Bridge, red and white, looking like the flow of blood in the body—life was moving, white cells before oxygen, red after. The rest of the world was moving on. I, on the other hand, was stuck. As a seasoned warrior, I knew at that moment that I had done everything I could possibly do, repeatedly seen every doctor I could possibly see, had done my own research, and was now at the wall, out of ammunition, my resources exhausted. Again I was living the real-life nightmare of screaming for help when no one hears you. This wasn't even like my previous experience of waking up on the operating table during surgery. I was awake, walking, talking, seeing and touching people, but getting no response, no effect, no help. I thought of the homeless, the insane.

I knew at that moment that there was no way out and that I was going to die soon. It was strange, but I felt a sense of peace. At least dying would be an end to the suffering and the horrific pain. I was beyond simple exhaustion—I was very sick. I knew that my spirit, let alone my body, could not go on much longer.

That night I said to God, "OK, I give up. Thy will be done." After that, I slept and went home the next day, a day early, to be with my family.

Not knowing what else to do, and since I couldn't sit still, I went back to work. Everyone told me that I looked grayish green. Every day I continued to spike a temperature and wake up with night sweats, and everything hurt. I went for my chemo at the end of the week. When they flushed the IV line with saline, I felt it gurgle in my neck. I told the nurse about the gurgling.

"Everything is just fine. We have a great blood return."

She didn't listen, didn't care. I didn't care anymore either.

I spent the weekend in bed. I felt physically toxic. Sunday night I had an amazing dream. An angel came to me and told me to remember to see my primary care doctor, Dr. Donald. I immediately woke up. I know I hadn't previously thought of calling him. I hadn't seen him since the diagnosis. Why would I, since I was seeing all these experts?

The next morning, a little uplifted, I called and went to see Dr. Donald. He examined me and said that my breast looked bad. It was hot, swollen to the point that the skin looked like it would crack open, and it hurt even to breathe on it. The scar from the lumpectomy six months before was now so thin that it looked like a water blister. He told me that he thought I should have the implant removed immediately. He ordered blood work "stat."

My white blood cell count was over 17 on chemo! Normally, my count would be 5 or less, depending on where I was in the chemo cycle. He said this situation was unacceptable and that he would call my oncologist and find a plastic surgeon in my health care plan to remove the implant as quickly as humanly possible. He would make all the arrangements. After that, all I could do was cry with relief for the rest of the day. Finally, someone was going to do something! Thank you, God.

Later that same day Dr. Donald called and gave me the name of the surgeon who was going to contact me and arrange to see me as soon as possible—that day or the next. He never got a chance to call. The next morning I could barely walk. My legs were so sore and stiff I couldn't walk. Doug was already at work. The nanny was out dropping off the kids at school. I rolled off the bed onto the floor and lying on one side crawled like a caterpillar to the bathroom where I pulled myself up the wall to reach the telephone hanging there. I called Doug and asked him to come home right away. By noon, that same day, January 24, six weeks after I stopped the radiation treatments, I was admitted to the hospital with Doug at my side.

Things got busy very fast. I met the new plastic surgeon, who was scheduled to operate and remove the implant in just a few hours. There were many blood draws for lab tests and an IV was to be started using the Port-A-Cath, since my veins were shot. While they were trying to flush the catheter, my breast surgeon, having heard I was in the hospital, came into my room. Again I felt gurgling in my neck, and I told her this. She felt my neck while flushing the catheter with saline. Before you could blink, I was sent to X-ray, where it was confirmed that the catheter had flipped out of the superior vena cava and was now in my jugular vein. Proof again that I was not crazy.

So before the breast surgery I had to be detoured to the cardiac catheterization department and sedated with Versed, a wonderful drug. Then the radiologist threaded a catheter through my veins from my groin up to my neck and brought the Port-A-Cath tube back to its proper place.

The Versed sent me to a tropical island full of incredible colors, the scent of coconuts, and the musical sounds of steel drums. I didn't care about anything.

Shortly after the catheterization was done and too soon after the drug wore off, I was back in my room briefly waiting with Doug until the breast surgery. While we waited for the surgery, the plastic surgeon that performed my reconstruction stopped by, as well as an infectious disease doctor and yet another partner of my oncologist. I thought, *Boy, news travels fast around here.* And as usual, my boss called the room.

In the operating room, the female anesthesiologist was very kind and caring. I wondered whether she was always this way or if my condition was that bad. The implant was removed. When I awoke, I noticed an immediate relief of the pain. The fact that the underside of my breast was left open with two huge drains hanging out of it was irrelevant on the pain meter. We soon found out that indeed the breast was infected. The plastic surgeon removed the implant, along with over 150 cc (5 ounces) of pus and necrotic breast tissue. The culprit was the staph aureus they had found a colony of earlier. I wasn't out of the woods yet. I was started on Vancomycin again, twice a day for twelve days, and would have to be monitored closely.

On the first day post-op, my new regular oncologist, Dr. S., came to see me. He sat on the foot of my bed, took both of my hands, and looked me in the eye in an emotional state.

"I'm so sorry."

I can't even say what that meant to me. I felt like a human again—not a case, not a thing. Over the next day, all of my doctors (except for the radiation oncologist) came by to check in on me. I felt like Dorothy in *The Wizard of Oz* waking up in her room after the horrible tornado with the farmhands all stopping by.

A couple of days later, I was discharged with an IV, drains, and a visiting nurse, still extremely weak, but alive. I arrived home to scores of cards, flowers, and plants. Lyn had asked me if she could let people know what was going on before I was admitted. I'd been reluctant—I didn't want to be pitied. Then she said something I will never forget. "Linda, you are not allowing people to receive the blessings they would receive if you allowed them to show they care. And besides, you could use the prayers, don't you think!"

Well, I admitted, I had never thought of it that way before. And not surprisingly, it did make a difference in every way. Soon, everyone in my life who knew what was going on was praying for me and asking everyone they knew to pray for me as well. Prayer chains were started by my sister Diane's and Lyn's Bible study groups.

After the glow of salvation wore off (about one week post-op), I sat and thought about what had just happened. I was angry with all of these doctors except Dr. Donald and the new plastic surgeon. I now knew that the symptoms I'd had were not from breast cellulitis, the subject of my research, nor was it radiation mastitis, the reductive diagnosis of my medical team. It was an infection, probably contracted in the hospital during the original lumpectomy surgery. I thought it was likely that the chemotherapy and then the radiation treatments—the final blow—had knocked out my breast's local immune system, allowing the staph infection to thrive. But what did I know? I was forced to be my own doctor without any of the tools of the trade or hospital and prescription privileges.

Later that week, I had an appointment with the radiation oncologist. He told me that my most recent ordeal was going to be presented at the weekly hospital tumor board for the physicians in attendance to review what had just happened, to evaluate what they could have done differently and, most important to me, how to locally treat the remaining left breast. He told me that, unfortunately, I was the statistical one or two complications his department had encountered in the current year. That characterization rang of *thing* to me.

I went home, drafted, typed, and sent the following letter:

FEBRUARY 3, 1996

Dr. M.

Dr. S.

Dr. P.

Dear Doctors:

I understand that my case is being re-presented at the Hospital Tumor Board due to the conclusion and hopefully successful treatment of the latest complication, my infected left breast. I applaud this step since I think everyone needs to step back and reflect on what happened here. I am writing this so that an important opportunity is not missed at this tumor board.

While I'm sure you will earnestly debate what came first, the chicken or the egg—was it radiation recall from chemotherapy, radiation mastitis, the implant, etc.—what this patient thinks is important is that you step out of your respective specialties and focus on what is important: *the patient, the whole patient,* and that you need to LISTEN to the patient, treat the symptoms but *find the cause!*

This ordeal has been hellacious and required much effort and energy on my part. Since mid-December, I have been complaining of inflammation, redness, excessive tenderness, and at times severe pain, and have been febrile on and off for almost six weeks. I have asked for a team quarterback and asked you to do research to determine why this was happening. I presented my own research and even said that my breast felt like it was infected. Could you imagine anyone being more proactive? The symptoms were treated by two rounds of steroids and painkillers.

Perhaps this was appropriate given the original culture result. It is not my job to second-guess all of my hired professionals. Someone needed to *focus* and get out of the rut of "was it the implant or the radiation?" Who cares! The "bottom line" was the patient wasn't getting better.

We have a saying in business, which I'm sure you've all heard: "K. I. S. S." or "keep it simple, stupid." I think you needed to focus here on being *doctors* first, specialists second, and even though my case seemed complicated, was it? In hindsight, it really wasn't. It was a simple infection. I also think you should remember symptoms are a manifestation of a causal problem. When a problem seems too complicated, I suggest you K. I. S. S.! In my opinion, this lesson is the real opportunity of the tumor board.

At my company I require excellence in the 40 or so accounting and finance professionals that report to me. I expect no less from my health care team. In order to feel comfortable with my health care team going forward, I am *requiring* that you *listen* to me. I will also be asking for explanation and support to my satisfaction for all treatments and procedures going forward, as well as copies of everything. If any of you are not comfortable with this, you'll need to let me know immediately so that my treatment is uninterrupted.

Let's get this team moving forward to get me well. Happy debate!

Sincerely, the manager of *this* health care team,

Linda M. Zercoe

cc: Dr. Donald

I did not expect any response, but I got two. One was from Dr. Donald, whom I had copied as a courtesy. He very kindly stated that he would "be happy to be a backstop. I'm not a quarterback, but hopefully a safety." The other letter I received was from the radiation oncologist acknowledging my request for communication and explanation for procedures, from which I concluded that he obviously missed the point of my letter or wasn't going to refer to it in any other way.

I returned to my group at the Wellness Community. I had so much to talk about—the trauma of two emergency surgeries, the fear, the abandonment, the frustration of nobody listening to me, the multiple doctor failure, my dream and my spiritual rescue. The word *lawsuit* circulated the room, reminding me of the mob's reaction when Pontius Pilate asked what to do with Jesus, proclaiming in unison, "Crucify him!"

I did give the idea of a lawsuit some time to roll around my head, but all I could think of was my therapist asking "So, tell me, how will this help in your recovery?" *Besides,* I thought, *where would I find the time or energy to put together another medical team?* Also, since the treatments were almost over, I could soon move on with my life. I knew without a doubt I would have had no hesitation in suing if my oncologist had not sincerely apologized to me once the infection was confirmed. So did I forgive them, or was I just too shell shocked, beaten up, stupid? Who knows?

I believed in my heart that these doctors were all good, honest people who really tried to do their best. In some strange way, I thought of them as victims as well. They were victims of a horrible insurance system where, at that time, they would receive maybe $45 per visit including the patient's co-pay. I knew that the economics of managed care unfortunately forced them to see an excessive number of patients just to break even. How would they have had the time to focus on anyone, except on a crisis-management basis? I thought of my oncologist's shoe.

My antibiotic treatment finally concluded after about a month. The pain was gone. The drains had been removed and the opening at the bottom of my breast was healing. When Doug and I went for the follow-up appointment with the new plastic surgeon, we discovered that his wife had recently died of breast cancer.

He was unhappy that my removed implant had not been placed beneath the pectoral muscle. "Breast cancer is too risky," he said, "and implants obscure the detection of a tumor, through both radiological means and by palpation."

That was not the case with me, since fortunately I'd found the lump anyway—although now I knew exactly where he was coming from. He recommended that I have another mastectomy; he considered breasts just troublesome "sweat glands." He also said that any reconstruction would be difficult since my skin had been so damaged from the infection and the short-lived radiation. Doug and I thanked him for his help and walked out of his office looking at each other with *All righty, then!* written on our faces. Did we just hear I now needed another mastectomy?

Well, I'm sure I couldn't even fathom the thought. Doug, tearful, turned to me, looked me in the eyes and said, "Poor honey." He took my hand and told me confidently, "Don't worry. We'll get through this as well."

CHAPTER 13

THE HUMP OF A LUMP

FEBRUARY–MAY 1996

N ear the end of February, after spending more than two months in the underworld, I returned to work. My chemotherapy continued, and my hair started growing back in patches—though not enough to stop wearing a wig.

Things at work were really changing fast. I found myself completely out of the loop. My department, as well as the entire accounting/finance function of the company, was embarking on a "reengineering" project, complete with outside, objective, and very enthusiastic consultants who would be sure to come up with dramatic recommendations and changes that were guaranteed to be commensurate with their desired fees. Seeing the writing on the wall, my boss decided that she was going to fulfill a lifelong wish to live and work in France and would be leaving within the next few months. Ever faithful to me, she was recommending me for her job. I felt honored, but many mountains needed to be scaled before we would even know if that job still existed.

At the end of the month, Doug and I went to a cocktail reception hosted by his company. This was the first time any of his associates had seen me since my second cancer diagnosis. We made our way around the hotel ballroom—me, complete with wig and a smiling mask. Not one person mentioned our ordeal or my illness, or asked how I was doing. I felt like the proverbial elephant in the room.

"You look great," many of Doug's colleagues insisted. *Get real*, I thought.

What did I expect? Maybe no one cared, but more likely either seeing me just made them feel too uncomfortable or they thought if they mentioned anything I would get upset. Once again, I felt like a leper—but then I immediately told myself, *Stop feeling sorry for yourself* and *Get over it.* By now, I was used to having complete conversations with myself. I, at least, listened to me.

At the end of the month, the tumor board met to discuss my case. Interestingly, only one member of my "team" attended—the radiation oncologist. The board's recommendations were that there should be no further radiation and I should either have another mastectomy or do nothing but maintain close surveillance. The latter course was considered difficult since the breast tissue had become firm from all the damage. This was yet another blow, but I tried to bring it into perspective—at least I was alive. I was absolutely not looking forward to another surgery. This would make the eighth trip under the knife in less than three years. However, I couldn't have the surgery until after the chemo was over and my immune system had a chance to recover. Figuring that would be sometime during the summer, I decided I would worry about it then.

In early March I discovered yet another—enormous—lump, in my left armpit. This area had been swollen after the axillary node dissection and hurt, along with everything else, when I had the breast infection. But now that the swelling had subsided, there it was. I met with my breast surgeon pronto. She was very concerned, so much so that she personally escorted me to radiology, where I had an emergency ultrasound.

The ultrasound found a solid, probably malignant tumor roughly one inch in diameter by a half inch thick that had not shown up in previous mammograms and ultrasounds. Surgical evaluation was recommended, and of course my surgeon would be happy to do it. Around this same time, I was told that I had a nodule in my right lung. I was also feeling pain in my left lower rib cage. This was all getting to be too much. It was crisis all the time. I thought, *When does it end?* Then as if someone was whispering in my ear, I heard, *Shhh, it ends when you are dead.* How's that for perspective!

I refused to respond reactively to these latest developments. Of course the surgeon wanted to do surgery—that's what surgeons do. I took a few steps back and tried to look at the big picture. *OK,* I thought, *what do we know?*

1. I'd just had a huge breast infection and a bout of bronchitis/pneumonia.

2. I was distrusting of my doctors after the recent debacle.
3. I was facing another mastectomy. How many more surgeries can you have before your brain turns to a puddle of mush?

By now, my medical history was anything but normal.

I concluded that I should seek another opinion, outside of this medical group, about how to proceed.

I arranged to consult with the comprehensive breast clinics of two extremely reputable university medical centers, Stanford and University of California at San Francisco. Preparing for these visits was no easy feat. Each facility required multiple copies of films, reports, pathology slides, lab reports, and medical records. Thank God, I was trained in crisis management in my nursing career and organizational skills from business school. I kept in touch with the office and tried to stay in the loop at work via cell and pay phones at the hospitals while collecting all of this data.

Doug and I arranged to go away for the weekend to Mendocino right after my first clinic visit. The second visit would be the day after we returned. Just the fact that I was able to get these appointments so fast—both within a week of the ultrasound—spoke to the potential seriousness of the situation. Or, who knows, maybe God just made the road clear to facilitate finding out, whatever the outcome would be.

We arrived at the first visit, at Stanford Hospital, with my neat shopping bag containing the Cliff Notes of my nightmare of a life over the past two and a half years. This was a teaching hospital. In addition to the seven doctors who were professors and associate professors of medicine, several students would be reviewing my case. They all came into the examination room en masse. I felt like I had been kidnapped for a freak show at Coney Island. Topless before all, one breast reconstructed and the other shriveled and damaged, visually examined, poked, and prodded, I was a humble broken specimen. This was what my life had come to be.

Then they left, saying they would be back shortly with their recommendations. Doug and I tried to keep things light while we were waiting.

After the complete panel had reviewed my case a few of them returned to present their conclusions. First, they recommended a CT scan of my lungs to determine if I had metastatic disease (*horror*). However, their radiologist thought that the questionable nodule on the lung X-ray was possibly an "artifact," like a blood vessel (*relief*). If the lung scan was benign, then they recommended a mastectomy and lymph node biopsy immediately (*horror*). The enlarged lymph node in my armpit could be a reaction from the infection, but they did not recommend a sampling biopsy of the lump in the armpit, since it still wouldn't rule out malignancy (*horror*). They also recommended that the lump be surgically removed (*horror*). They definitely would not recommend further radiation treatment (*relief*). I was also informed that, after their review of the pathology of the breast tumor, they felt there were not clear margins, further indicating the need for a mastectomy (*horror*). And finally, if the lymph node proved to be malignant, my prognosis would not be good, since it would mean that the cancer had continued to grow despite the Adriamycin. Therefore, I would not even be a candidate for high-dose chemo and a bone marrow transplant (*horror on the magnitude of receiving a death sentence*).

In stunned silence, off we went to Mendocino. For the entire weekend, I had to look death in the face once again. Although at that point in my life contemplating my own death was not a new experience, this time it was fraught with thoughts of horrific physical pain, and then of the *me* of me disappearing and leaving my children without a mother. I grieved the most for the last.

I talked, prayed, and cried to Doug for the entire drive and most of the weekend, until I had nothing left to say. He didn't say much the whole time. He didn't dismiss my fears or offer false hope, and for once he didn't make things worse by starting a fight. He just listened intently, touched and held me. He gave me just the type of support I had always needed, and I loved him for it. This horrible time was worth it—just for that moment.

Once again, while looking out at the western horizon with the waves crashing against the rocky Mendocino coast, I said, "I give it to you, God. Thy will be done."

On Monday we met with the other breast oncology clinic at the University of California, San Francisco. This visit required contact with just one professor. Their breast tumor board also concluded that radiation was not a good option. This was coupled with another confirmation of positive margins on the tumor pathology (meaning the surgeon didn't get it all). The board recommended a mastectomy after the chemotherapy treatments were over. They also thought that the lesion on the lung was probably an artifact, and that a follow-up X-ray and subsequent CT scan, if necessary, would be helpful to rule out a tumor once and for all. They recommended that, since they thought the lymph node enlargement was probably a reaction to the infection, a core biopsy of the lump in my armpit would be a reasonable course of action.

Wow, what a difference in approaches, I thought. This recommendation was much more optimistic and less invasive. I liked this plan. Therefore, we had a plan.

MARCH 12, 1996

Well, this morning was fun, having the core biopsy done. It felt like you have a broken bone and someone was hitting it. I couldn't stop shaking and crying. I pray the results are good. I'll know tomorrow. Nothing else is scheduled yet.

I slept today. My friends at work sent me flowers again. I'm getting embarrassed now. It never seems to end. It helps to see that people care. Tomorrow is Kim's birthday. She's pretty excited. I can't believe she is 15 already.

Writing in a journal helped before. I hope I can keep it up.

MARCH 13

Great news, the lymph biopsy was negative for cancer. The tide has turned, my luck has changed. We've turned the corner. I'm so excited. I have a couple of hurdles more, but this was the biggie. I'm looking forward to getting the report—just to see NEGATIVE finally in writing!

Alane and I scheduled La Costa spa treatments for during our stay on "sister" vacation in a few weeks. So many people called. They had their family and friends praying too! It works! I'm so awed and thankful!

Kim's birthday went well. She seemed to like her cake, gifts, etc.

I spoke with my boss tonight. She told my potential new boss that I'll be back full time in a few weeks and wants us to meet next week. We'll see. I'm afraid that it is pushing things a bit. One day at a time.

MARCH 15

Well, we dodged all the bullets. Yesterday's CT scan showed atelectasis (collapse) of my lung, no tumor. It showed a spot on my liver. So then

they did an emergency ultrasound, which showed cysts—nothing
to worry about. I had the bone scan today, which on the computer
showed "hot spots" (increased blood flow) on my rib where it hurts.
The radiologist said everything looks fine. This radiologist was the
doctor who read my ultrasound and MRI and noted nothing special
when I had that bad breast infection. I don't trust him, so I'm having
my oncologist or my surgeon request that someone else look at it.

I'm going to stop all these tests when I'm through here. The more
they look, the more they find, so they do more tests, only to find out
it's nothing. What a roller coaster.

I took Brad and Kim out for dinner. Kim is so smart and has a lot of
common sense. We had a nice chat. Brad was very good.

MARCH 17

Well, things with Doug *were* going fairly well. He seemed to be there
during the crisis. Now he's started his shit again. Previously, he had
mentioned he was going to get counseling to help him be more in
tune with me. Now he's not going to do anything. This environment is
so bad for my health and the well-being of the children. I want peace,
quiet, kindness, certainty. I'm tired of trauma and turmoil.

I'm sitting in the backyard now. It is a beautiful spring day. There is
a gentle breeze, not a cloud is in the sky. I'm sure I can get the events
of the past week behind me, although I need to have a chat with my
oncologist tomorrow.

MARCH 19

Today I was at work from 10 until 4:15. I didn't get that blown-out
feeling, but my time there was very busy. The commute home was
horrid, 1 hour, 20 minutes. I'm getting worried about all that I'll need to
know and all I don't know now in my future/current job. I haven't been
focused there, and I'm not sure that I want to be. I know I'm too into
the detail and I need to learn how to manage my time better.

I had a fun time with Brad tonight. He is so attention starved. Kim is
having problems in Science. We are going to need to see her teacher.

MARCH 20

The oncologist called tonight. The bone scan was fine. Still, I am so
irritable. Doug is being antagonistic. Kim is in a bad mood. The nanny's

car is broken down and she's doing "poor me." I can't wait to get out of here next week. I feel too put upon and I'm tired. Kim got another tardy slip today, which means detention on Saturday. She doesn't think it is a big deal.

MARCH 23

I had chemo yesterday—10 down, 2 to go. They are getting harder. I feel sick for longer. It helps to stay busy, not to think about it. My stomach feels like I'm going to be sick from both ends. I feel green.

I went to a mindfulness meditation class today. I think I can do that. I took Kim and her male friend to the mall. He asked her out. They were heavy-duty sucking face in the backseat of the car on our way home.

It is such a struggle to get her to focus on her studies. She's grounded and getting an F in Science. She tries to use the easy way out but doesn't realize that she's not learning anything and will lose in the long run.

Whining and still depressed!

MARCH 30

Well, today is day five at La Costa. I arrived here an uptight, knotted, stressed-out mess and am now starting to feel myself unwind. Spending time with Alane has been very enjoyable. We get along fabulously. We've always been so close, and now, even though she has plenty of stresses of her own, she is still so supportive of me. I have been chilling out, reading an entire Terry McMillan book, appropriately entitled *Waiting to Exhale*.

I can't say I've relaxed this much on any vacation in the past couple of years. This is just what I've needed for a long time. I've had two full body massages, a neck and shoulder massage, a facial, a back facial, thermal mineral body scrub, and a pedicure. What pampering! Alane and I even took a class on mindfulness where we spent 20 minutes experiencing a raisin in our mouths as an exercise in living in the present moment. We laughed over dinner every night.

Believe it or not, I miss my family. Especially Brad. He has had chicken pox all week and is finally getting better. Doug seems to be managing.

Doug hasn't gone back to counseling. But I'm starting to figure out the pattern. When he's tired or after a trauma, he can't cope. That's when he gets mean and stupid. I'm getting better at ignoring him.

I know I'm battle fatigued and weary. I'm learning to do less and getting better at not wanting to do as much. Someone else can do it! Now, I'm on vacation! For now I need to focus on this moment. This place is really pretty, lots of birds of paradise, bougainvillea, lilies.

APRIL 3

Back home, back to work. I'm still fairly relaxed, but it's being tested. The kids are great. Kim went from an F to a B in Science. Brad is over the chicken pox and is back to school. I've been to work every day for at least six hours. Work is a zoo. My boss was offered the job in Europe. I don't know yet how this will affect me. She's made some promises but nothing is formal yet. One of my peers doesn't have a job anymore—watch him become my boss!

Doug always reminded me of the tortoise—"steady as she goes," more than occasionally hiding his head in his shell, getting clobbered, lashing out at times. He navigated the course with conviction, plodding around obstacles, seeing the goal, always taking the long view, never wavering. I was the hare, racing through life and bouncing off the walls, expending enormous amounts of energy. How did we wind up together?

Doug always knew and never asked why. I always asked why and never seemed to know. It seemed cancer was making our differences more clear.

CHAPTER 14

JOB

MAY–AUGUST 1996

U p until the breast infection I was able to envision chemotherapy as therapeutic. Through meditation I could visualize the chemicals attacking any remaining cancer cells. But now my infusion appointments seemed more like going to the gas station for a fill-up. I was ready to move on with my life. What I really needed to do was to get back and focus on my job.

My boss already had one foot out the door. As it turned out, the consultants were more annoying and numerous than ants at a picnic. I felt absolutely out of the loop and unqualified to discuss with them what was going on in my department. It was simultaneously interesting and horrifying that the people in my department appeared to be perfectly able to get by just fine without me. In truth, I had given no more than a 20 percent effort, on average, for the last few months. Now that I was back, I was just another layer of bureaucracy.

The new "decision maker" had a technology systems background and knew nothing about what we did. We went out to lunch. I wore a red power dress and a sporty chemo crew cut; he, an empty suit. At lunch, by asking questions and interpreting his cryptic responses, I learned that the plan was to roll up all the accounting, finance, and reporting functions into a "shared services" department. It would have five or six senior officers, probably reporting to this man, whom I assessed to be very political. The team of consultants was in the process of interviewing everyone in my department. My interview was scheduled for later that week.

He also told me that Jacqui had indeed recommended me for an important role, but he wasn't yet sure how all of this was going to shake out. I was now on the front line of a new battle—the battle for my job.

In the middle of May, the chemotherapy ended without much fanfare other than collecting my twelfth teapot. By the end of the month, Mr. Decider told me that I would have a key role, that I needed to think broadly, and by the way, how would I feel about having so-and-so reporting to me? I felt hopeful. The next week I shared with a colleague—who no longer had a job—that I had been told I would know what my role would be by Memorial Day. My colleague told me he would be throwing his hat in the ring for the same position I was up for. That meant that now there were five or six people, including me, in contention for just one senior officer position. I should have kept my big mouth shut.

Our nanny informed us that she was moving back home to Colorado. She missed her family and had just broken up with her boyfriend. She was going to leave at the end of June, when we were scheduled to take a family vacation to Disney World. We were all very sad. She had become part of our family and was the human glue that had held it together for the past year, all at the tender age of 24.

Deep breath, I thought, *time to find another nanny*. I asked, no begged, Doug to take the lead on finding another nanny. The poor kids would have to deal with a stranger for the summer. By now I realized that it ends when you are dead—so stay focused, positive, and just deal with it.

The stress was fierce. Every night after strategizing, executing, and campaigning in the workplace all day, I began to have increased symptoms of a feeling that had accompanied the later part of my course of chemo. When I was overly tired, which was frequently, I would feel indescribably blown away—just hollowed out in my gut. Now this feeling became so intense, it felt as though I was not just emptied out but that my life force, or chi, was pouring out of my center into a puddle on the floor. I didn't know what was going on.

In early June, I was informed that I wouldn't be told what my role would be until after the new organization was formed. I knew from this that things did not bode well for me. If I was a significant player, I would be on the inside, helping to form the organization. By the middle of the month, Mr. Decider informed me that my colleague had indeed thrown his hat in the ring. It wasn't hard to figure out what was going on; I knew that my colleague had almost certainly got the job. The following week I was officially informed that my position was going to be eliminated and that I didn't get the senior role in the new organization.

Hearing this was the final straw. After two breast cancers, two real or imagined near death experiences, numerous bouts of physical torture, loss, and impending loss, I became hysterical, sobbing in my glass-walled office for the entire world to see—broken.

Days later, my new boss (his name began with *D* so I'll just refer to him as Dick) offered me a consolation prize—any of several other positions in the new organization in areas that didn't interest me, were not senior roles, and might or might not be a demotion. Even though I previously had some regard for Dick, I had to wonder how he'd gotten the job. I didn't think he'd even gone to college (neither had Mr. Decider), and he certainly didn't have a CPA designation. I surmised it was the usual "old boy network," although I had to admit that my having been MIA at various points over the past year could have been a factor. I hadn't been able to contribute much to the organization, and maybe my health history made me seem like a risk. In any case, there was no job posting, no formal interviews, just a few casual conversations with Mr. Decider, and absolutely no discussion around the decision points—absolutely no whys or wherefores. What happened to the published human resources policies?

Even though nothing had yet changed in my responsibilities, I met with Dick regularly to get a sense of the logistics of the transition, if for no other reason but to update my staff—to little effect, since he didn't have a plan. At one meeting we discussed that his wife's position had been eliminated at this same company many years earlier, and that she had subsequently changed careers and was doing just fine now. (*And how is this relevant?* I thought.) Then he told me that his mother had had breast cancer and was a survivor, so he understood how difficult it could be to deal with. I remember thinking, *Does he mean as a patient, and your point is?*

In any case, I considered the discussion—while probably well intentioned—inappropriate under the circumstances. I was personally and professionally offended by his condescension.

Before we left for Florida in June, I initiated the process of negotiating an exit package. I was scheduled for the second mastectomy in the middle of July. I couldn't imagine returning to work between my vacation and the surgery, to my all-too-public glass office or whatever smaller space that would replace it. Besides, the thought of reporting to this person was absurd.

We left for vacation with nothing settled. We returned from vacation and still nothing was settled. I used up my paid time off in the days before my surgery thinking, *Here I am relying on this unqualified person to execute the necessary conversations and paperwork on my behalf.* I was determined to leave this job and wanted the best severance package I could get without quitting outright and thereby getting nothing. Suddenly it dawned on me, hadn't I prayed that God would make it abundantly clear whether or not I should continue work? Now, lo and behold, here I was in a situation where my position was eliminated and all options presented to me were intolerable. But, even though this was exactly what I'd asked for, I was angry about how things happened. I felt cheated and believed that the process used to decide who would get the job wasn't objective; therefore, this was a case of flagrant discrimination.

I wasn't sure but perhaps this new sense of purpose and focused anger helped me to face what I had been dreading, the mastectomy. Once again, I was laid on the gurney and wheeled into the operating room, this time to lose my second breast. There would be no reconstruction. I was in the hospital for just a couple of days. Physically, I recovered quickly, but mentally and emotionally, I was not well at all.

My parents came out again to help us. They needed to feel like they were doing something; staying home in North Carolina was not an option. My mother spent the entire time sewing draperies for our living room and dining room, a project she enjoyed and that helped her feel productive. I appreciated my parents' desire to help, but I realized immediately that my mother couldn't handle the visible loss of my breast. She wouldn't talk about it; she couldn't even ask me how I felt. My father was even worse. He wandered around aimlessly, not knowing what to do, or just slept to escape.

By this time in my life, I understood that they loved me the only way they knew how. During this visit, I started to view them differently, as older and weaker. I was able to forgive them for the disappointments

I had felt in the past and love them for who they were—my parents, flawed, human, and incapable of openly dealing with the mutilated horror that was their perfect baby daughter.

It took a while to get used to the new "me" with the amputated breast. Doug tried hard to be loving and supportive. My insurance covered a breast prosthesis, a breast-shaped silicone blob that I could wear in a special bra, but I needed to go to a medical supply warehouse in an industrial complex to be fitted and covered under my plan—a cold and impersonal scenario. I decided instead to go to a store that specialized in these matters, unhindered by the cost. I was lucky to have such an option.

It was astounding to me that the owners of this store, a mother-daughter team, were among thousands of entrepreneurs that owned businesses providing only this service. I felt far from alone when I saw the quantity of options and sizes, bras and bathing suits. These proprietors took a hard and ugly situation and turned it into something warm and bearable. For the first time, I also realized the epidemic of breast cancer was more than a statistic but an *industry* supporting an entire economy of clothing and prosthesis manufacturers, storefronts and catalogs, not to mention the pharmaceutical manufacturers, doctors, hospitals, and therapists whose entire livelihood was derived from this disease. It was a sobering thought.

Doug hired another nanny, but she was really more just a housekeeper to help us for at least the summer. Although she was nice, she could only deal with one or two items on a to-do list without winding up in tears before the end of the day. She didn't last.

In August, I finally received my severance package. Now I finally had the time to think about myself.

That summer was a complete blur of heat and haziness. Somehow, I got through the days, but along the way, the feeling of being physically emptied out increased to the point that there were times that I just couldn't breathe. I was given medication for anxiety, Ativan, which I had to take around the clock to relieve the symptoms. Since the medication seemed to help, I figured I now had an anxiety disorder. Although I was never officially diagnosed, I believe I had a nervous breakdown. When I started to think about my life, I just couldn't bear it. I became a walking, talking zombie.

At some point our friend Janet came to visit from New York for a couple of weeks. Nancy also came. Both of them, as well as other people who called or stopped by, casually offered the same comment—"Your life reminds me of the Book of Job."

"Great," I responded.

I felt like I must have done something horrible, or that I *was* so horrible, that I must have deserved to have all this loss and suffering in my life. I constantly questioned what I was doing wrong, what the message was that I wasn't getting—how many times did I need to be hit with a scud missile to get it? I didn't believe that this was all just random bad luck. Maybe I just needed to search deeply to give meaning to all that had just happened just to avoid hurling myself off a cliff.

In the Book of Job, Job loses his family, his wealth, and his land and is left in an instant with nothing except his faith. His cynical wife survives, and chides him for not cursing God. But he continues to be held by God as a righteous man, even though all these things had been taken from him.

Job says, "We accept good things from God; and should we not accept evil?"

When he is then covered in boils, his friends come to sit with him and give him comfort. In front of his friends, Job laments and curses the day he was born, but the Bible says, he "never sinned against God with his lips." Eventually "even his friends were convinced that Job had brought this suffering upon himself through wicked deeds or sin." They urge him to repent to end his suffering. For Job, the greatest trial is not the pain or the loss; it is not being able to understand why God allows him to suffer.

Well, I certainly couldn't say that I was focused on God like Job, but I believed I did have a strong faith. I also believed that, while I was far from perfect, I didn't deserve this. But I had to wonder why all this was happening to me. What meaning was I to derive from the events of my life to date? God wasn't answering. It was all too much for me to deal with, so, I concluded, maybe it wasn't just about me.

At this point, Doug and I were not getting along well—again. I began to blame Doug and our relationship for everything. The emotional pain, feeling unloved, and the despair of abandonment that I now believed created the cycle of illness for me. Cancer was not something tangible to blame. My rage multiplied to borderline insanity and was appeased only by my overwrought outbursts, frequent lamenting, and ranting of "he this" and "he that" in whatever venues were available to me—usually to close friends over lunch or on the telephone. My ego couldn't imagine that I was anything but the victim here, and as usual Doug was at fault.

What I didn't know at the time was that the chemotherapy had done a real number on my ovaries. I hadn't stopped ovulating from the chemotherapy, as I'd been told would happen, so I didn't think about it. But I had been hurled into severe hormonal upheaval—peri-menopause in the extreme. In an earlier period of history my irrational, mercurial behavior would have gotten me locked up in a wing of the house or an institution, or even burned at the stake for witchery. Fortunately, Doug saw it as just another difficult period in our turbulent marriage, a period that he had referred to as a "bad patch."

Now I was the one who became Dr. Jekyll and Ms. Hyde. Doug didn't know who I'd be when he got home, how I would react to anything he said, or why I would fly off the handle at just about everything. When he was home, he tiptoed around land mines with bombs and bullets flying around his head. Somehow though, he knew that it wasn't always going to be like this. He offered his arms for comfort, sex for closeness, was open to do anything to help. He was met with a head spinning 360 degrees, vomiting pea soup.

CHAPTER 15

WHO AM I?

SEPTEMBER–DECEMBER 1996

In September, Brad began first grade, and Kim, her sophomore year of high school. Kim was learning to drive. How did that happen? Over time my panic attacks became less frequent. I still was not feeling great mentally or emotionally, but I felt I could hang on until we went to Kauai for our planned vacation later that month, where I knew that I would be in an environment that I would find peaceful and healing. We hired a cleaning service and let the nanny/housekeeper go.

Now that I was over the shock of not having a job, I felt decidedly discriminated against in the way things went down at the end of my employment. I met with an attorney, who said that this could be a case of discrimination based on a "known medical condition." He described the many steps that were involved and explained that we would be fighting my former employer's legal department as well as their outside counsel, basically making me David against BofA's Goliath. He mentioned the American Civil Liberties Union and an Americans with Disabilities group that might help in this matter on my behalf.

After giving the situation some time to roll around in my head, I decided not to proceed. The first reason was that this was not how I wanted to spend my precious time. Second, I thought the stress would be unhealthy. And finally I thought that since, businesswise, San Francisco is a small town, a lawsuit might affect Doug's and my future careers. Still, although the stress probably would have killed me, I also thought it might have been a healthy way to deal with all the rage. What *do* you do with all the rage?

Meanwhile, I became a full-time mother, complete with a master schedule filled with child-oriented activities. The scale was tipping into the male domain of Cub Scouts, karate classes, boys coming and going, classmate parties, boys' gifts to buy. Kim's activities, in addition to everything that she had been doing before, also now included evening drama classes, PSAT prep, and study skills classes. Also, since I didn't believe that teens should "hang out" at the mall or in town, since it could lead to nothing but trouble, I insisted that Kim start a part-time job at the local senior center for a couple of hours a day after school. An added bonus of all this activity was that Kim had plenty of opportunities to practice driving us around on her learner's permit.

I soon found out why my mother would hit the imaginary brakes and hang on white-knuckled to the door of the car while cursing under her breath when I was learning to drive. I'd always wanted to blindfold or strangle her. Now I knew firsthand what it was like to be perpetually trapped on Mr. Toad's Wild Ride. I wondered, *And how is this good for my health?* How did other parents do it? I found screaming at the top of my lungs helped—slightly.

Doug and I called a truce and went to Kauai using frequent flyer miles and hotel points. As I had anticipated, it was wonderful. This was a new island for us, much more quiet and peaceful than Maui. We had a chance to talk about a lot of things. We decided I could plan to take Kim to Europe for her upcoming sixteenth and my fortieth birthdays the following summer, and I would ask Nancy if she wanted to join us. We also discovered that I had feeling again on the left side of my chest around the mastectomy scar. It didn't look pretty but this was certainly an unexpected surprise, and a gift. Who knew ribs could be a turn-on?

After our vacation, I quickly discovered I was now a member of an entirely new community. We lived in an area that was relatively affluent. Many of the wives I knew had the privilege of staying at home and raising the children, while many of the husbands were executives that traveled quite a bit or worked long hours. All of these women were very intelligent and had lives that were filled with their own activities when they weren't focused on their children. It seemed as though everyone played tennis, was a member of a country club or some civic organization. Even though I already knew many of them from my book group and various neighborhood activities, I had no idea where I would fit in.

When I wasn't maintaining the house, I was doing laundry, shopping for food, paying bills, picking up after the children, or driving them somewhere. For many years, our nannies had done much of this, so it was new to me. But it didn't take me long to realize that it wasn't any fun. I worked from morning until night and *still* had no time for myself. I wasn't paid, in either money or thanks. The job was boring, not intellectually challenging. I had little time to shop, and I felt guilty about spending money now anyway.

For so many years, my work had helped to give my life meaning. It was a huge part of my identity. In working, I felt valued and challenged, and was socially engaged. As the autumn matured in all its Bay Area brownness, I began to get more involved in my children's schoolwork and activities. It wasn't long before they realized that their type A personality mother wasn't any fun and began asking me when I was going back to work. *If only it was that easy,* I thought.

My exit package from my former job included career counseling. So I made an appointment to see what it was all about. After a barrage of personality and interests tests, I learned who I was—at least on paper. The tests showed I was a leader, intuitive, sensing, introverted. Introverted? I had just been through years of being out on stormy seas, fighting for my life, and I knew I certainly wasn't an introvert. I assessed that the tests were picking up on my current tendency toward reflection and perhaps the chronic depression from sorrow and grief. I decided to scrub the entire process and revisit it in the spring, thinking that maybe with time to heal, mentally at least, I wouldn't be depressed or introverted—blue on paper. I concluded that the career counselor's summary and the accompanying color-coded pie and bar charts weren't really who I was—at least not by nature.

When I had a few spare minutes, I continued working on my dollhouse. I started making dates to have lunch with some friends that I enjoyed spending time with, thinking I should take the time to get to know them better. Before you knew it, my calendar was filling up. I volunteered to help teach reading in Brad's class, since I had never really done this before. I became a class field trip coordinator and chaperone. I volunteered to work in the school library.

Even though I was busy with outside activities, I was still spending more time inside my house than ever before—at least conscious time. I hadn't been there that much since we moved in other than recovering from one thing or another or just sleeping. I decided I really liked the house, even though it needed work. I liked lighting the fireplace—we had never thought of lighting it before. My house was becoming home, *my home,* after living there more than three years.

Since the cancer, I had a regular schedule of follow-up doctor's appointments. By October, I was down to a quarterly schedule of tests, visits, and more frequent Port-A-Cath flushes. I still wasn't sleeping well, continuously having symptoms of a bladder infection, or "bladder irritability" as they called it, and still extremely agitated emotionally. Every time they did a urine culture, it came back negative for infection. I didn't know if I was suffering from the aftereffects of the breast cancer ordeal (post-traumatic stress syndrome), my new identity crisis, hormone fluctuations, or what.

My oncologist's office group had a PhD who was a therapist. I met with him. He suggested, after listening to my litany of symptoms and complaints, that I *was* depressed and I should see a psychiatrist, who would be able to prescribe antidepressants. The psychiatrist was handy with the prescription pad and prescribed an antidepressant and something to help me sleep at night. I needed a pill to get through the day and a pill at night to counteract the day pill so I could sleep through the night.

I kept thinking of the lyrics of the Jefferson Airplane song "White Rabbit":

> One pill makes you larger
> And one pill makes you small
> And the ones that mother gives you
> Don't do anything at all

The fact that this was what my life had come to made me even more depressed. I began to think about how much of my depression was situational, hormonal, chemical. Was there a difference? Could a pill fix all of these things? I doubted it. I thought, *Why wouldn't I be depressed? Wouldn't anybody be under the circumstances?* I decided to just keep busy and to spend as much time as possible staying involved with people. I became a member of the "ladies who lunch" crowd.

I was fortunate. I had many friends to spend time with, time that I really enjoyed. Now that I had more time to spend with her, my friend

Clara was fast becoming another soul sister, in addition to Nancy, Lyn and my sister Alane.

Clara and I had met a few years before when her daughter Diana and Kim became close friends in middle school. Clara was a native New Yorker, a true Manhattanite, down to her fondness for black attire, serious glasses, and comfortable shoes. She'd moved to California with her husband and two daughters within a month of when we did. She was a retired history teacher, a prolific reader, and a consummate volunteer with a strong interest in politics. She was such the opposite of me in many ways. She was hot when I was cold. She was very touchy-feely, a comforting shoulder, a raft in the storm. I was a whirling dervish. She kept the home fires burning. She was a thrower; I was a saver. She was practical, a planner. I was a scatterer of birdshot.

I also had my other friends from around the country to talk with on the telephone, and of course, my family. Instead of feeling sorry for myself, I tried to focus with gratitude for all the blessings I had in my life. I made lists every day of the ten things that I had to be thankful for. Each new day I tried to come up with ten different things. Within a week it really worked to shift my mind out of the continual funk.

I decided to host a thank-you luncheon in the form of an English high tea for the people who'd helped my family during my illnesses. I researched the brewing of tea, bought books on the tradition of formal afternoon tea, planned a menu, baked breads, and made everything from scratch. I filled the house with fresh flowers, made calligraphic place cards, and had sugar cubes with flowers on them. I called Clara to come early when my aggressive menu of tea sandwiches wasn't coming together fast enough. Cheerfully, she threw herself into the assigned tasks while soothing me with a humorous story.

The tea was so much fun. Alice, the March Hare, and the Dormouse weren't there, but the Mad Hatter might have been. I was learning that having a purpose or project was positive for me mentally, and it limited the time I could spend brooding.

My father instilled in me a deep appreciation for music. I knew music could evoke feelings of happiness, sadness, joy, or tears. Singing was a release, and dancing was a euphoric. I believed that music was the poetry and dance of the soul and one of the most divine gifts for humanity.

Listening to music always helped to make me feel better, so I made it a point to remember to spend my days at home listening to the music that made me feel good. Music also helped lift my spirits out of my funk.

I went about my busyness with a Walkman strapped around my waist, listening to music, even when my family was home. It was an effective tool for avoiding family skirmishes. I would put the Walkman on, but not turn it on, just so I'd appear engaged. It trained me to allow others to work things out for themselves. I started learning how to check out and think about myself just a little. I now understood the attraction of my father's music room and his weekend headphones escape.

By November, my bladder symptoms had still not abated. I felt the same pressure I had when I was pregnant, but I knew that wasn't possible since Doug's vasectomy. I had a pelvic ultrasound and was told by my gynecologist that there was a large fibroid on my uterus about the size of a small lemon, equivalent to a sixteen-week pregnancy, once again confirming that I really wasn't crazy. Even though he assured me that fibroids were usually benign, all I could think was, *Another growth—and since when did normal apply to me?* He recommended a myomectomy, a surgery to remove just the fibroid. He didn't think I should have a hysterectomy; I didn't need to lose any more body parts.

I decided to get it over with and behind me as soon as possible. I was scheduled to go in in early December, three years almost to the day since finding the first lump. This would be my ninth surgery since then. I started getting worried about what was wrong with my body. Why was I continuing to grow all these tumors?

I went to the hospital for the pre-op consultation, which included signing a consent form. Reading the consent, I was appalled to find out that the surgery of removing a "normal" fibroid could possibly include a hysterectomy, removal of the bladder, ovaries, rectum, and colon. I was upset. I told the nurse that I wasn't signing the consent since my doctor had not discussed these possibilities with me and I would need to talk with him personally before I would sign.

Shortly after I got home, the doctor's office called me to say that the surgery was cancelled since I wouldn't sign the consent.

"I'm still planning to have the surgery but I can't sign a form noting 'informed consent' if the doctor hadn't discussed any of these possibilities or scenarios with me. Please have the doctor call me this evening to discuss these things."

"OK, but your surgery has already been removed from tomorrow's schedule."

What a nightmare. I had been treated badly before, but this was insane. I wasn't being difficult—the doctor hadn't done his job. Having a history of the unlikely happening, I wanted to be sure that I wouldn't wake up the next day to more than I could bear. I wasn't prepared to lose all of my pelvic organs to cancer.

I called Clara and told her what was going on. She tried to assure me that this was probably just a misunderstanding and that everything would work out just fine.

I explained, "The situation is already tainted. How am I supposed to trust this doctor during the surgery if he failed in his duty to discuss with me the contents of his 'informed consent'?"

"Maybe it was just an oversight."

Why wasn't *I* able to be reasonable? I was a mess. I thanked her and told her I would call when I knew anything. Meanwhile, all my childcare arrangements were on hold until this doctor called.

Finally, about 7:30 p.m., he called and *he* was angry. I explained that he never discussed these possible scenarios with me and I needed not only for him to explain the likelihood of these things happening but that I wanted to have a say in how many body parts could be removed.

"This is a boilerplate consent for uterine surgery, and I can't proceed unless I have your permission to save your life if you start to hemorrhage," he explained.

He assured me that he didn't foresee any of these things happening. What he didn't know was that my friend Terry at the Wellness Community had died from misdiagnosed metastasized cervical cancer, and this was all I could think about since I read the "boilerplate." We agreed that he would see me in the pre-op before the surgery to go over the consent form.

My decline of confidence would never have occurred if he'd done his job right in the first place. I'm sure he thought I was crazy. Nonetheless, I decided to proceed, knowing full well that he would soon be removed from my list of doctors. At this point, I thought one mechanic was just as good as the next. I decided that, for me, it took more than surgical ability or specialized training to be worthy of my team. While I appreciated the skill involved, too many times it was evident to me that there needed to be substantial training on how to connect with the person known as "the patient." Unfortunately, so far in the journey, doctors who could connect were exceptions, not the standard.

In the morning, signing the consent went off without a hitch, while the gynecologist stood by my side answering all of my questions. I was wheeled to the OR and woke up with a catheter (not explained previously) and a new incision (crooked). No hysterectomy. I was discharged the next day. I recovered very quickly, amazingly so. And my bladder symptoms, with the associated feeling of fullness and pseudo-pregnancy were gone.

At the post-op appointment, I learned that they had found two fibroids. The smaller one was just a fibroid, a benign tumor, not uncommon, but an anomaly nonetheless. The large one was abnormal. The doctor also informed me that the pathology on the larger mass had already been sent to Stanford for a second opinion. The upshot was they all concluded that this fibroid was a "symplastic leiomyoma."

"What exactly does that mean?" I asked.

"It's a rare case of a fibroid gone bad but not enough to be considered a sarcoma, uterine cancer." Since this had been completely removed, the treatment was over and the chances of it recurring were rare. Again I heard *rare*. What the heck was going on here? Why was my body growing so many different tumors—cancerous, benign, not quite cancer, pre-cancer, rare?

I decided to put all of this out of my mind and focus on creating the most special and happiest family Christmas we would celebrate in a long time. I thought that once again it was time to count my blessings. After all, I was still kicking and not in the throes of pain, doom, or despair for the first time in four Christmases. I baked breakfast breads, made candy and cookies, went full bore on the Christmas decorating, and listened to holiday music all day long. I handed out specially wrapped homemade cheer to friends and neighbors, even sending out holiday cards with the first (and only) annual family newsletter. And the cash registers were ringing.

Brimming with the spirit of Christmas cheer, I thought, *I like being home.* Was it a case of "There's No Place like Home for the Holidays"?

No, it wasn't. It dawned on me—I liked really knowing what was going on in my daughter's life. When I kissed Brad at bedtime, I realized that just yesterday Kim was this small. Where had the time gone? I was happy and grateful (most of the time) to be spending this time with them. I enjoyed being involved in the classroom and their activities. Maybe it would be OK to just stay home and be a mother, just a mother. Why shouldn't they benefit from the best of me instead of only seeing me when I was exhausted from working all day?

But the elves were very busy buzzing in my ears that holiday. *Wait, what about your career, your dreams, your goals, money? No, what about time for yourself, time to be the kind of mother you want to be, to be there when the kids come home to ask each of them, "How was your day, darling?" Why can't you just* be? *Why do you have to* be *anything? Why can't you just* be *happy with who you are—right here, right now?*

That last one was a concept that I had no way to understand in the context of the life I had led thus far, but somehow these thoughts still entered my mind.

Doug was very happy this holiday. He settled into his role as sole provider, coming home to his castle, the smell of bread baking, children caroling (on the stereo at least), traditional life circa *Donna Reed,* and a happy wife (relatively speaking), apron not included.

CHAPTER 16

ENSNARED AND EMBROILED

JANUARY–OCTOBER 1997

JANUARY 2, 1997

At the moment, there is no crisis. I'm feeling pretty good, happy even! I went back to the gym today. I can finally relax and focus on what makes me happy, focusing on my health and the kids. I'm still go, go, go. On the road a lot.

MARCH 26

I now go to a Bible study once a week on Wednesdays. I am learning so much, and it is helping me to be increasingly peaceful. The women there are wonderful. So far, we've studied St. Paul's 1 Corinthians and are now on 2 Corinthians.

I went with Lyn to the local hospital last week where we committed to volunteering in a federally sponsored breast cancer early detection program for the underserved community. I'm very excited about getting involved. It's a weird feeling returning to the hospital as a worker again and not a patient. I thought this would be a good place to start my involvement with the other side of breast cancer.

Things are going well with Doug. We seem to be getting along so much better. He thinks he is right on track to make partner in two months. He bought his boat, a little 14-footer, and just got a truck—he's in kid heaven.

Kim seems to be doing better emotionally since she started seeing the therapist; her headaches have seemed to diminish. She is much less irritable. She appears better able to manage her course work since I've limited her telephone time. She auditioned and made the concert choir this week. I don't think I've seen her this happy in months. It was very positive for her. She was one of 12 out of a class of 30-something students that auditioned. So, needless to say, now she sings all the time. I'm very happy for her.

Brad has been a bit sassy lately. I guess that is what you get with a teenager in the house influencing his behavior. I just have to keep him channeled positively.

Today I finally saw Dr. Donald (my angel) for my horrible allergies. It's great to have a normal medical problem. Also, I have decided to explore the feasibility of reconstructing my left breast. Hopefully they can do it before the summer. The prosthesis is so hot and sweaty.

APRIL 2

Where is the time going? It just zips by. I looked in the mirror today, and I'm getting old. It's so weird, I still feel 20 mentally, but I don't know physically (I'm pretty out of shape). I'm told that I look great for my age, but I think I look old and weary. I'm going to be 40 this year. I was 16/17 when my mom was 40. Wasn't that just yesterday? Now she's 64. If my next 24 years go by this fast, it really makes you feel like we are only here for an instant. You have to wonder why we are even here at all.

The kids are off this week. Kim is attending a lifeguard training class all week. We have our nephew visiting. Today was a great day. I had to drop off and pick up only Kim. Other than that I was home with the boys, stenciling, refereeing, doing laundry, etc.

My allergies seem better on the new medicine, and now I have an appointment with a plastic surgeon to explore breast reconstruction.

We had a wonderful Easter visiting with family. Brad is getting so big. Sometimes he is so playful and funny. Other times he can be such a wise guy. I need to pay more attention to him and play with him more.

One morning, I received a telephone call from the guidance counselor from the high school.

"Good morning, Mrs. Zercoe. I won't take but a moment of your time. I'd like to know if you wrote the note that I have in my possession excusing your daughter Kimberly from school for the afternoon."

Stunned, I asked, "Could you read me the note?"

"Sure Mrs. Zercoe, but I have to tell you that I have an entire folder of notes like these in Kimberly's folder."

I thanked her for the information. I wasn't an angel as a teenager. But by high school I'd settled down. When Kim got home that afternoon she made some excuses and was grounded again, this time for forging my signature and skipping school. She told me that it seemed as though she was always caught anytime she crossed over the line.

"So stop crossing the line," I said.

The remainder of the school year was a whirlwind of activities. A local plastic surgeon was not very optimistic regarding possible reconstruction of my left breast. He told me that the skin was extremely thin in the mastectomy area so he didn't think a saline implant was a good option. He thought he could possibly do a type of reconstruction called a latissimus dorsi flap, named for the muscle from the side of the back, which is detached and then folded over to the front of the body to rebuild a breast. But before that procedure, he would first need to surgically place and then gradually stretch the muscle with an expander implant. This type of reconstruction would also probably require skin grafts from other parts of my body, like my thighs, after I had grown a temporary boob on my back.

I was very discouraged since it was not an appealing procedure. I was concerned it could leave me weaker on the left side of my body, and I was left handed. I also thought of the Scarecrow in *The Wizard of Oz* when he told how the witch had taken this part of his body and threw it over there and then took that part and threw it over here. How much could you rearrange someone's anatomy?

On June 1 Doug finally made partner. We celebrated in style at the local Chinese restaurant. The spouses were invited to the new partners meeting in New York the following month. In the middle of the month Kim and I went to see *Madame Butterfly* in San Francisco. I started crying from the moment the first act opened, and escalated to outright sobs by the end of the last act.

Yes, it was a sad story, but what I realized was that the Colorado River's white water of my emotions was being dammed up by all my damned running around. I wasn't allowing myself to think about anything that day or any other day. Instead, I would always say to myself, à la Scarlett O'Hara, "I can't think about that right now. If I do, I'll go crazy. I'll think about that tomorrow."

This expression, or one very much like it—*If I think about it today, I will surely die*—had served me well for many years and helped me survive. But the incident at the opera was yet another clue of the approaching emotional tsunami I had thus far managed to keep in check.

July was an exciting month. Doug and I went to New York for his "induction ceremony." We stayed at the Plaza Hotel by Central Park. The wine was flowing. We had plenty of schmoozing, a trip around the island of Manhattan on a boat, complete with an artist doing caricatures of the passengers. Every night, at the end of the day's festivities, there was a gift from the partnership awaiting us in our hotel room. The gifts included flowers, a silver Tiffany picture frame, a basket of fruit, chocolates—so lovely. The formal black-tie signing ceremony came complete with a silver pen, photos, dinner—and the news that, in the case of divorce, the spouse needed to sign documents waiving the right to sue the firm for 50 percent of the new partner's capital in the firm, present or future.

Incredible.

If the spouse refused to sign, the potential partner couldn't be inducted. So what are you supposed to do? You sign and think, *Boy, are you an idiot.* So here I was, once again totally dependent on my spouse and screwed to boot. (No lawyer booths were available for on-site consultation.)

While we were in New York, Doug and I drove out to Long Island to see my Aunt Barbara, who was receiving home hospice care for pancreatic cancer. She had been diagnosed only months before but was already nearing her death. She lay in a hospital bed in the living room of the house she and my Uncle George shared. I could see that she was wasting away from the cancer. An epidural pump trickled morphine or Dilaudid into her spine for the pain, in addition to the morphine drops that were being given under her tongue. *How many years was it since I was last there?* It was hard to see her like this, still so young, so recently vibrant. I went over to her bed and held her hand. She knew I was there and said hello and how happy she was that I came. But it was hard to hear her.

I was speechless. What do you say to someone who is dying? It's not going to be OK. Do you ask if they are comfortable? I racked my brain trying to think of what to say that might be appropriate. I could think of nothing except how sorry I was that she was going through this and how much I would miss her. I looked down at her bony hand with tears in my eyes. After a long while of saying nothing, I stood up, bent over her bed, carefully trying to put my arm around her, and whispered in her ear, "I love you, Aunt Barbara." What else was there?

I missed her funeral.

I felt very emotional while I was in New York. Seeing friends and family saddened me since we lived so far away and missed sharing our lives more intimately. After being in Manhattan, I also realized I was still mourning my career and my former relative independence. I worked hard to feel better before the end of the trip, remembering that New York was just a plane ride away. I quickly rationalized that I *was* successful, having come through to the other side of the cancer ordeal. I had new friends in California who had supported me, and I had been supported both in person and by telephone by friends and family from the East Coast. I concluded that there's more than one kind of success.

When we returned home I turned the big four-oh. Doug had planned a surprise luncheon for me and twenty or so friends at a local restaurant. He ordered beautiful flowers for the table and remembered every detail. My gift was a diamond heart necklace that he'd bought for me in New York, plus a trip to London and Paris with Kim, where we were going to meet up with Nancy at Heathrow Airport. It was the fourth anniversary of moving to California, three and a half years since the first breast cancer, two years since the second, and one year since losing my job and my second breast.

Kim and I met Nancy, who of course had also just turned 40, at Heathrow. I was worried out of my mind when she didn't arrive when expected. We waited at the airport, flopped in chairs, exhausted, watching the parade of the Middle Eastern women shrouded in burkas followed closely behind by airport porters carting their Pierre Cardin or Louis Vuitton luggage wrapped in clear plastic. Nancy finally arrived, a little tipsy, having just met a wonderful man/drinking buddy on the plane.

We spent a week in London seeing the sights. I was the tour guide, planned the day's sightseeing, meals, shopping, teas, and whatnot. Kim and Nancy were the ducklings. Then we took the Eurostar high-speed train through the Chunnel to France, where we were going to stay with my former boss from Bank of America, Jacqui, at her apartment in Paris.

Jacqui was a very gracious host. She cooked some meals for us and accompanied us on a few of our outings. One of my favorites was going to the open-air market to shop for food. There was a little shop for everything—a fishmonger, a wine merchant, a butcher, a patisserie, a cheese shop, a baker, a produce market and maybe even a candle maker. Jacqui was fluent in French and whisked around the streets with ease. She was also taking cooking classes at Le Cordon Bleu and having a gown custom made for a short trip to San Francisco later that year for the opening of the symphony.

I starting thinking about all the things that I'd wanted to do since I had cancer. But the fact was that I couldn't do anything but the same old thing and now had even less freedom than before because I had no job, much less money, and no childcare. All this made me feel provincial, stupid, and trapped in my current life. I was jealous of Jacqui. I consoled myself by viewing her as a role model of what life could be if you set your mind to making your dreams come true. The problem was I didn't know what the dream was anymore.

On the days when we were on our own, not understanding the language, the ducklings opted for McDonald's or some other American fast food chain. This was not what I had in mind when I came to the culinary capital of the world. The trip started going further downhill for me when Nancy and Kim weren't interested in spending any time at the Louvre.

We traveled by train to the town of Giverny to see the artist Monet's home and gardens. I absolutely loved the beauty of France, and I was thinking I wanted to move there as well. One day we went shopping at Le Bon Marché, where I spent hundreds of dollars on beautiful French lingerie that I could wear with my breast prosthesis. In the dressing room, I remembered that I was still angry and sad about losing my breast. Spending all this money on underwear wasn't going to help me to feel prettier or happier, even though I had never seen lingerie more beautiful! I was becoming more determined to find a way to reconstruct this breast. By the end of the trip, I was finally saying *Au revoir!* instead of *Bonjour!* when taking my leave, albeit with a New Jersey accent.

We celebrated Brad's seventh birthday. The fall began with Doug taking a work trip to Hawaii. I couldn't go. Doug went to New York. I couldn't go. Doug went to Los Angeles. I couldn't go. I was busy keeping the home fires burning and shuttling to soccer practice, games, and Cub Scouts. When the weekend rolled around, Doug used every opportunity to go camping with Brad, his brother, and our nephews. So when was there time for us?

There wasn't. I began to think this was by design. I was unhappy again, felt unloved, unvalued, and not special in any way. Nothing was clicking on the job front, or the relationship front. I felt disgusted and absolutely stuck—no options. Needless to say, attempts to try to discuss this with Doug went nowhere, support was absent, our relationship desolate. My questions were met with evasion or sarcasm. When I would withdraw between skirmishes, Doug would parry with gibes and antagonism, even making faces at me and sticking out his tongue. Then he would suddenly act as if nothing happened. I thought that this was all crazy making. If I was depressed before, it paled compared to how I felt now.

I continued going to church and to Bible study. Obviously I was still missing something because I was definitely not at peace, nor happy— not even happy that I had survived. I thought, is this it? Is this what my life is supposed to be? I thought that maybe as a couple we had lost sight of everything that mattered. I proclaimed that we were just roommates who didn't get along.

Near the end of September, I got the name of a Christian-based counselor from Lyn, but I told Doug that he needed to call. I thought he needed to show some effort to meet me somewhere along the path toward improving the situation.

He did, and we met with this man four times. He told us that our relationship was toxic. (I knew that already.) He told us that we had poor communication skills. (I knew that too.) He didn't think there was anything he could do to help us since our troubles were enormous. It was his opinion that Doug and I were both very angry people and we were both apathetic about changing our behavior.

Finally, he recommended a Catholic-based marriage encounter program called Retrouvaille. He told us that this was more or less the end of the road, but that sometimes even after a couple is separated this could help, if we were willing to do the work. Around this same time in the Sunday bulletin at church, there was a little section on Retrouvaille and a telephone number. I had never seen this in the bulletin before or since this time. Was this what God wanted?

At this time, I was beginning to seriously contemplate the work of getting a divorce. How did we get here, divorce or Retrouvaille? In either case it was the end of the road and it would be work—more work— which I resented after everything else I had been through. I opted for Retrouvaille, but I wasn't optimistic. What if that failed too?

Meanwhile, I was referred to a plastic surgeon in San Francisco to explore breast reconstruction options. I was interested in pursuing a graft from my backside, the last option, since two doctors had already told me that I could no longer have a simple implant due to the infection damage in the area. I really liked this new doctor. We consulted, and he didn't think that the gluteal flap was necessary. Besides, he said, "Why would we want to ruin a perfectly good ass?"

I thought he was funny, and I trusted him instantly. Most of his practice was correcting congenital or accidental injuries to the face. His waiting room was always filled with patients of all ages in varying states of repair.

He did not think there would be any problem putting an expander implant under the damaged skin, stretching it, and replacing it with a permanent implant down the road. It would mean, however, that I would have to have two more surgeries.

"All right," I said, "I need some good sleep anyway." We scheduled the first procedure, the placement of the expander, for December.

I recommitted to working on my dollhouse again. I took a three-day class to make a miniature Christmas tree. Kim was testing for college admissions and got her driver's license. When she began driving other girls from the neighborhood to school, she told me that she couldn't hear them talking in the car. She thought there was something wrong with her hearing.

Her doctor referred her to an audiologist, where she was tested and diagnosed with an auditory processing disorder. This meant that she could hear only noise in one ear and had to overcome the noise while still trying to hear everything with her other ear. The audiologist said that typically people with this problem had trouble learning foreign lan- guages and learning in a lecture-based environment. She said Kim had to be very smart to compensate for this disability as well as she had.

Now I knew why I'd needed to spend thousands of dollars on tutors and that Kim hadn't just been slacking off since we moved to California. She couldn't hear and process the information once the style of teaching changed in middle school. Interestingly, since this was considered a handicap, she would be allowed to have a tape recorder or a human note taker in all her classes. She was also told that if she wore an earplug in her good ear she could perhaps train her other ear to hear. In the infinite wisdom of adolescence, she opted to do none of the above.

Around this time, I learned that my uncle had colon cancer. His mother, my maternal grandmother, had died of ovarian cancer at the age of 82. I questioned my parents and cousins on my father's side of the family about my paternal grandmother, who had also died of cancer, at 57. I had always been told that it was metastasized bladder cancer. Now my Aunt Gertrude was telling me that she may have had ovarian cancer instead.

In 1990 and 1994, respectively, the breast cancer mutation genes, BRCA1 and BRCA2, had been discovered, and were often in the news. Apparently, there was an additional risk of breast cancer in women with a family history of ovarian cancer. Given the new information of my younger grandmother dying of ovarian cancer, I thought maybe I should see a genetic counselor to determine whether I might have this mutation. Maybe this test might explain the breast cancer—and I had Kim to consider.

By the time I went for a follow-up appointment with the oncologist, he agreed that seeing a genetic counselor would be appropriate. Meanwhile, I was once again experiencing bladder symptoms although a follow-up ultrasound showed no new fibroids. The doctors attributed these symptoms possibly to low levels of estrogen, which they did not recommend supplementing due to the breast cancer risk, even though the invasive tumor in my left breast had been estrogen-receptor negative, meaning that, supposedly, estrogen did not make it grow.

Aside from all the extracurricular and social activities, plenty else was going on—too much, as usual. My career was seeing doctors and specialists. My marriage was on the rocks. My daughter was at the pinnacle of adolescence, hampered by an auditory processing disorder, but newly empowered by the freedom of driving. Brad was in second grade and doing well, when he wasn't mimicking his father's behavior.

That fall, Doug registered us for the Retrouvaille program. It consisted of a weekend retreat followed by six weekly meetings on weekends. The brochure advertised that the program was designed to
provide the tools to help put your marriage in order again. The main
emphasis of the program was on communication between husband and
wife. As the counselor had told us, Retrouvaille was Catholic in origin
and orientation.

Isn't God perfect? I thought.

CHAPTER 17

REDISCOVERY

NOVEMBER 1997–JUNE 1998

We had our Retrouvaille retreat weekend at the beginning of November. I looked at Doug, seated next to me during the opening activities in an auditorium that was absolutely packed. His face was filled with childlike innocence and apparent determination. It seemed to me that he came to this weekend with a sincere heart. When I saw that, I thought I would try. What else did I have to lose at this point?

After getting a quick orientation to the events of the first day, we began classes about personality types, relationships, communication building and styles, problem-solving techniques, dealing with conflict, etc. Then we each wrote a letter focused on answering specific questions, and later came together to discuss the responses. The questions included: What were my reasons for marrying you? When have I experienced romance in our relationship? Disillusionment? How do I feel about compromise?

What did I learn over the weekend? I learned I was grieving, always grieving. I was angry—maybe from the process of grieving—but I was also bitter, which caused me to focus on Doug very critically, seeing mostly the negative. I was disappointed in the hand of cards I had been dealt and disappointed in the way I felt I was cared for during all the loss and trauma of the past few years. I learned that I wanted a dog.

I realized that Doug and I came from similar backgrounds. Emotional abandonment, trauma, and abuse are common features of the childhoods of people with one alcoholic and one absent parent. We also shared other issues. We were both highly sensitive but in different ways. We had both learned to become very self-reliant. I learned that Doug focused on logic and had a hard time getting in touch with his feelings. He avoided feeling, and when in danger of feeling bad, would either throw a bomb or flee. He had no tools to draw upon; he said his role models came from watching television in the 1960s and 1970s.

We knew we loved each other and were bonded. It would take a long time to recover and heal, and a long time to master better communication skills. We were optimistic we would have the chance. The new dog was going to be on hold. Doug wasn't ready for that particular commitment and wanted me to wait and be sure.

After the seven weekends of sessions ended, did Retrouvaille solve our problems?

No.

But what it did do was afford us the opportunity for a truce and give each of us a better understanding of the other. We both learned that the only thing we had the ability to change was within our own selves.

Thanksgiving came and went, and, yes, we certainly had many things for which to be thankful. Hopefully, my health, our marriage, our lives were on the road to recovery. In the midst of the flurry, Kim's cutting classes reached a crescendo when, while sitting in the line of cars waiting to pick kids up at the end of the day, I saw a couple of teens making out on the hill above me. I remember thinking, *How would the parents of these two feel, knowing that all the parents waiting in their cars were observing this spectacle in full view?*

Then I saw that it was in fact *my* daughter on the grass with some boy, and that she was cutting class for this interlude.

When Kim got into the car and I confronted her, she excused her behavior by saying she missed her biological father and her boyfriend was helping her to deal with all that was going on. *How manipulative,* I thought. That might have worked in middle school, but no more. I told her to knock it off and grounded her.

On December 4, I had the surgery to place the expander implant in my left breast, surgery number ten. It required an overnight stay in the hospital, and if everything went well, the doctor would continue to inflate the expander with saline at regular intervals to stretch the skin. Another surgery would be required eventually, to replace the expander with a regular implant. At least it would ultimately fill a bra, they assured me. I would no longer have to use the breast prosthesis, which was hot, heavy, and cumbersome. In some small measure, I would finally be somewhat physically "whole" again.

The Christmas season was full of festive activities. We saw the San Francisco Symphony and Choir for the performance of Handel's *Messiah*. We went to the Christmas pageant at church, Kim's holiday choral concert and various holiday parties. I had my breast expander topped off.

I also had the first of three appointments with a genetic risk counselor. I thought maybe there was a genetic reason these things had happened to me. I was concerned that my ovaries and not my breasts were the real ticking bomb.

Recently, my mother's brother, who was in his sixties and already had been diagnosed with early-stage colon cancer, had also been diagnosed with prostate cancer. My mother had had three precancerous polyps removed from her colon in 1990. Most frightening was my cousin Anthony, a first cousin, the oldest child of my mother's oldest sister, who at age 49 was diagnosed recently with lung adenocarcinoma, which had metastasized to the lymph nodes in his left armpit. His tumors were large, and he died within a few months.

I wanted to be certain that I was doing everything I should be doing as well as taking advantage of all the medical information that was currently available. The genetic counselor discussed the BRCA-1 and BRCA-2 gene mutations at length, and she thought I would be a good candidate for this testing. The real issue was not necessarily my ovaries but the possible implications of a positive test result for my sisters, my daughter, and possibly my cousins and even mother. In other words, if I had the test and the results were positive, how would the rest of the family respond to this new information? I decided to discuss it with them first, and defer any testing until after the new year.

As part of the preparation for the visit with the genetic counselor, I had my cousin Patty send me a medical consultation report from my grandmother May, the one who died in her fifties, six months before I was born. After reading it, I felt like I had a glimpse into her life. She had been chronically ill with asthmatic bronchitis and emphysema. She had double vision, high cholesterol, hypertension, and edema of both legs. I felt such empathy for her. She was so young, yet felt so horrible. This was two years before her diagnosis of cancer. I remember wishing I could be with her and hold her hand. Was she a happy person? Why did she get sick? Was my grandfather nice to her? There were so many unanswered questions that would never be answered, including one that might affect me—*Did I inherit her poor health?*

Over the holidays, we were called by the school district. Brad's name had come up to number one on the waiting list for an alternative program at another elementary school in our school district. It was a continuous learning program designed to help high-potential students excel. He was in the middle of second grade, not a perfect time to change, but we decided that for him the change would be for the best in the long run.

So when school began again in January, after the holiday break, Brad started at a new school. Fortunately, he had a wonderful new teacher and saw a few familiar faces that he recognized from church and Cub Scouts. Later that month, he was tested at school and determined to be eligible for the gifted and talented program, confirming for us that we made the right decision to change schools.

The growth of my new breast continued with additional infusions of saline every two weeks. Checkups with the oncologist and the gynecologist continued. Other than the reminder of abnormal Pap smear results, life began to take on some semblance of normalcy, even for us. Our calendar was loaded with many wonderful activities. I was feeling very grateful and hopeful. Our entire family was doing well, all at the same time. Cousin Anthony's death had reminded me that life—especially the life of some—was way too short. I needed to find joy while I still had time.

Doug was doing well at work but was always very busy. But he was positive, as I was. We were getting along much better. I made a conscious decision to notice and appreciate all his efforts. I had to remember that if I focused on the positives and blessings in my life with gratitude, things felt so much better. Medically, I was on cruise control. Therefore, now more than ever was the time to savor life. I wanted to celebrate. Through all of these years I had been the subject of so much attention—maybe now it was time to do something special for Doug.

In June, Doug was going to turn 40. I decided it would be nice to recognize him with a fun surprise party. Beginning that winter, I began to plot. I found out that this was the year that Motown and the Grammy

Awards celebrated their fortieth anniversaries. That knowledge led me to come up with the theme for the party. Of course, the party would need a musical focus, so I decided to have a karaoke party with a DJ and invite everyone to come dressed as their favorite performer. There would be prizes for best performances by a single, duo and group, both male and female.

During the planning, I started involving some friends in my hunt for appropriate vintage clothing from the 1950s, 1960s, and 1970s. We had so much fun scouring the Bay Area for hats and polyester. A group of five of us, already good friends, members of the same book club, living in the same neighborhood, began to celebrate each other's birthdays and with the upcoming party as another unifying bond, our group, the "Hidden Assets," loosely named for where we lived, was born. The group consisted of Lyn, Mary, Jane, Kelly, and me.

We began to plan our karaoke act for the party. We decided to impersonate the Supremes and sing their hit "Stop! In the Name of Love." With the merriment and silliness of teenagers, we choreographed and planned the costumes for our performance, which meant more trips to the vintage clothing stores, lunches, and rehearsals.

My sister Alane, a talented graphic artist, made centerpieces for the table, using the head of Doug from a high school photo and the body of John Travolta from the cover of the *Saturday Night Fever* album and shipped them from the East Coast. We created nametags from Doug's baby pictures and even came up with musically inspired names for the food we were serving at the party. It was difficult containing my excitement and keeping the plans from Doug.

Fortunately, he was away on business when my parents arrived and final preparations were being made. He thought my parents were just out for a visit. Doug had no idea what I was doing for all those weeks, and he didn't ask.

Doug was overwhelmed with surprise at the party. As soon as he walked into the backyard, he was given his party identity, Elwood Blues from the Blues Brothers, complete with hat and skinny tie, while the song "I Can't Cut You Loose" from *A Briefcase Full of Blues* played in the background. My parents even got into the act as Johnny and June Carter Cash and sang "Jackson": "We got married in a fever. ..." It was great fun to see neighbors dressed as Howard Stern, Tina Turner, Diana

Ross, 1950s greasers, '70s hippies, and the like. Even the caterers joined in the festivities, singing "Red Red Wine."

The party was a smashing success. Friendships were cemented and new ones forged. For months at subsequent get togethers, our group of friends watched the party-highlights videotape and retold stories about the evening.

For Doug's actual birthday present, I surprised him with a trip to Seattle, followed by a few days in Victoria, British Columbia, and then the ultimate for Doug—three days of salmon fishing with a guide on the Campbell River while staying at a fishing lodge.

In the midst of party preparations, I went for surgery number eleven, the placement of the permanent implant. It was no walk in the park, with drains hanging out for a week, but finally, the saga of my breasts was over.

Kim was finishing her junior year of high school, taking the SAT exam for college entrance, taking acting classes at a theatre conservatory in San Francisco, voice lessons, dance lessons, and getting involved in the local musical theatre community. Brad was active with the Scouts, camping, and dissecting bugs in the yard with his friends.

Now that we were both 40, Doug and I began to feel young again.

CHAPTER 18

RAISING HELL

JULY 1998–APRIL 1999

B y the summer of 1998, at age 41, I could tell that my hormones were starting to act up. I had a constant feeling of bladder irritation that manifested itself as frequent trips to the bathroom, especially at night. I was beginning to have huge mood swings again, accompanied by insomnia. I knew there was something chemically wrong. I went to see a doctor in San Francisco who was recommended by a friend. He was a "climacteric endocrinologist," someone who was supposed to specialize in menopause.

I thought his specialty name said it all, *climacteric*—a year in which important changes in health and fortune are thought to occur, a critical period. Ancient philosophers, such as Plato and Cicero, believed that the climacteric occurred in a person's life every seven years starting with the seventh year of life then 14, 21, 28 ... 42. The age 63 was especially associated with death. These years corresponded to the ages of man—7 was the age of reason; 21, adulthood; etc. To me, though, the word *climacteric* sounded like *climate*, as in weather—pressure, temperature, precipitation, sunshine, cloudiness, and especially winds, storms, tornadoes, cyclones, any and all extremes. My life was all about climate, now it was climacteric, requiring that kind of specialist.

The doctor took a history of my symptoms and ordered laboratory tests that confirmed I was "very perimenopausal." He recommended an herbal supplement of plant estrogens, which he had coincidently co-developed, to attempt to mitigate the symptoms.

That August, I also attended a women's seminar on menopause hosted by a local hospital. The speaker was a female gynecologist, Dr.

A., who specialized in menopause and spoke on the roles of many hormones, including estrogen, progesterone, and testosterone and the thyroid's function during the pre-, peri- and post-menopausal periods. She included slides in her lecture that highlighted the cycles of the different hormones during each of the pre-, peri- and post- periods and the chemistry of the hormonal precursors, hormonal conversion, hormone receptors, and the effects of these hormones in the body. Finally, she walked the audience through the various scenarios and spoke about the supplements she would recommend to mitigate symptoms.

After attending the talk, I decided that I needed to educate myself more on this topic and began to read the current books on the subject of female hormones, hormone replacement therapy—especially after a diagnosis of breast cancer—as well as books on menopause.

I was continuing to have Pap smears about every three months with an occasional cervical biopsy thrown in for good measure. A pelvic ultrasound done in early September revealed that my ovaries were now cystic and the "nonrecurring" fibroid was back. I started considering a hysterectomy in order to be done with the whole thing, but decided to wait and see for the time being.

SEPTEMBER 8, 1998
Today was the first day of school. For me, the beginning of a new year always seems to start in September, which is ironic since it is also the beginning of fall, the decline, the initiation into the death cycle.

Kim started her senior year. I'm not sure how I feel about her starting college next year. I love her and will miss her. Even though the last few years have been trying, I don't feel ready to let her go. Yet I know I must.

Brad started third grade. He doesn't seem to like growing up. Does he have a Peter Pan complex already? He is getting so big.

This school year I am going to try to slow down and focus on what I enjoy in the home and on dance and music. Tonight is my first tap dancing class. I stopped taking phytoestrogen yesterday, the one that was prescribed by the climacteric guy. In six weeks I've gained weight, feel fat, and am not sleeping or feeling better. I'm going to wait and see what Dr. A. has to say.

SEPTEMBER 28

Schedules are starting to get crazy. The tap class has been quite a hoot.
I start ballet next Monday. I went back to the gym—dance aerobics—
trying to get back in shape. I feel old and my body has gone to hell in
the last six months with all this hormone upheaval. Dr. K., the ob-gyn
finally called me today and put me on an estrogen-testosterone
combination, Estratest HS, a half tablet every day.

Hopefully, the mystery of my misery will be solved. I am hoping to
see an improvement in my energy, my sense of well-being, my libido,
my mood, my irritability, etc., etc. All this is to come from one half of a
pill! Things are now pretty calm with Doug. It is amazing when we go
out and spend the time—we have fun and get along fairly well. We went
dancing this weekend and out for dinner.

I'm pretty busy with Brad's activities as a field trip mom, religion
class assistant, den mother, and working in the classroom. Kim found
out yesterday that she got the part in the show *Little Shop of Horrors*
produced by a local musical theatre company. We are all so excited.
However, it appears she has broken up with her boyfriend (good!).

It really feels like fall. I love fall. It rained this weekend. I still miss
the East Coast colors.

OCTOBER 18

We started planning the college fairs and trips with Kim. She thinks
she would like to go to college for some sort of performing arts. Brad
started guitar lessons and is playing club soccer. He is also taking
a class at the Lawrence Hall of Science in Berkeley once a week. I'm
now also involved in coaching Brad and some of his classmates for
Destination Imagination, which is a worldwide competition later this
year.

I don't know how people with four children do it. I feel like a
logistics planner with a master schedule. Who has time to make dinner
or rest? How did I ever work? Doug escapes to fish in the lakes and
reservoirs of Northern California every chance he gets. I guess my R&R
is a bikini wax. I don't know why I'm whining when I sign my own self
up for these things.

NOVEMBER 11

Last Saturday I found another lump. Upon further checking, I found a second one, one on each side. Needless to say, I have the well-honed vacillation between hysteria and "It's nothing" syndrome.

First thing Monday, I called my surgeon and scheduled an appointment. The best I could get was Nov. 17, eight days later. No such thing as frequent shopper benefits with this crowd!

The bigger lump, the one on my left side, is near my sternum between two ribs. It seems to roll a little, so I thought, well, maybe it is a gland or fat. But when I went to see my plastic surgeon on Monday afternoon, he told me that you don't typically get lymph nodes in that spot. He seemed gravely concerned, and that really frightened me. I was seeing him to discuss the final procedure of my reconstruction, the nipple construction and the tattooing of both sides. Now, we are on hold to see first what we are dealing with.

We are into Kim's college application process. She is anxious, hostile, and nasty—stress in a teen. She is rehearsing for her show *Little Shop of Horrors* scheduled to open Nov. 21. Brad varies between whining and hostility. Why are my children this way? Is this how I communicate? Do I resent having them? Do I not meet their needs? This behavior, I can tell you, is a real pain in the batoongies.

Today was Veteran's Day, so my lovely darlings were home from school. As den leader, I took Brad and 7 other boys (with 3 other moms to help) to the local paper to see how a newspaper is made. It was an interesting tour. Then we went to Burger King (I'm on liquids today). All this fun only for my son to say, "So, I don't see what the big deal is. It was boring."

I gave up my career for this?

I am managing to hang together for one reason—*Gene*, my new obsession. Gene is a '50s era fashion/glamour doll. A few months earlier I was in town to buy someone a gift at a gift shop and my love affair with a doll began. As I was browsing, my head snapped to the right, and there in the lighted shelves stood Gene—not just one but many Gene dolls, all of them different.

In her backstory, "Kathryn Gene Marshall" was born in 1923 in Cos Cob, Connecticut. At 17 she became a model for the Chambers

Model Agency. As in every Hollywood fairy tale, she was discovered and quickly became a star of stage and screen. Her career spanned the decades of the 1940s and 1950s.

A version of the doll came with an outfit for every screen role, premier, glamorous party—and of course attire for every aspect of her personal life.

Some dolls came with different hair styles to go with their costumes; there were different colors and different unique costumes. All the dolls and costumes were limited editions. Each came with a booklet containing a detailed description of the attire down to the fabric and style along with the backstory of the outfit and Marshall's role when she wore it.

The clothing was magnificent, the fabrics glorious, the accessories detailed down to the size of a bead. I began collecting. It was hard not to want everything. I signed up for presales, requested the lowest numbers in the limited edition certifications. I snuck them home, delighted and feeling wicked at the same time.

Slowly Gene started showing up around my house dressed in different outfits. She was in the living room, the bedroom, the foyer, the dining room. As the months went by, each room acquired multiple Genes, and I started to arrange them in scenes by theme—the Mexican Hacienda, Wild West, Classical Quartet Concert—complete with props and backdrops. Each month every scene would change, as would the dolls' outfits, sometimes related to the holidays that month. It could take days to make the monthly change, hunting, gathering, designing, creating this world of fantasy.

This doll invasion did not escape my husband. "What the hell are you doing?" he asked.

"I don't know. Playing?"

The remainder of the year included, along with the normal holiday festivities, the scare of a triple-elevated cancer antigen, another abnormal Pap smear, the findings of a new fibroid, and an infected supraclavicular incision caused by the dissolvable sutures that had not dissolved after a recent hasty surgery to remove the lumps I had found. The lumps had turned out to be "normal" lymph nodes. To say that I was getting sick and tired of all of this would be an understatement. I was running low on hope. The future loomed bleak—time-bomb ovaries, problematic cervix, lumps growing here, there, and everywhere. I was getting more and more ready to get out that machete to clear out the underbrush to protect the forest.

The new year started off with our hosting a small New Year's Eve party—an appetizer and dessert buffet, dancing, and of course music, including that of the artist Prince to herald in 1999. Kim had follow-up voice auditions for the colleges she applied for. Not only did Kim pick the top six colleges with a musical theater major, including New York University, Oberlin, University of Michigan, and Indiana, but also she refused to apply to any schools that were not considered "most selective." She needed to compete on grades, test scores, essays, and the audition as well. It was certainly an interesting process, similar to the reality show *American Idol* today—except that you don't receive any feedback until you are accepted or rejected.

In January I had a follow-up appointment with my gynecologist. After having been evaluated for genetic risk but still procrastinating on having the actual test, and having two grandmothers with ovarian cancer, my own funky fibroids, cystic ovaries, and weird Pap tests, I decided that the best thing to improve my chances of survival was to have it all removed. I rationalized that if I had a hysterectomy, I wouldn't feel like the specter of death was looming over me all the time. I just wanted to get this whole cancer trip behind me and start to live again. Drastic times called for drastic measures.

One morning, I made three phone calls. I scheduled surgery for a total hysterectomy including ovary removal for early March just as I would have made an appointment for a major service for the car, the expensive but unavoidable one. Then I called my parents to ask them to come to California to help with the kids. When they said yes, I phoned the airline and bought their tickets.

FEBRUARY 5, 1999

Well, I'm back in counseling. I guess that makes it the fifth start for individual (second for marriage), and that doesn't include the Wellness Community. What's interesting is that the therapy is not about cancer, grief, or work. All that does come up—but not as much as our relationship. Maybe the marriage is the scapegoat. I'm sticking with it this time to get to the bottom of this situation once and for all. I hope to have major growth—for a change.

My parents told me today they don't want to get in the middle of anything. They don't want to come next month for the surgery if we're fighting; it stresses them out. I told them I guarantee nothing. I told my mother I will not be discussing this with her nor do I want her advice. She will have to trust that I am intelligent and have good judgment and that I know what is best for me. My mother's historic reasons for staying in this marriage were verbally abusive too, focusing on my flaws. Maybe that explains why I've put up with it for too long! Mom says:

"You're too sensitive."

"You blow everything out of proportion."

"You always need something to complain about."

"You're never happy."

"You're making a mountain out of a molehill."

And the best one yet: "What are you complaining about? He's a professional, makes a good living, you do nice things, he doesn't sleep around, he doesn't drink or beat you—you should be happy."

Should I? Of course, I'm the failure because I'm not.

FEBRUARY 10

I feel a little hope. I found a note with a list of the things Doug is going to do to improve the situation:

1. Read one book (self-help) every 45 days

2. I will be kinder and gentler and stay in tune to my wife

3. Spend 2–3 hours per week doing an activity that gives my wife pleasure

FEBRUARY 22

Things seem a little calmer right now. But I'm still depressed. My upcoming surgery is depressing. I feel sure it's the right thing to do, but I don't like it. I'm tired, very tired, and weary. Most of all I dread the recovery and the fact that it means that I'll feel lousy physically, emotionally weary, and still have to juggle. I almost wish I could stay in the hospital for a couple of weeks, not have to deal with the whining, yelling, and the lack of engagement, interruptions.

I need space, quiet and time—lots of it. I never come close to getting anywhere near what I need to process all of this. I have a fantasy of being in a white bedroom with white linens, no decorations. There is a large multipaned window with a chair for gazing outside. I sit in the chair to view the rain on the lush green lawn. I stay in that room, am fed meals, get clean linens, no visitors are allowed. There is time—just time to think, time to cry, and time to heal. I think it might be at an insane asylum.

FEBRUARY 26

Well, it's official. I've been diagnosed as depressed, not clinically depressed but depression caused by "exogenous" forces. I believe *much* of what I feel is hormonal. Since when don't I have the capacity to stand up and take on the challenges life brings my way? I started back on Wellbutrin. I've come full circle on the hysterectomy. I think I've been suffering from this hyster- thing in hysterectomy—namely hysteria. Doug was surprisingly supportive last night. I wonder what will happen. Will we look back and say *God* that was an awful time but look how much we have grown. I hope I live that long. I am going to do this. Breast cancer was the warning. What if I already have ovarian cancer? One day at a time.

A letter came from Indiana U.—doesn't look good from the size of it. Poor Kim. (Where is she anyway? She should be home.)

The counselor says my Gene doll thing is very good for my peace of mind—a healthy escape. Yes, I know—a fantasy.

MARCH 1

I feel a bit better. I would love to know, is it my cycle, increasing my hormones, starting on Wellbutrin? I even feel pretty good mentally considering that I've been up since 3:30 a.m.

I think a big reason is that we had a relatively quiet weekend. Warriors game Friday, *U.S.S. Hornet* with Den 10 on Saturday, party Saturday night, errands, church, quiet Sunday—even though Doug griped, slammed, complained, and almost killed a cyclist rather than wait for him to be out of harm's way.

I noticed Doug has quite a temper and can get downright ugly at times—no patience. I feel good that I did not get sucked into *his* problem.

MARCH 4

I have this eerie sense of calm about the upcoming surgery, although I'm not too fond of the surgeon. He has too big an ego and is another one that doesn't listen. I have been saying the Rosary, especially focused on the mysteries. I am particularly attracted to the sorrowful mysteries, which focus on the passion (agony in the garden, scourging at the pillar, crowning with thorns, carrying the cross and the crucifixion). It helps me to have perspective. Also I was happy to receive anointing of the sick and reconciliation on Tuesday. It helps. I have to remember to stay focused on what is important.

I pray that Doug does not make my recovery harder than it has to be, that he has empathy for my pain and that I don't have ovarian cancer. God, I really want a break. I'm afraid. Poor grandmas.

MARCH 8

We are home. It is over. No news is good news. The doctor says everything looked OK. He will call with the lab results. What's taking so long? Things have been relatively quiet. Doug has been pretty good. I would define it as quiet strength, I guess. He hasn't had a whole lot to say, and I certainly don't feel connected, but at least it has not been brutal.

My tummy is swollen and red. I seem to have feeling below, which Doug did ask me about today. I chuckled inside. I have enough gas to power a thousand ships.

MARCH 10

I am sad. I feel loss. A part of me is gone. Gone is what gave rise to and housed my growing babies. All of a sudden I feel old, no longer a young woman but a mature one. Kim is going to be 18 in just a few days. I remember when I was pregnant with her. That person is still in my head. When will I feel connected? Maybe this is being connected. Maybe this is all there is.

We found out yesterday that there were no signs of ovarian cancer. I don't understand why I had this symplastic fibroid again. Why do I keep producing them? He said the pathology of my cervix was dysplasia. What a mess. How did I become such a mess? I need to slow down my life and enjoy more. Start looking away from trouble.

I'm still very sore but it's getting better and the swelling is getting smaller. I haven't had any drastic hormonal upheaval yet. I do have pronounced hot waves though. It's kind of like a feverish furnace and then it subsides. I feel mellow to melancholy. If this is as bad as it gets, then I think I'll be OK.

MARCH 14

Even though I was sore, I dragged the family, even Mom and Dad, to the Del Valle Dog Show in Pleasanton to see the papillons. After a papillon named Kirby won the Westminster Kennel Club Dog Show and after doing research, I've decided that this is the type of dog I want. Of course when I told Doug, he said to get a "real" dog. But this dog will be for me. At the show I started talking with breeders about how to obtain a puppy. It sounds harder than adopting a baby. There are waiting lists. They won't release females, or males for that matter, until they are big enough to decide whether the dog will be pet or show quality. Everyone in the family, except maybe Brad, thinks I'm crazy to want a dog. I don't care what they think.

For a few hours it was nice to escape into another world even if I felt like I was dragging around balls and chains. I think finding a puppy will be a fun long-term project.

MARCH 16

I went through a few days last week with horrific hot flashes. I felt that if this were to continue in frequency, I'd hurl myself off the Golden Gate Bridge. We're talking a furnace—gasoline poured on me and lit on fire, drenched, no escape. I upped my Estratest HS to an additional half pill. That seemed to do the trick.

I'm still not sleeping even after taking Ambien (a sleeping pill) last night. My parents arrived last Friday night. I'm trying really hard not to be too cranky. I'm really trying hard to be accepting and ignore their little foibles. When the going gets tough, I go to my room (frequently).

I am enjoying some of the time being with my parents. I know they really love me, but I realize they are getting old. My dad has been very sweet and helpful. He likes to have projects. Mom is helping, but she has horrible rheumatoid arthritis pain now and complains about it all the time. I feel guilty.

Kim turned 18. Wow. She is an adult now, her own person. We still have no news on colleges. It's in God's hands.

MARCH 17

I discussed with my parents and Doug at dinner that I'd like to write a book. It's amazing how consistently I am pooh-poohed. Well, once again, so much for having any expectation of support. They all agreed— why would anyone want to hear about my miserable problems, citing that everyone has problems. I'll call it *The Breast Cancer Chronicles*. I'm starting next week, an hour or two a day. If nothing else it will be a history for my children. I'm really excited about going to the Breast Cancer Conference in May. I will be getting more involved.

MARCH 18

How ironic that I had this surgery to save my life and now I just wish I were dead. I'm sick that I don't have the courage to just blow my brains out. All I can think about the last two days is how I wish I were dead and all of the different ways to kill myself. I hate myself for having no guts.

MARCH 22

Well, this horrible depression is decidedly my hormones or lack thereof. Fortunately or unfortunately—depends on the moment—I'm still here. I've never been so depressed. I'm so irritable, lashing out at everyone. I'm alienating my whole family.

Mom and Dad left yesterday, and I feel guilty about their visit—and of course Doug has all these negative comments about my feelings and behaviors that just make me feel worse. Thank God for Clara. She came over last week and rescued me from myself. For three days she sat with me locked up in my room. She helped me to feel like my mental state wasn't just the hormones but also dealing with having my parents here and them ignoring that anything was wrong. I couldn't even be near them without feeling I would be mean, biting their heads off or saying something nasty. They are too old and needy themselves. They tried, but this was an extremely difficult situation.

We all went to *Tony n' Tina's Wedding* before they left, to celebrate Kim's birthday. It was interesting, a little raunchy. But Kim and her latest boyfriend, Zach, seemed to enjoy it. I can't seem to get anything done.

Doug says I need to focus and have an attitude adjustment. Leave it to him.

MARCH 23

I went to the doctor today. I wrote a quick list of how I feel, and they actually wanted to keep the list. The doctor put me on Premarin in addition to the Estratest. I've now gone from .625 mg to 2.5 mg of estrogen. As Clara says, "trial by error," when hearing my daily tales of woe in dealing with the doctors.

I feel like the guy is torturing me. He is concerned about HRT (hormone replacement therapy) with my breast cancer history. What difference does the long-term risk make if I don't want to live through today? Is this just grief? I feel like I have nowhere to turn to stop the pain. Clara has been helping me a lot.

MARCH 27

I'm feeling a little better but not great. Very tired. Brad had something in his eye and we wound up having to go to the ER at 1 a.m. for these huge pimple-like things on the inside of his eyelids—conjunctivitis. Friday I spent the day with Brad and was fine, except for having to fight him to give him the eye drops.

MARCH 29

I had a much better day Saturday and Sunday. I upped the Premarin, now at .625 mg Estratest and .625 mg Premarin in a.m. and 1.25 Estratest and .625 Premarin in the p.m. I slept great on Saturday night but only 3½ hours on Sunday. Today, even though I have less patience and have still a bit of depression, I almost feel normal. It is still hard not to do too much.

Friday night I made a list of what was bothering me—always there, but just magnified, especially in the evening when tired:

> Beat husband up for failing to meet my needs
> Feel low self-worth
> Feel depressed, hopeless, unloved
> Focus on failures/mistakes
> Feel sorry for myself
> Feel easily angry at people
> Too reflective

Too analytical

Can't shut down or relax

Unable to focus and accomplish

I took Kim to see *Rent* yesterday—very good. Kim has been depressed. She hasn't received good news from any of the colleges she applied to. I guess she will have to go to the junior college and try again next year.

APRIL 3

As this past week has progressed, I'm having more and more energy. After not sleeping again and again, I upped the estrogen—one Estratest 1.25 plus 1.25 Premarin. I'm not having the mood swings and my depression seems to be lifting a bit. Beginning to be a little energized, but I'm still cranky when I'm tired. I have got to stop doing so much. I am a broken record. I can't stand the gynecologist—what a jerk.

My counselor has suggested that I go see an acupuncturist/ Chinese herb medicine person for my sleeping problems and anxiety. Supposedly Chinese or Eastern medicine works with the body's energy meridians. The energy is called chi. Acupuncture and the herbs help to remove the blockages that cause disease, open up the pathways to healing and restoring balance. Wouldn't that be something? This medicine practice is thousands of years old. You are diagnosed by your history, how your tongue looks and your pulses. Your body systems are different from those in Western medicine. You have a spleen, liver, and kidney system. You are damp, wet, or dry. You are wood, water, wind, metal, or dirt. I should give it a try. What do I have to lose?

Also my therapist assigned homework. I now need to take myself to the movies at least once a week to relax. The family falls apart when I'm not well. I guess I have to stop thinking about myself. So where do the movies fit in?

CHAPTER 19

THE INFINITE LOOP
APRIL–SEPTEMBER 1999

APRIL 12, 1999

Thursday, Kim went to the emergency room. I wasn't around when it happened as I was out to dinner with a friend. A dog she was caring for latched onto and tore open her chin. The ER doctor was an asshole. He didn't call in a plastic surgeon and closed up her wound with black exterior stitches. He put her on an antibiotic that is not effective for dog germs. He treated *her* like an animal. He didn't bother to give her something to calm her nerves. He yelled at her, referring to her chin as "hamburger meat."

Her boyfriend, Zach, was much the hero. His mother, who owns the pet-sitting business, felt so bad. It was an accident.

Friday was supposed to be my pamper day. Instead I called my plastic surgeon to see if Kim could be seen. His nurse said that he will not look at her chin until it is healed (in approximately six months) and gave us some tips the ER doctor failed to do. I missed my waxing appointment and rescheduled. Then Kim and I went to see her doctor. He changed her antibiotic and chastised the ER doctor and said, "Do not go to that hospital ever again."

APRIL 22

We went camping. In the morning I bought myself a pack of cigarettes and had one. Why? To feel better or fulfill a death wish, who knows? When we got home, I went to see a Chinese medicine doctor/herbalist/acupuncturist. The consultation was disturbing. He hit many nails on the head. I felt like he knew me. He commented on how he didn't know how I was alive—because most people he claimed would have given up. He said I have a strong will to live, like a tiger. But this will is also preventing me from healing. He thinks that I have a "wood personality" and am blocking my liver somehow.

He also told me that part of my spirit has left me and I need to get it back. He knew a shaman. It was overwhelming. He gave me some herbs. God knows what's in them. We'll start acupuncture next week. He didn't seem to think insomnia was my biggest problem. He told me that the liver blockage was forcing energy into tumor formation and growth.

I went to book club. A club member wanted to hold my hand and asked me, "Can you stop getting sick now?"

APRIL 26
Friday was the day of Kim's boyfriend's junior prom. I gave her a pedicure and manicure. We did her hair and makeup. It was nice. Mary came over, and on two glasses of wine, I was ripped. I'm reading a wonderfully helpful book entitled *Close to the Bone: Life-Threatening Illness and the Search for Meaning* by Dr. Jean Shinoda Bolen. This book is so true. I can't believe it. I really want Doug to read it. He won't, and even if he did, he'd say, "So, what's the big deal."

Yesterday I bought some suits to interview in, but now I'm thinking that I should wait until September to start working. Last Thursday the University of California called regarding the chief treasury officer position I applied for months ago, wanting to know where I've been for the last three years. I told them home and I haven't heard from them since. Oh well. By the way, I got conjunctivitis over the weekend starting at Saturday night's Warriors game with the Boy Scouts. Now Doug is hinting around that he wants a boat motor for his birthday.

MAY 22
Kim had her senior ball yesterday. This week has been nonstop harassment about the after-prom activities. Her first proposal was renting a van to go to Santa Cruz, then her second idea, a sleepover with Zach and other friends, culminating with staying out all night. I'm worried that Zach's stepmother doesn't really know what's going on.

I've been having repetitive dreams about leeches sucking on me. Whatever the situation, I find out later I have some obscure itch and check the cause, a leech, and then many leeches. I start screaming to deal with the horror as I painfully try to rip them off my body. Talk about symbolic.

I'm in the air, off to Washington, D.C., for the Breast Cancer Advocacy Conference. Outta here, alleluia. I'm so glad to be getting out of there.

MAY 23

Robert picked me up with his friend Katherine. It has been so good to see him. Sunday, Katherine picked us up and we went to some dive for breakfast and then to an open-air flea market with lots of junk.

Back at the hotel that afternoon I went to my first session of the conference. It was fantastic. So many people were there and all so energized. I met a film producer from California. She's a busy activist.

This evening, Robert, Katherine and I went to a restaurant on the waterfront of the Potomac River. It was such a beautiful and balmy night. It feels good to be away and feel alive.

MAY 24

Full day at the conference—session one on Tamoxifen, luncheon with Susan Love, MD, as speaker, then session two on "Is Project Lead for you?", then a session on "The Environment and Breast Cancer."

It seems to me that the more they know, the less they know. They discover new information and data points, but they can't prove conclusive correlation. For example, cigarettes cause cancer, but why do non-smokers get it too? The mystery increases with each new theory or research finding. When I get home, I need to get copies of my X-rays, information from the oncologist on tumor assays and progress notes, and be certain they save my tumors.

I am pretty excited about getting involved. This evening there was a cocktail reception with dancing to a live band.

MAY 25

Today was "Lobby Day." We got up early, got on buses, and headed to the U.S. Capitol. We had a rally in the morning. No one was there other than the conference attendees. We didn't fill the mall. We didn't even cover the landing platform before the steps. I don't understand—where was everyone? You would think breast cancer wasn't even an issue!

For the rest of the day we toured the congressional office buildings, visiting representatives, their aides and assistants. At 4 p.m. some of us, residents of California, met with the top aides in Senator Diane Feinstein's office.

The senior aide welcomed us and said, "Let's go around the room, and it would be great if each of you could tell us if there anything in particular that we can help with in our role in Congress."

When it was my turn I said, "I think there is a problem with getting second opinions outside of the network if you are in an HMO. Insurance doesn't want to pay for it, and even in network it is difficult."

At the end of the meeting, the top aide asked if he could contact me in the future for more information.

"Senator Feinstein is aware of this issue. Your story may help in the case she is making to get insurance reform, especially with the HMOs."

I gave him my number.

I had good and bad observations about the experience of Lobby Day. The good ones were that in some cases it appeared that our visit may have made a difference. In others we had to meet with very young people (interns, aides). It appears to me that these young people analyze the information, summarize the information as they see fit, and then make recommendations to the senator or representative. Pretty scary. One of the legislators that we were scheduled to meet with was wrapped up in the China weapons theft issue and another one was dealing with agricultural appropriations. There was a reception, where we met Nancy Pelosi. She gave a short speech, and afterwards there was lots of handshaking.

MAY 26

I slept well last night, but unfortunately I had to get up at 5:30 a.m. for a 7:15 bus to the National Cancer Institute. I attended a lecture session from 9 a.m. to 12 p.m. given by the head of the National Cancer Institute, an overview of what they are doing in cancer research, some of which was very interesting.

I especially enjoyed the session of one molecular scientist researching mutations, metastasis, and the relationships of tumor suppression genes and oncogenes expressed in malignancy. She explained how a breast cell changes to cancer and how the cancer spreads. It appears from her studies that the breast cancer cell first "tricks" the body while in disguise as it migrates to the pathway of blood or lymph vessels. Then the "cloaked" cancer cell escapes detection by the many immunological factors in the pathway environment. It survives until it plants itself in a foreign organ. Finally, it mimics the host organ cells to protect itself until it takes root and triggers angiogenesis to feed itself. It sounds like an alien invasion. This was very disturbing.

It appears as though the cancer cells are very intelligent.

MAY 29

I'm on Continental flight 1957 en route to Houston and on my way home. I had a glorious week. I slept great and feel energized. I can breathe again. I am looking forward to getting home. I plan to focus and get some things done. I am looking forward to eating lots of produce. I enjoyed my visit with Robert and the peaceful interaction. It will be interesting to see how long it takes to feel the toxicity again. We'll make a note.

JUNE 12

I am sitting at a picnic table at a campsite at Hell Hole Reservoir near Lake Tahoe. Doug and Brad are out fishing. I think I am the only woman, possibly the only human, for miles around. Why did I come? I guess I thought that if I stayed home I'd be painting the trim in my bedroom or stripping doors, working. At least here it's quiet, peaceful, nothing except me and the mosquitoes.

Kim graduates from high school next week. I feel so sad and glad. I'm sad because she's off, about to embark on her own life. I'll never see her anymore. She will be doing her thing, working, going to junior college, shows. She's all grown up. I'm glad because it's less of a burden on me. Boy did that go quickly. Doug and I have had two fights since I have been home. It is so draining. Although I still feel pretty good since my trip, it is amazing to see how good I feel when I'm out of a draining environment. But what do you do, abandon your family?

It's so quiet here just birds, fog, and the whir of mosquitoes. I do hear a boat or a plane in the distance.

School is almost over for Brad—the end of third grade already. He was so funny this week. He had to give an oral presentation on a term paper he did on "Aircraft of the World." The morning of the report he totally freaked out. He was so nervous. He didn't want to go to school. He couldn't eat. He was certain he was going to throw up. It was sad, but funny too. Since when did he become so unsure of himself? I went to his class for his presentation. He did just fine. Afterwards, he acted like nothing had ever happened—go figure.

I have heard twice from Diane Feinstein's office regarding medical second opinions and dealing with insurance companies. This sounds exciting. She wants to use some of my stories to introduce a bill regarding coverage for second opinions.

I am still sleeping pretty well off the Trazadone. I think having my hormones in balance really helps, as well as not having to listen to Doug snore, since he has taken up residence in another room.

CHAPTER 20

SMOKE AND MIRRORS

OCTOBER 1999–MARCH 2001

Kim was busy with her first year at the junior college, dating, working, and performing in the theatre. She also applied to a few more colleges so she could transfer for the next academic year. She was rarely home and was not going to account to us for anything involving her life. I stopped waiting up for her or for the phone call in the middle of the night. I was letting go.

Y2K wasn't the Armageddon predicted. It wasn't anything that even blipped.

I started smoking again on Valentine's Day 2000. On the way home from our romantic dinner I wanted a cigarette, so we stopped at the market. When we came home I lit up, sitting out on the back deck. It was relaxing. I noticed starting to smoke was something you have to really work hard at to like. The first taste was horrible, improving with each subsequent cigarette. I don't know what I was thinking—addictive personality disorder, part of letting go, learning to relax, giving up the fight, all of the above? At first I limited my smoking to two cigarettes a day, then four. I didn't smoke enough to be chemically addicted but I became addicted to the behavior.

It was interesting to note that to have a cigarette, I had to stop what I was doing, go outside, and commune with nature. I had the time to stop and think, which I believe for me was a drug-induced form of meditation. Certainly there was no social aspect to it, since no one knew I smoked and I knew no one else who did or would admit to it anyway.

In March, Brad and I drove up to Grass Valley to purchase an adorable 6-month-old male papillon puppy from a breeder we'd met at a dog show in San Jose. He was my new baby. Doug had told me that if I wanted to get a dog, then get a "real" dog. This wasn't in that category, but too bad. I liked this breed because they were smart, self-grooming, their hair didn't mat, they were great companion dogs, and they were small.

Brad and I named the dog Indigo since his hair was a bluish black and white. He became my new best friend and was a great companion. I am sure my decision to finally get a dog was in response to no longer being able to have children. The good news was there were no diapers, laundry, temper tantrums, or answering back, just unconditional love and companionship. He really brightened my days and my spirits.

Shortly after he arrived on the scene, Doug grew to really enjoy him. Kim and Brad seemed a little jealous. Indigo never became their dog, probably due to my possessiveness, who knows. As a result of getting a puppy in conjunction with the beginning of spring in California, I began taking longer walks and spending more time in the yard for house-breaking purposes—which naturally led to more smoking.

As Indigo was exploring the backyard, I began to imagine a body part cemetery with white crosses in the corner of the property up on the hill. There would be one for each breast, my uterus, two fallopian tubes, and two ovaries, seven in all. Wow, I realized, there was a cross for every body part that is associated with the body as female. Was I even a woman anymore? Did I now have to take hormone pills to be artificially female? Does being a woman come from a bottle of pills? I felt like I had been a male, a warrior, for so long, I really didn't know what being female felt like. I wondered if on some level that functioning as a male—a sole provider, ambitious professional, cancer warrior—had made the female parts of me become diseased, rejected, discarded, violently removed for some unconscious reason. I knew I enjoyed being a mother, although not a very touchy-feely one. I enjoyed home endeavors, crafts, sewing, embroidery, my Gene dolls, friendships, flowers, color, music, talking on the phone, shopping, clothes, makeup.

Were these some of the attributes of being female? I presumed I had two X chromosomes in each of my cells, does that make one a female? Yes, it does, by medical definition. Also, I still had my genitalia. So I concluded I was still female. I rationalized that nobody else could see the erasure of the now missing critical pieces of me, obliterated forever.

The XX part of me gave some fantastical notion of the idea of having a funeral service for these parts, complete with some burning (candles, campfire) and other women dancing, chanting in circles with flowing dresses as part of a grieving process, signifying the end of some era in my life. But it was brought up short by the strong current of male yang within me that said I was being ridiculous, *Snap out of it.*

In spite of the yang, I still felt heartsick and sad. Why was it that even though my former breasts were referred to as nothing more than sweat glands and their reconstruction good enough to fill a bra, I missed my breasts, their softness and excitability? And now that the uterus and associated reproductive organs were removed—the cause of melancholy, nervousness, depression, and hysterical fits, at least in misogynistic historical circles—I still felt all those things. Life is too bizarre!

My trips to the backyard also helped me wrestle with the notion of my sexuality. I finally deduced that sexuality was "all in my head" and therefore hadn't been removed. However, my interest in sex depended on the state of my marital relationship. When it was good, I felt sexual; when it was bad, I felt asexual. But I thought that was probably true for most people. I thought, *Too bad that it wasn't mostly good, because when things were good, the sex was great.*

I continued playing with my dolls. The collection by this time was obscene. I had multiple dolls in each major room of the house; I continued to change each doll's outfit based on my mood and the season. I delighted in costumes like Champagne Supper, which the preferred customer catalog described as follows:

> Romance blossoms during an intimate candlelight dinner in London. How could he resist her in this sumptuous gown of rich copper satin with fur collar and cuffs on the hourglass jacket? Cream roses accent the uniquely cuffed bodice, while two under-layers of gold crinoline add feminine fullness to the skirt. The outfit includes topaz rhinestone and golden jewelry, lined clutch purse with hand strap, gloves, seamed hose and shoes—Circa 1957.

I collected outfits like Hello Hollywood, Hello and Goodbye New York. I couldn't resist Love Letters, which included the costume's story in the booklet:

In the film "Love Letters" pen-pals plan to meet. He writes: "How will I know you?" She responds: "I'll wear something red." What an understatement! *Love Letters* is a two-piece cocktail suit in an explosion of vibrant red, circa 1947, trimmed with red bows and a red organza rose. Includes trimmed red hat, red bead hatpin, red gloves, handbag and shoes (all with red crystal beading), seamed hosiery (not red!).

I created a doll townhouse complete with all the official Gene furniture and doll props on the shelves of the armoire in our bedroom. (Armoire needed but purchased with Gene in mind.) The credenza at the front door was a doll scene that continued to change monthly. Doug said nothing of this. He was actually very tolerant.

Kim was accepted into Philadelphia School of the Arts' Musical Theatre department as a transfer student, so we headed to Philly to check it out. She met with numerous faculty members and was even offered a monetary scholarship. In the end, though, she decided that she wanted to take more academic classes and not just classes in performance, dance, and voice. She decided to finish her associate's degree and then transfer to a four-year college for some yet-to-be-chosen major.

I went to see a psychiatrist and was started on yet another antidepressant. I also started seeing a cognitive behavioral therapist. If I needed to pay someone to listen, I thought maybe this would be a new twist, to find someone who could help me change some of my patterns of thinking, anger, depression, sadness. I just wanted to feel better, sooner rather than later.

I kept myself busy, my usual modus operandi. Nothing was clicking on the job scene after several interviews. I started working on crafts, mosaics, painting flower pots, and adding whimsy to the house on the order of Mary Engelbreit. I refurbished my childhood toy box and stenciled the laundry room.

During the spring I was co-coaching Brad and his friends, seven 9 and 10 year olds, for a Destination Imagination competition. The children selected a "challenge," constructing a roller coaster that would maximize the number of oranges that would successfully make the trip in the time allotted. This had to be built on a limited budget and within very tight parameters for size, height, weight, etc. We visited the roller coaster exhibit at the Tech Museum in San Jose. We visited hardware stores. The kids had to come up with all the planning and solutions to the problem at hand. It was hard to be quiet and not lend advice, but without intervention they negotiated, planned, designed, and executed their solution. The other coach's garage became the construction site as the prototype for the project emerged—between our lessons on tool safety.

On the day of the competition we all drove up to UC Davis. The energy and excitement in the car was effervescent. At the competition, they completed the egg portion of the program, successfully transferring an uncooked egg seven times around a circle using a spoon (after numerous not-so-successful practices and clean-ups).

When their team was called to assemble and compete with their roller coaster, I held my breath and then cheered once the buzzer started the action. The kids worked together like a pit crew for NASCAR. There were a few glitches, but they calmly picked up and moved forward. Each of the team members had a job to do. Every orange went through a roller coaster course, and the fruit that successfully made it to the collection box at the end was worth one point. The gymnasium sounded like the Final Four, all for the grade school kids. Doug quietly stood manning the video recorder.

Brad's team came in fifth for the State of California. Brad was so happy, proclaiming, "This is the best day of my life!" Being part of that day and his joy made my living worth whatever it took to stay alive.

That summer was five and a half years since the first breast cancer diagnosis and four years since the second. When I wasn't overscheduled, I continued to ruminate in the backyard. What was wrong with me? Why couldn't I see my life as a huge gift, and cancer, as the spinning of straw into gold, making lemonade out of lemons, the turning point? Was I just happiest being miserable? I knew somewhere in those years I had lost my sense of humor and my love of life.

Cancer may not have killed me but it killed a part of me that wasn't in the body part cemetery. The problem with this war is that you can't identify who is the enemy and who shares the battle cry. The war is with your own self. Every instinct is to hate the enemy, but when the enemy is your own body, the anger turns inward, and becomes depression. The surge of battle is intuitively thwarted at the onset. There is nowhere to run or to hide. The problem with all these questions, questions, questions is that there doesn't seem to be an answer. Therefore, Cancer is the ultimate rhetorical question. The question, always the same with the Big C, is *why?*

The sickest part of all of this was that the rest of the world, including most of my closest friends, knew nothing of the demons chatting up a storm inside my head or the clouds of smoke billowing in the backyard. I believed the rest of the world saw me as fun-loving, having a zest for life, sometimes even wild and crazy—someone who was making the most of her life. But as Doug told me, "They don't really know you."

During the summer my upper back began to bother me. I assumed that I must have pulled a muscle, or that maybe it was stress and tension. Then I thought maybe it was due to the different sizes or weights of my reconstructed breasts. When it didn't seem to be getting much better, after weeks of Advil and heating pads, I went to my primary care doctor and was referred to physical therapy. They worked with deep heat, ultrasound, moist hot packs, and massage, and we pinpointed the focal points of the pain as primarily in the right rhomboid muscles under the shoulder blade and a few intensely painful areas along my spine. After a few sessions without seeing any improvement, they told me that they didn't know what else they could do. After seeing how upset I was, they decided to keep trying.

Pain wears you down and makes you very cranky. I was on one antidepressant during the day, a different one at night, hormone replacement therapy, and non-steroidal anti-inflammatory drugs for the pain. This was in addition to all the vitamins, antioxidants and herbal supplements I now took every day.

My love for my children, my dog, and the make-pretend world of my dolls was all that seemed to keep me going. The cognitive behavioral therapist wasn't helping in any recognizable way. I was just paying him $100 per hour to listen to my miseries.

Since I avoided all the darkest corners of my mind, I decided that some of my depression might be due to living in such a dark house. I felt that there was something wrong with the energy of the house. Feng shui was starting to become popular, so I hired a feng shui consultant to help me set things right. She told me that our house layout was all wrong but in feng shui theories there were remedies using crystals, water elements, plants, color, and mirrors. These were things that reflected light, redirected energy flow, and created balance. According to the consultant we had a problem with our career and money center. All the energy was rushing in a line through the front door, hitting the wall, and going nowhere. Our love corner was all wrong. We needed to add red for empowerment and to improve the career center, use carefully placed crystals to focus energy, buy a fountain, and other assorted remedies. I implemented some of her suggestions and became determined to remedy the entire house and to "feng shui" my life. But that would take time.

In October, I flew to Chicago for the annual Gene Doll convention. The theme was "A Toast at Midnight" to celebrate the new millennium. It was amazing to be with hundreds of people with the same obsession. My eyebrows were raised by the scores of people—including men—who were wearing exact, life-sized replicas of the doll's clothes and had not just one, but numerous costumes. The "Meet the Doll's Creator" seminar was like a mosh pit at a rock concert.

During the workshop on making luggage for the doll, I pinched the sewing needle between my teeth to pull the thread through the imitation leather and seriously chipped my front tooth. Here I was indulging on the order of Marie Antoinette with this doll obsession and now looked like I should take up residence in a double-wide down by the railroad tracks. What the hell was I doing? I decided to stop spending all this money on a doll and become a living doll myself—spend more time on my appearance and care for myself. Why didn't I think of this before?

Somewhere between the trip to Chicago and the repair of my tooth, I had a dream. I was in heaven with God, saint that I was. Everything was golden, glowing, and joyous. Doug had just died on earth.

God turned to me and asked, "Well, what should we do? Should we let him in?"

I didn't have to think about it for more than one second. I said, "Of course we should."

I woke up realizing with profound intensity that, when all was said and done, love wins and I loved him. I think this was a message of hope and helped me to relax a bit, realizing that in time I'd feel better about everything, including Doug. I needed to start focusing on the big picture of life and remember the many positive qualities my husband had. Then

I purchased a new car, a two-seat roadster convertible with personalized license plates. I sold my mommy car and said thank God and good riddance.

The trips to the cognitive behavioral therapist and physical therapist continued, without much, if any, improvement being noted on either front. In December, from out of nowhere a huge pimple-like thing erupted on my face, growing from nothing to Krakatoa on my left cheek within a week. It didn't seem to be a normal pimple; it was an eruption of another kind. After Christmas I went to see my plastic surgeon, somehow knowing this thing had to be removed. He did so immediately, sent it to pathology and informed me it was a keratoacanthoma. This news, which would probably be no big deal for most people, sent me reeling. This was yet another "-oma," a low-grade skin malignancy. What else was going on that I couldn't see? I couldn't stand it anymore. I was teetering close to the event horizon of the black hole.

The beginning of 2001 bumped along. I tried to focus on the steps necessary for Brad to apply to private middle schools, the testing and school visits. I called an architect to begin working on formulating a plan to remodel our house to fix the feng shui.

In early March we found out that Brad didn't get into any of the schools to which he applied. I was heartsick. I knew that he wasn't particularly motivated about the testing. Who knows how he was on the school visit? My experience with Kim at this age was that this was the age where the garbage starts. I thought he might have purposefully sabotaged himself.

The night of March 31, Doug and I went to San Francisco for dinner with friends. Our friends knew the chef at Moose's restaurant in North Beach and we were showered with special dishes and wines. The next morning, Doug and Brad left for Tahoe to go skiing for the day.

That day I fell into the black hole.

PART 3

CHAPTER 21

THE CATACLYSM

APRIL–JULY 2001

APRIL 10, 2001

I awoke the morning of April 1 in excruciating pain—a 10 out of 10. I could barely breathe. It was like I'd been run through from my upper abdomen to my spine with a spear and was left hanging on the wall.

I used the "hissing" and "heeing" breaths from Lamaze classes I took years ago to somehow get through the day. I also alternated between the usual feelings of hope and utter dread. Without eating or drinking and staying very still, I lived until Doug and Brad got home from skiing in Tahoe.

Over the next 24 hours the pain dissipated somewhat but it was now radiating under my right shoulder blade. Even still, I managed to resume normal duties and I didn't know what to make of what was happening. Over the next week the pain continued to subside, but I made an appointment with my primary care doctor, Dr. Donald, anyway, to see what he thought about this latest development.

After examining me, he thought that I might have had a severe gall bladder attack and ordered blood work, including pancreatic enzyme tests for amylase and lipase. He called me at home a couple of days later to see how I was feeling and to tell me that these pancreatic enzymes were still significantly elevated, a week after the initial attack. When I told him that I was still experiencing abdominal pain as well as a nonstop headache, he said that he wanted me to go to the emergency room and be admitted to the hospital for tests. I couldn't imagine what could be wrong but I knew it couldn't be good.

APRIL 11–16

After being given adequate pain relief in the emergency room, I realized how much pain I'd been enduring for weeks, even months. After doing numerous scans in the ER, they admitted me to the medical floor. I was a nervous wreck, squeezed in between two roommates, one moaning loudly in the process of passing a kidney stone, the other having some noxious intestinal problem. After much complaining to doctors about unrelenting migraine headaches (probably due to caffeine withdrawal), I was transferred to a private room for some peace and quiet and given caffeine in an IV drip, since I wasn't even allowed ice chips.

After the acute episode appeared to have been subdued with painkillers and forced starvation, the oncologist told me that the CT scan revealed a large (8 cm) tumor in my spleen that was not related to the cause of the pain. The visiting oncologist said that the large mass on the spleen was probably lymphoma.

Before discharge, I learned from the doctors that the probable cause of the pain, which had now been named "pancreatitis," was gallstones, possibly stemming from excessive doses of hormone replacement therapy or (they implied but I emphatically denied) a drinking problem.

I was discharged from the hospital and instructed to schedule and attend numerous follow-up appointments with specialists and to get more lab work done.

MAY 14–17

The severe abdominal pain continued. The only thing that helped was not eating, which has resulted in my losing 15 pounds. I located a gastroenterologist affiliated with Stanford Hospital and scheduled an appointment for a consultation, but before that could happen I was back in the hospital.

I was moved from a semi-private room to a private room after, again, being plagued by headaches and insomnia. Then, while I was outside smoking, I suddenly became very weak and would have collapsed had it not been for Doug holding me up. In between scheduled radiology tests, I was informed that something was wrong with my blood and I would need to be tested for hepatitis, HIV, and other viruses and would then be seen by the hematology experts. Initially, my diet consisted of nothing other than an IV drip.

My blood tests weren't good (hematocrit of 35.4, a white cell count of 2.5, and a platelet count of 79). They said it might be a recurrence of the Epstein-Barr virus that caused the mononucleosis I'd had in 1972, or I could have a parvovirus. Everything else was negative. When no qualified hematologists could be found (due to the entire department's attendance at some out-of-state conference), the residents descended, complete with a cellophane-wrapped smoking cessation kit, which was abruptly refused, citing that I was already dealing with enough.

A CT with 3D reconstruction study of the pancreas revealed a prominent pancreatic duct with small "vague low attenuation in the region of the pancreatic head." I was told no discrete mass was identified.

At this point, they were thinking that the mass in my spleen might be a hemangioma (a benign blood tumor). After a couple of days of fasting, my diet was changed to clear liquids to replenish my now scant blood supply, much of which was currently located in the lab, still undergoing tests.

Clara came to visit. In between interruptions from medical personnel, we shared the following moments of temporary sanity and laughter:

The attorneys have been called!

This is the best medical care in the world?

The victim has left the building!

Who's in charge in here, anyway?

In what other industry do you have to pay top dollar to be abused?

$10,000 a day—a bowl of Jell-O and not even a pedicure?

I hope it's contagious!!

Who are the ones who are really sick?

How wide does the crack have to be?

Physician, do no harm, do nothing. Patient, heal thyself!

Zero: What we knew yesterday. Zero: What we know today. Zero: What we will know tomorrow.

"You picked a very bad time to be sick"—according to the attending physician.

I was discharged with instructions that included a diet of clear liquids and Boost. I came home to the end of fifth grade for Brad, the graduation of community college for Kim, an extended visit by my mother-in-law, and Doug's return to work. This left me juggling all the balls with arms so weak I could barely hold a cigarette to my lips.

MAY 24

I met with my oncologist today. I am appalled to learn that the mass on my spleen has been there—in its current size—for at least 5 years, but it was never reported despite repeated prior testing.

"Just how large does a mass have to be to be seen by radiology and appropriately noted?" I asked. My oncologist looked like a deer in the headlights. Apparently an 8 cm tumor was not worthy of note in 1995.

I am fearful of falling through the cracks, especially since I have now shrunk from a size 10 to a size 6. I feel another war is coming. The enemy chatter has been monitored; the word tumor blatantly and repeatedly appears on the screen, missed by all intelligence (perhaps an oxymoron) for years. The enemy cells are deeply embedded. I am frustrated and very depressed.

MAY 25–26

My anxiety was curiously under control as I was prepped for the ERCP (endoscopic retrograde cholangiopancreatography) procedure. I was semi-conscious while they inserted a vacuum cleaner–type hose down my throat, through my stomach and duodenum, and into the common bile duct. I noted that it was very unpleasant. I had previously been told that this procedure could incite an acute pancreatic attack and I would therefore be staying overnight in the hospital to be monitored. I awoke feeling very beat up.

The next morning, after no episodes of pancreatitis occurred, I was visited by the gastroenterologist, Dr. Y. Doug was there when I was told that the test was inconclusive. He said there was no cytology confirming a cancer but that during the procedure he was unable to get a wire the size of a strand of hair through the stricture in the pancreatic duct, therefore a stent insertion was impossible. When I asked Dr. Y. whether he thought I might have pancreatic cancer, he was evasive. He made some allusion to "shades of gray" and then added, "It's a mystery."

After Dr. Y. left the room, Doug looked in my chart, found the report and looked at the photo taken during the procedure. In a breaking voice he told me that the report confirmed there was a large light brown mass blocking the pancreatic duct and the radiologist's impression was the worst, a pancreatic tumor was suggested.

I was discharged with a referral to a surgeon and prescribed diet of clear liquids, saltines, rice, pasta with no meat, and pureed fruit—but only if tolerated.

I am shell-shocked, still walking and talking, but feeling suspended from reality and not really here after being hit with a 20-megaton bomb.

MAY 30

I met with the surgeon. Clara came with me for support. Even though I was the patient, I was horrified throughout the entire appointment for the person having to undergo this operation. This physician, Dr. H.W.T. was pleasant and knowledgeable about his craft. He confirmed that there was a tumor blocking the pancreatic duct that needed to be removed.

He described the surgery, the "Whipple procedure," drawing pictures to help explain it. They remove the head of the pancreas, the entire gallbladder, the duodenum (the portion of the small intestine between the stomach and the jejunum). Then they open the tail of the pancreas and attach the stomach, the remaining portion of the pancreas, and the liver duct to the jejunum. Basically, they reroute most of the digestive system.

"Luckily," Dr. H.W.T. noted, "you are young and in good physical shape."

He informed us that they were also removing the spleen. He agreed to do a straight vertical incision rather than a curved one. I told him of my concern about disrupting the pedicle flap from the breast reconstruction. He agreed not to use staples.

He casually informed me that I would receive an epidural during the procedure to help control and minimize the immediate post-operative pain. The hospital recovery would be around a week to 10 days. Initially after the surgery, I would be fed with a feeding tube placed into the jejunum to allow the new stomach-jejunum attachment to heal. I would have several drains.

His schedule had an opening for 5 days hence. I agreed to the timing and walked out of hospital, but my mind went further out of the building to somewhere over the rainbow. I was imagining myself again as Scarecrow in *The Wizard of Oz* complaining about the mischievous winkie monkeys taking parts of my body and throwing them here, there, and everywhere. But the question was, where was the attachment connecting the brain? Sometime in early April my brain left my body.

MAY 31

Notes on Implementation of Operation Code-Named "Whipple":

Today—D-Day minus 4 (D-Day: day of massive assault/possible date of death).

Snap Out of It.

Pull yourself up by the bootstraps.

Prepare tactical offensive and defensive preparation for major combat. The Whipple procedure (not operation) is a whopper with a high mortality rate.

Stop feeling sorry for self.

Begin drafting the troops.

Secure the perimeter. Inform parents they are not coming to help since the general does not want to refocus on taking care of them instead of taking the hill.

JUNE 1—D-DAY MINUS 3

Celebrate Doug's Birthday.

Eliminate nonessential communications.

Assign Alane to post of Communications Director for tactical communiqués and family tree debriefing.

Assign Lyn to post of Assistant Communications Director for friends and California contingency debriefing, including the recording of daily communiqués on answering machine. Lyn to care for Indigo.

Arrange with Clara for all essential care of Brad.

JUNE 2—D-DAY MINUS 2

Arrange base fortification, including laundry, food supplies, settlement of financial obligations for during time of MIA.

Secure post-operative help through sister Alane.

Initiate reconnaissance with God through the receipt of Sacrament of the Sick and prayer circle at church, mass intentions, prayer chains at other churches.

Write letters to children and Doug to be opened in the event of mortality.

JUNE 3—D-DAY MINUS 1

Prepare mindset for war, hijacking of the body, and being held deep inside enemy territory with assumption of enemy control of body for prolonged period.

Remember to breathe.

Discuss last wishes with Doug and give him sealed letters.

Enjoy last rations of clear liquids, cold chocolate Boost.

Take 2 mg of Ativan for sleep.

D-Day

I was prepped for surgery while functioning in a state of nonreality. I talked, answered questions, made jokes, played games of cards with Doug, and appeared cooperative without actually being present. I was busy contemplating the abyss, reconciled that I'd been charged, found guilty, sentenced, and was awaiting my deserved execution.

After saying good-bye and I love you to Doug and Kim, I was wheeled to the operating room. My vague memories of the preparations in the cold operating room included insertion of an epidural catheter, signing my consent for participation in some prebiopsied pancreatic "tumor" research, placement of anti-embolism stockings, burning in veins.

I awoke immobilized, a POW inside the enemy lines. I heard women talking in the background, fussing with some of the tubes around me. I attempted to make contact with these people, to express the severe pain I was experiencing.

I was ignored. I passed out.

Time passed. Intermittently conscious, I repeatedly tried to contact the enemy to express my distress. Finally, I was told by the guard that I shouldn't be having pain since I had an epidural.

Apparently it wasn't working. Hours drifted by as I fainted in and out of consciousness. Finally, when I started moaning loudly—or maybe just screaming, the anesthesiologist came in and realized that the epidural must have failed. He began to administer some pain medication, the first since the surgery. Divine mercy had intervened on my behalf. I realized I wasn't literally in the hell of a POW camp but in the recovery room after the surgery.

Once I'd been moved to my room and given a button connected to a machine to self-administer pain medication, I dosed and dozed in and out of consciousness, never more than 25 percent relieved of the pain. Many days later, Doug told me I was barely recognizable. My head was the size of a large pumpkin; my tongue was engorged, cracked, and very sore. He sat with me throughout the night, pushing the painkiller button when I couldn't and gently wiping my tongue with glycerin swabs.

The next morning, I was conscious enough to realize I had survived but didn't know what they found. My body had become the war zone. I had a central venous line in my neck, IVs in both arms, was on oxygen, in a bed that pumped air, had a catheter for urine, a tube draining my stomach with a puncture hole, a tube going into my small intestine with another hole, a tube and associated hole coming out of my liver, a couple of Jackson Pratt drain tubes, more holes and an incision running down the entire length of my abdomen—with no staples, thank God. It felt like someone had broken my back in three places.

As I became more alert I realized that I couldn't see well and asked for my glasses. They were missing and assumed lost somewhere post-admission. I was in a haze of disbelief, spared execution but now awaiting the next round of selection, the results of the pathology.

On day two, the surgeon told me that my spleen, which they had removed, had completely become a rare benign blood tumor called a hamartoma. I remembered the resident saying that there were approximately 185 documented cases of this type of thing. I was asked to sign something giving them permission to study this fine specimen. Their enthusiasm for this "gift" of my body part reminded me of the character Renfield from *Dracula* and his obsession with procuring and delight in eating spiders and flies. Maybe I should have sold it on eBay to the highest bidder.

The results of the pancreas pathology revealed that I had a small tumor, a new primary adenocarcinoma. We were all still waiting for the results of testing the rest of the tissue.

The nursing care on the post-op floor was exceptional. Apparently the rules of the Geneva Convention were applied there. I had never been that needy, totally dependent on the good graces and the compassion of others. Days drifted by. I was made to get out of bed and start walking. Doug arranged for me to have a massage in my room to help with the pain in my back. The masseuse who came couldn't even touch it. I asked whether I could have an infection from the epidural or if it could be from organ nerves being cut during the surgery, like the phantom pain after an amputation.

The cruelty of the patient-controlled analgesia, or PCA, machine is that you can press the button for pain medicine all you want, but you will only get the prescribed dose, at a designated interval. After that dose, nothing happens until the machine says you can have more.

A pain management team was consulted and finally, after some adjustments were made to the medication, I started to feel some relief. I was sent for many X-rays of my back, culminating finally in an MRI. For that, they had to clamp the tube that was draining the acid from my stomach, so while in the tunnel for the MRI, my stomach was filling up. I had to stave off vomiting until reaching my room, where I just made it to the sink in time.

By the end of the first week after the surgery we learned from the surgeon that there was no metastasis.

"You are a very lucky girl," Dr. H.W.T. said.

He was going to be getting back to us in the next few days to see what further treatment was required. I was a very lucky girl, indeed. The small tumor grew in exactly the right place to cause symptoms. Too bad I felt nothing except unlucky that I had yet another cancer, the third primary cancer. This was the fourteenth surgery since 1993, four more body parts to add to the cemetery of me, which now totaled eleven. And I was probably looking at another round of chemotherapy.

The anesthesiologist came by to see how I was doing. The head nurse in the recovery room interviewed me for an incident report that she was filing on the two nurses who ignored me in recovery. Security came by and filled out paperwork to file a claim for the missing glasses.

After a week of staying with me, Doug left for home, and my sister Alane took his place in helping to care for me. She helped me bathe, walk, learned about the care of all the tubes, the flushes, and the feedings that were going directly into my intestines.

While she was caring for me in the hospital, Doug helped Kim move. She had been accepted by the University of California at Santa Barbara, had rented a room in a house of women on a street overlooking the ocean, and was ready to start looking for a part-time job before classes started. She had accomplished all of this completely on her own. I understood that she needed, finally, to get out of the house, away from the gloom and doom and away from cancer. I was sad, glad, horrified, and proud of her all at the same time. She was gone, my baby.

Over the next week I was gradually able to decrease the pain medicine, go to the bathroom, shower with all the tubes, and walk the halls with all my baggage in tow. While walking through the halls I saw several pancreatic cancer patients who had had the same Whipple operation, but only to relieve some of their pain. They were jaundiced and didn't have a good prognosis. They were going to die, soon.

I started feeling a little bit lucky. I guessed it was all a matter of perspective. The intermittent chatter in my head repeated, *What are you complaining about? Think of all the people in the world with no arms, no legs, worse off than you, stupid!*

The surgeon told me I was scheduled to consult with an oncologist in a few weeks, and I was discharged after almost two weeks in the hospital. I had a painkiller patch of Fentanyl and many instructions. A nurse was scheduled to show up at the house later that afternoon with all the equipment for my care and feeding. The ride home from the battlefield—in what felt like the equivalent of a Humvee—was treacherously bumpy, as was the next week of recovery interspersed as it was with equipment failure and clogged tubes.

Alane's help was followed by a week of Nancy's care. By then I was more able to get around. Some of the tubes were removed by the surgeon. I couldn't get over the length of these tubes inside me. I felt so much better with them out, all except the remaining J-tube for continued feeding. I was getting stronger every day.

After doing much research and reading up on the topic of pancreatic cancer, Doug and I met with an oncologist at Stanford. He had been recommended by the surgeon. We were told that since pancreatic cancer was so aggressive, even though I had a small localized tumor, I should consider receiving 5-FU through a continuous pump into my abdomen for a few months, followed by radiation therapy. This was their standard treatment for adjuvant therapy (for preventive purposes or cure of remnant cancer cells), and this doctor was their top gastrointestinal oncologist. I thought the treatment protocol was a bit antiquated, based upon our research, and I was horrified at the thought of having a thing coming out of my stomach for months.

He mentioned the survival statistics for my case. I remembered hearing I had a one in five chance of living five years, the same for living one year with or without treatment. My head was spinning (a possible 20 percent battery life remaining, only if you want to believe it). I wanted to see an expert. He recommended Dr. T., a doctor at UCSF Medical Center whom we had already read about in our research. She was an expert on the little they knew about pancreatic cancer other than what everyone knew—it was aggressive and fatal. I was being sent to the front line once again.

In San Francisco, the doctor explained that it was extremely rare for a pancreatic tumor to be found at stage I. There were no treatment protocols for this scenario, since there had never been enough people to study at this stage. However, she thought I might want to consider a chemotherapy regimen that used a relatively new promising drug combination called Gemzar and Cisplatin, or else Gemzar alone. The course of treatment would be around six months, I wouldn't lose my hair and I shouldn't feel too horribly incapacitated. She did not recommend radiation in my case, since I'd had such a reaction from the radiation years before. She also added that the pancreas is hard to isolate without "sterilizing" the surrounding tissue. I noted to myself that we were still in the cut, burn, and poison stage of medical science, so barbaric, a type of scourging.

Nobody could answer why this was happening. Did I have a genetic syndrome? Was there some sort of immunological treatment? It was so frustrating hearing "not yet." I prayed even harder for grace, *not strength* anymore, *not patience* anymore, just grace.

Doug was hanging in there. He was in shock, having just been given his next set of marching orders. His answer to everything was "in sickness and in health," implying that that was the vow he made. I wondered, exactly when the health part was coming. *Well,* I thought with a feeling of sadness, *he drew his lot when he chose me.*

CHAPTER 22

VICTIMS AND HEROES
IN THE AFTERMATH

JULY 2001–JULY 2002

Che war had definitely escalated. The nuclear bomb of a pancreatic cancer diagnosis had just detonated in the core of my body. While the prognosis indicated relative containment, the significance of what just happened was not yet knowable. How could I ever feel safe again? I was involuntarily redeployed for another tour of duty. I made the decision to receive the Gemzar chemotherapy treatment alone and have it administered close to home. But I would be followed by Dr. T. at UCSF.

Before treatment began I went down to UC Santa Barbara to visit Kim and to attend the parent orientation for transfer students. I was emotionally numb and could barely walk, lightly tiptoeing so I wouldn't feel as if my insides were ripping apart. Kim informed me that she had decided to pursue a women's studies major. I managed to help her with her class scheduling and really enjoyed seeing her, but she would be truly on her own once again. Mommy was checked out.

When I returned home, we drove Brad to Aviation Challenge Camp, and Doug and I spent a few days in Yosemite. I usually needed the ocean to put my life into perspective, but Doug needed the mountains. The majesty of the Sierras, the timelessness of the Yosemite Valley, the uncorrupted vistas of millions of years, helped me to realize that I could get through the next six months of treatment. After all, I thought it was a drop in the bucket in the scheme of eternity. I refused to focus on the fatalism of my prognosis. I continued to pray for grace.

Chemotherapy treatments scheduled for every three weeks began in August. In between my first and second chemo treatment I underwent the surgery to place a vascular access port in my chest, since my veins were shot. This was the fifteenth time I was rolled into an operating room in seven and a half years.

Brad's school year began at about the same time, with all of its associated busyness. Doug decided to be the head coach for Brad's soccer team, which would involve evening practices and weekend games. In between driving to school, preparing meals, and going to doctor's appointments, I was dragging. I felt horrible from the chemo, exhausted. As usual, everyone else's life had moved on, the parades were over.

I turned to prayer with renewed vigor in an effort to find some comfort, peace, and quietness of mind. I returned to Mary by praying the cycles of the Rosary ever more fervently. "Hail! Mary, full of grace, the Lord is with thee." Mary, the ultimate mother, the mother I needed to get through this. Mary, mother of Jesus, my loving mother, pray for me, pray with me, be by my side, help me to not go insane or abandon the ship.

Mary answered me. *You are a mother too. You can still be the mother your children need and I will be there for you.*

I needed to live for my children.

Oh poor, poor Mary, the mother of Jesus, having to watch in horror all of the events of her son's passion, being at his side for his death. This was the worst thing that could happen, the pain and suffering of having a child die, regardless of their age. This was to me, the horror of the most horrible. This perspective helped me remember that I would look to the future, knowing that this particular time, like all the other trying times, would pass and that there can still be good times. I wanted more good times.

My friend Robert came for a long weekend visit after my third chemo treatment. His visit was just what I needed to raise my spirits. I was blessed to have such great friends. Then, early on Tuesday morning, while Doug and Robert were en route to the airport for Robert's return flight to Virginia, my sister Alane called to tell me to turn on the television. A plane had just crashed into the World Trade Center.

I turned on the TV and watched in disbelief as the spectacle of 9/11 began. I called Doug on his cell phone to tell him to turn around and come home, since all the flights had been grounded. When he and

Robert returned, we all watched in horror as the disaster unfolded. It was unfathomable to see the first tower, and then the second, implode into a smoldering heap of twisted metal while belching an immeasurable ash cloud of incinerated concrete, glass, and steel. Even worse was the knowledge that in the ruins lay particulates of the occupants, the workers, the victims, who had spent their last seconds of life on this planet there.

Robert and I spent the next few days and nights transfixed, our hopes waxing and waning for reports of survivors. We felt a sense of loss for the devastated families of the victims and were shocked as we learned the details of the terrorist plot. We were paralyzed in utter shock that the Twin Towers, those icons of America, had been destroyed forever. Doug and I used to work on the floors where an entire brokerage company, Cantor Fitzgerald, lost almost every employee. Intermittently, and then increasingly, the stories of tragedy were replaced by reports of heroism, charity, coming together, and rallying, demonstrating that hope still remained in Pandora's Box after all the malevolent forces had been unleashed on the innocent.

It was providence that Robert and I were able to be together while these events occurred and that I was too sick from the chemo to do anything else. By the end of the week he was able to return home. Even when time seems to stop and we are suspended in suffering or move away from difficulty, the clock keeps ticking, the world keeps spinning, and we all eat, sleep, laugh, cry, love, and die.

SEPTEMBER 18

I received a call from my mother, who told me the news that my cousin Claudia's firstborn son had died in a motorcycle accident. Claudia, her husband, and her son were out for a ride together. She'd watched in horror as his body was smashed and mangled. She found his severed foot in the woods and brought it to the rescue helicopter. She wasn't allowed to go with him. He was taken to the hospital without the chance for her to say good-bye.

I called her as soon as I hung up with my mother. She was beside herself with grief and self-blame. Life for her would never be the same. The worst that could happen—for her, did.

This was a time of great introspection. The World Trade Center site, a place associated with a good time in my life, was now a pile of ash and rubble. It had represented my youth, my career, my good health, my hope, and a new beginning after Dave's death. Now Ground Zero seemed like a metaphor for my life.

While I rocked back and forth on the back deck, looking out at nothing particular, I thought back to a time when as children my mother brought my sisters, baby brother, and me to a beach in Long Island called Tow Bay. It was on the bay side of the island, not the ocean side, easier and far safer for four children, even though we weren't allowed to put more than a toe in the water. All day long my sisters and I gathered these little balls with golden specks in them from around the sand dunes. With these balls we built an imaginary city, an empire of gold, using some of the gold balls as imaginary people in our utopian civilization.

Near the end of this day of great fun, my father met us at the beach after work. We were so excited to show him the empire of gold we created. He asked us where we found all of this treasure and we pointed to the sand dunes. He laughed and proceeded to inform us that these pellets were rabbit turds. Instantly, our entire world of gold turned into a heap of shit. Life, even an imaginary one, could change in an instant, gone in a flash.

I was living in Cancerland—surgery, treatment, and recovery. But at least I was still alive. With the poor survival statistics I had been given but refused to believe, I was keenly aware that my life too could be gone in a flash. I decided that I'd better start to live life like I meant it, to start doing some of the things that I wanted to do and to get my mind off cancer. I made plans to join the choir, because I loved to sing, but also because it would make me committed to attend church every week. I started going to rehearsals for the chamber choir hoping that singing "For the Love of the Lord" would help me to feel better. Choir rehearsals were once a week in addition to singing at the 10:30 Mass on Sunday.

My angel, my primary care doctor, surprised me with a call at home to let me know he was retiring to care for his wife who had Alzheimer's disease. He wanted to wish me the best and tell me that he had been honored to know me. I felt so special that he would take the time to call me, let alone tell me that. At the same time I was sad that the "safety" was leaving my team. Who was going to replace him?

I finally met with the genetic counselor at UCSF. She told me that I met the criteria for a few genetic syndromes that they knew about and discussed each of them and how my blood and tissue samples would be sent to the various labs and universities where the studies were being done on BRCA 1 and 2, for Peutz-Jeghers syndrome and Cowden syndrome.

"There's probable certainty that your cancers are part of some genetic syndrome," she said. "And even if these particular ones turn out to be negative, it just means researchers have not yet identified your particular syndrome."

Having some answers might be good, since the implications for my family—children and siblings—were enormous.

I decided to go ahead with the testing finally.

On the night of October 26, after the fifth chemo treatment, I spiked a fever of 104.5 degrees and could barely walk. I called my local oncologist and was told to meet him at the hospital the next day. In the morning, I asked Doug to take me to the hospital, but he said, "I can't, I have to referee a soccer game."

I called several friends until I found one at home. My friend Mary took me to the hospital.

I was on the oncology floor of the hospital for two days, though nothing conclusive was discovered even after several tests. I decided that at my next appointment with the oncologist, I would be telling him *I was done* with chemotherapy. I thought that it might kill me, a heavy price to pay for some assumed but not statistically proved assurance that I would live. And I could no longer live with that.

In the aftermath of 9/11 and pancreatic cancer, I began to wonder, do we always need to have an enemy? Looking at it another way, does having an enemy ultimately make you a fighter? The daily news was filled with Al Qaeda, terrorists, anthrax scares, and the Department of Homeland Security. My own war was being fought in my mind. I wondered if there always has to be a duality—good versus evil, black versus white, God versus the devil, "us" versus "them." If there is always this sense of duality in our culture, then it would stand to reason that there would always be a hero and a villain.

The current heroes were the Americans, the victims of 9/11, the rescue workers, Mayor Giuliani. The known villains were the terrorists,

Osama Bin Laden, the radical, anti-American Muslims of the Middle East. But in my war, what was I? Was I a hero? Was cancer the villain? In my marriage who was the hero and who was the villain? Was I the hero because I was the victim? Or was Doug the hero because he had a choice to flee or to stay? Wouldn't the identity of the hero and the villain all depend on what side you were on?

Maybe each person's life is the life of a hero, sometimes recognized, but mostly not. But then I had to wonder, by whom do we want to be recognized? Do we even need to be validated by others, as are athletes, movies stars, politicians, our modern day heroes? What was the "golden fleece" for all the rest of us—the trophy, the memorial, the tribute, the medal, the ribbons and statues for the mantel, the reward and recognition? What is that saying—"If you're not a somebody, you're a nobody"? There are no parades for surviving cancer, beating the odds, or living with any chronic illness for that matter. But isn't each of us longing to be honored, loved for being special, uniquely able to navigate through each day?

I wondered who is it that punishes the villain—God, the Fates, karma? Are we all like the World Trade Center, punished like the phoenix, burned to the ground, only to rise up from the ashes over and over again? The unceasing cycle of death and rebirth begins again, I decided, just more frequently for me. I had to wonder just what exactly I was being punished for. I was not able to make any sense of it.

I decided that maybe the point is nobody truly ever gets it. That might be why there are myths, religions, wars, stories of human and supernatural dramas to help us to understand, ultimately, the basis for all the duality. I wanted to understand the ultimate question—What is the meaning of all of this?

I felt so lost, so alone, so I wandered further back to the church, to Bible study, needing to find something more concrete to believe in. If I was being punished by all of this horror, I wanted to amend, repent for whatever I did to deserve this. Maybe I was bargaining, who knows.

Lyn and I got a few women together for a healing prayer circle at church. It was a very intense experience. In a very loving environment we all began to pray; eventually a couple of the women began praying in tongues. I remembered vocalizing that I could not see the light or love of God inside of me, barely a faint flicker. For the next ten minutes or so we all focused on this. One of the women told me that God's love for me was enormous but that I needed to love that part of me, myself. I suddenly felt that for eighteen years I had been punishing myself for Dave's death and for living after having sworn the lover's oath that I would die if anything ever happened to him. I absolutely knew at that moment that his death was not my fault and that I lived for our daughter. The emotion of the release of all of that imprisonment was very intense.

Later in the prayer circle, now in a meditative, contemplative state, I saw myself in a small sailboat in a very calm lake. There was no wind so I couldn't tell in which direction the boat would go. I decided to leave it up to God. I was safe in the boat, floating, not sinking or struggling. The lake was calm. Maybe I could begin to forgive myself for self-punishing and stop the storm within my mind.

Since I had quit the chemotherapy, knowing in my gut that it was the right thing to do to begin to recover, I needed to put my house back in order. That meant addressing the mountains of doctor and hospital bills that had accumulated over the course of the past six months. In that time there were four hospital admissions and too many tests and appointments to count. I soon discovered that this was one of the reasons that my path had led to becoming a CPA, since it required that methodical, auditing mindset to make any sense of all of it.

After weeks of sorting out the mess I noticed some shocking business practices. The numerous mistakes in billing, overbilling, the declining balances over months of statements for bills that had yet to be paid was mind blowing. I couldn't imagine how anyone could deal with the magnitude of this mess if they were really sick or not an auditor. I spent hours on the phone making calls to doctors' offices, hospitals, the insurance company; spent hours on hold and debating poor accounting practices to get correct statements.

Fortunately, I was very well insured through my husband's company. The bottom line was that my expenses were capped. However, many business managers of my health care providers that were "contracted" with the insurance plan argued that I was responsible for amounts above the rates they agreed to accept as part of the contract.

Knowledge is power, and I knew they were wrong. Success hinged on being prepared (homework done, understanding the plan) and being a fighter (not easily intimidated as well as properly equipped—that is, armed with telephone and a fax machine).

The most astounding news of this ordeal, other than finding out that an erroneous $84 balance had been turned over to a collection agency, was that for the year of 2001 my total (billed) health care expenses were well over half a million dollars. The Whipple admission alone was more than $330,000. I realized in horror that if I didn't have the "good" and very expensive insurance I had (a preferred provider, freedom of choice), I would have been billed even more than the insurance company had to pay and most certainly would have had to find a way to come up with more than $500,000.

If I didn't have insurance, I probably would not have gone to the doctor and most certainly would have fallen through the cracks. My breast cancer or my pancreatic cancer would have grown to kill me. I wondered if anyone predicts mortality rates based on types of insurance plans, options, and health care provider choices versus just not insured. I felt very lucky and very blessed. I realized if I was someone else, my future would look very different. I know I would have already been dead.

By Christmas I woke up to the fact that one result of the past six months was a substantial deterioration in Brad's behavior and his grades. He had become very testy, pushing limits to the point of exasperation. He was only 11, but the situation was already getting out of control. He was a former straight-A student who was now in academic jeopardy. He'd been offered opportunities for advanced math and foreign language classes at the high school for the next year but was now failing those subjects. I didn't know if he was afraid and losing his self-esteem or just crying out for attention. He was sorely in need of some rescuing, and it felt beyond my abilities. Brad had become part of the collateral damage from the most recent campaign of my war.

My prayers were answered when a good friend told me about an educational psychologist who ran a clinic that had helped her son with similar problems turn around. I scheduled all of us for an appointment and Brad for testing in January after the holiday break. Marching, getting shot at, getting up, moving forward, I felt like a soldier in the trenches. Fortunately, I had not yet been mortally wounded, though I had taken plenty of shrapnel. I started beating myself up for letting Brad slip, but I was taking steps to fix the problem.

Christmas came and went. Alane and Cameron visited for the holidays. New Year's Eve, heralding the onset of 2002, was a black-tie affair (complete with karaoke) at Mary's house. Kim came with her boyfriend. She was doing well in school, safe, and out of the line of fire.

When Brad's school term resumed, we met with the educational psychologist, Dr. B., and found out from the results of testing that Brad was practically a genius, equally on both sides of his brain. He had no learning disabilities and was having to work hard at not doing well at school.

Dr. B. set us on a program of accountability for Brad, with rewards and consequences based on how hard he worked. We established a "contract" in which undesirable behaviors were previously agreed on by all parties, and consequences for poor choices took the form of Brad's picking a card from a deck of chores. This program took so much pressure off me—the highly invested, disciplinary parent, who no longer had control of anything. Several times a week we had to go to Dr. B.'s for check-ins, homework planning, study skills, and a weekly wrap-up. Coming home to make dinner was a five-mile drive in hell having to listen to my son, letting off steam—to put it mildly. But slowly, like the train chugging out of the station and then building up steam, Brad started getting back on the right track.

The results of the genetic testing revealed that I had no known genetic defect. The company that held the patent on the BRCA 1 and 2 gene testing billed me close to three thousand dollars, and our health insurance wasn't going to pay for it. I thought it was absurd that a private company owned the rights to test for a genetic defect. I couldn't understand how this could make sense since I had the view that the point of doing genetic research was for the betterment of mankind. In June of 2000 the completion of the successful rough mapping of the entire human genome had been announced. I wondered how much of the genome had already been privatized.

How could a company hoard segments of the universal human DNA or a disease-related DNA? I couldn't understand how diseases of genetic origin like diabetes or cancer could be studied if most of the population couldn't afford the tests because they are patented and considered out-of-network, out-of pocket expenses. I thought the United States was making bad policy here. My fury with this situation ticked me from a tropical depression to a Class 5 hurricane.

In any case, we found out that the retesting of my breast tumor revealed that it was 3+ positive for HER2/Neu overexpression. I would have been a candidate for Herceptin if it had been discovered and available in 1996–1997. The retesting confirmed that the tumor was estrogen and progesterone negative. The pancreatic tumor was tested and also found to be negative for estrogen and progesterone receptors. It was negative for epidermal growth factor receptor and the HER-2/Neu oncoprotein overexpression as well.

For the next few months, the family was on autopilot. Brad continued seeing Dr. B. Doug started seeing Dr. O., a psychotherapist. I saw the entire alphabet of doctors and had my regularly scheduled three-month scans, MRI, and blood work. Kim was dealing with her issues at school and working at the Women's Health Center.

I decided I wanted to have a party in July to celebrate the fact that I apparently was going to make it to the one-year anniversary milestone since the pancreatic cancer diagnosis. In all the fun of preparation, I was back to normal—other than having regular stomach aches and some back pain. My strength was returning. I couldn't understand how I could feel so well physically with so many body parts missing. Why did we have these parts if we really didn't need them? I was still on hormone replacement therapy, an antidepressant, and a tranquilizer for sleep. But I began to believe that life had a chance to be good again.

CHAPTER 23

SURVIVOR

JULY 2002

In a mood of optimism, I sat down with Doug and asked him what he thought about the party idea. "Let's do it," he said. I began planning. At the time, the revival of the reality show genre was still in its early days with the recent debut of *Who Wants to Be a Millionaire. Survivor* was in its second or third season. Though I had never actually watched it, I knew enough—between the name and the concept of competing tribes—to use in planning a theme party. We would hold the party outside in our yard and tribes of guests would perform group karaoke. The decoration theme would, of course, be island tiki.

The date was set for a weekend in late June. We invited around forty guests plus my family from the East Coast. Alane was going to come from North Carolina with her son, Cameron. Nancy was going to come from New Jersey with her boyfriend. My parents were coming as well, though even after a couple of years, I wasn't exactly looking forward to seeing them.

A week before the party, my parents arrived, hobbling slowly up the gate ramp after their cross-country flight. Wow, did they get old. Mom was only 68, Dad 73, but they seemed at least a decade older. When she saw me, my mother, as usual, sighed with her typical slouch and look of exasperation as she handed me all of her bags, before I even had a chance to kiss or hug either of them hello.

My dad seemed happy to see me. As he smiled a little sparkle appeared in his eye behind his glasses smeared and coated with flakes of skin from his eczema. He had shrunk in height, leaning to one side, and had grown a bigger belly. His pants pockets still looked like they were each filled with a sandbag containing every worst-case-scenario-planning artifact, a holdover from his Boy Scout days run amok. He unburdened himself temporarily of his carry-on bags to hug and kiss me, shrunken and crooked, his burdens embodied.

When we arrived back at the ranch, they settled themselves in Kim's room, unoccupied while she was away at college. They covered the double vanity in the attached bathroom from end to end with all sorts of necessities and contingency items. How all this stuff could arrive in two small suitcases was beyond me.

At this point, even though it was cool outside, our house air conditioner mysteriously was now set at 65 degrees. Hot water was suddenly no longer available. All utility meters spun at warp speed. This was all to be expected. It was an invasion, not house guests but complete occupation.

A visit from my parents required putting on my imaginary armor as well as constant vigilance—getting myself centered through meditation, breathing exercises, prayer, visualization exercises; discussions of pre-visit can and can't do lists with Brad; anything and everything imaginable to avoid a level 5 core nuclear meltdown of me. I had saved several projects to keep Mom and Dad busy and out of my hair for most of the week, including making the table centerpieces, helping with decorating, and adding to preselected playlists that were to be burned onto CDs.

For the table centerpieces they had to cut out the "Island Man" I'd copied from the *Survivor* logo and stenciled onto black foam sheets. Then they had to cover cardboard tubes with fabric using a glue gun, add the cheap fake fern for the top of the "palm tree," mount all of this onto a Styrofoam base, and add a "tiki-torch" candle.

At first, my mother seemed happy to be doing this, but soon the muttering under the breath began, followed by repeated huffing, and then outright complaining.

"I don't know why I even came, if all I'm going to do is work."

Everything wound up involving my direct participation anyway. *So,* I thought, *why did you come, Mom?* I wanted to scream at her, *You are here for you and only you, Mom.* Instead of confronting her I got a perpetual stomachache, which cramped further with her every huff and mutter.

Meanwhile, my dad seemed to have developed undiagnosed narco-lepsy sometime over the years and was constantly falling asleep in the middle of something. I'm sure this condition developed as a survival mechanism. Dad would fall asleep in the middle of a sentence, or while holding something at a weird angle, even while he was standing, and especially when he had the remote for the TV in his clutches.

That week, when I realized that he was MIA on a regular basis, I sometimes discovered him "napping" in bed propped up on several pil-lows—with one foot on the floor, just in case—listening to talk radio (Rush Limbaugh or the like), through an ear bud plugged into a portable pocket radio in his shirt pocket. Or he could be found scratching his eczema-patched head in front of our home computer ostensibly work-ing on the CD burning project but in reality searching the web for some obscure whatnot or trying to figure out why the computer just froze up.

Dad was harmless, and I could really enjoy him when Mom wasn't around.

But she always was around, and by 3 p.m. every day was screaming "BRRUUCCEE" from across the house. When he timidly appeared, she switched into exasperated prima donna mode, and as if she'd actually done something that day, demanded, "Make me a drink."

Being well trained, he obeyed. "Ice or no ice?"

During the final party preparations, Mom watched the live dress rehearsal of the Hidden Assets (my girlfriend group from the neighbor-hood) doing the self-choreographed routine of Shania Twain's "Man! I Feel Like a Woman!" while sitting in a lawn chair. Then she was attacked by the automatic sprinklers and retreated into the house.

We finished decorating the backyard, stringing tiki mask lanterns across the span of the back deck, wrapping the middle post with brown burlap, adding clusters of ferns to suggest a palm tree, and finally secur-ing the purchased coconut decorations that looked more like a large, hairy brown scrotum.

This back deck was situated behind our living room and master bed-room. It was covered by the roof, was thirty feet long and about six feet deep, perfect for the main event, the karaoke competition. The sitting room off the master had a doorway out to the deck, the perfect entrance for the Hidden Assets' act. The deck had a couple of steps down to the concrete walk and then the lawn. At the end of the house, the walkway continued to the playhouse nestled under the redwood trees. The play-house, built for Brad years before, was converted into a "tiki hut" where the bartender we hired would be making the party signature drink—frozen piña coladas—as well as serving beer, wine, and nonalcoholic beverages.

The night before the party, the rental equipment arrived. Just as we were finishing the decorating details, Doug hit the scene in the kitchen with bags of groceries purchased on his way home from work, all nec-essary to prepare the food for the party. He had researched his menu for days, planned his "secret" recipe for pulled pork sandwiches, dirty rice, cole slaw, barbeque chicken, and grilled veggie kabobs for the main event. Sushi, coconut shrimp, mixed fruit salad in a carved watermelon, chicken satay with peanut and teriyaki dipping sauces would be the appetizers. No one would leave hungry.

Leaving Mom with her drink of vodka and Wink, thinking she was talking with Doug while he chopped, sautéed, slammed, banged, and ran the garbage disposal intermittently, Dad and I snuck down to Brad's room to finish burning the CDs for the cocktail hour music for the party. Dad had showed me long ago that the music can make or break a party. He also taught me you could have a party with the right music without actually ever having anyone over.

We included an eclectic mix of rock, pop, country, doo-wop, Elvis, Frank, Hawaiian, and some Chicago blues. We timed the music to cre-scendo just as we would initiate the first tribal karaoke challenge. Dad and I had fun picking the music and singing along. I learned more about my dad's love of doo-wop music, his favorite being the 1955 jump blues song "Speedoo" by The Cadillacs. My dad was a great singer, but I'd never heard him just let it rip. He especially loved Nat King Cole and the Mills Brothers.

Later that evening, Brad and I went to the airport to pick up Alane and Cameron. Alane and Linda reunited, Linda and Alane, soul sisters. Brad and Cameron, cousins, buds, and the builders of worlds in the land of the Sims. Once back at home, this was an intolerable situation for Mom. You could just feel the heat rise; the ions in the air change, the skies darken throughout the whole house. It was Pompeii—before.

Fortunately, beds needed to be made, towels provided, sleeping bags opened while Mom's version of the vodka tonic quenched the eruption for the moment. Unfortunately, my stomach rivaled any USGS seismo-graph for geologic sensitivity, and my stomach ache wasn't getting any better.

The morning of the party, Nancy and her boyfriend Bill arrived from their nearby hotel. Nancy expected nothing less than to be immediately put to work, intermittently providing an escape for me and Alane from Mom-zilla for one of our favorite high school pastimes—passing a ciga-rette back and forth in the garage or behind the playhouse, laughing and making fun of our parents, relieving the tension.

The weather was sunny, mid-70s, perfect for a party. The roses were in bloom. We had a beautiful large yard, just a small lawn but wonder-ful terraced gardens bordered on both sides by majestic redwood trees standing sentinel. Behind the deer fence at the back of the yard was a sprawling California valley oak on the hill that ran into the open space that was part of Mt. Diablo State Park. The yard also had an in-ground pool with just enough decking for several four-person bistro tables. We had a sense of seclusion from our neighbors, but since our yard was a natural amphitheater, I was sure the noise would bounce back off the hill in back and be heard around the neighborhood.

Early in the afternoon, I ran out to pick up the tropical-colored bal-loons and arrived home just as the karaoke system was being set up and the servers and bartender arrived. With so many details to attend to and instructions to be given, this meant I had not quite finished dressing when the first guests started arriving. They were all good friends so it didn't matter that my safari shirt was buttoned up the front unevenly for the entire party and never completely tucked in.

In addition to the Hidden Assets—Lyn, Mary, Jane, and Kelly—and their husbands, ex-husbands, and boyfriends, we invited my fellow ten-ors from the choir (all men) and their significant others; neighbors; and friends, especially people like Clara and her husband Don who had been such incalculable support over the past year. At least a dozen people were preselected for each of the four tribes of the party. Everybody was given a "Survivor" name tag upon arrival with their tribe identity indi-cated on the bottom.

Everything was perfect. Everyone seemed to be having a great time, slowly but surely relaxing into the island party atmosphere. Kim arrived from Santa Barbara with a male she introduced as a friend and was in a happy mood. Doug joined the party looking like a Hemingway version of the Crocodile Hunter, dressed up with construction boots, thick gray hiking socks with a red band on top, khaki cargo shorts, a multi-pocket khaki fishing vest with his broad-brimmed canvas hat purposely snapped up on one side to complete the look. I was reminded once again how creative he was, for a CPA.

The piña coladas were flowing, though some partiers opted for straight rum on the rocks. The time came for Doug and me to open the karaoke with Queen's "We Will Rock You." Shortly after we began singing, I knew Doug had probably started drinking a while earlier, so our performance was bad enough not to intimidate anyone. Doug immediately followed that number with his solo performance of ZZ Top's "La Grange", playing an inflatable plastic guitar and jumping all over the "stage." It was especially funny considering his six-foot-three build and his normally quiet and reserved demeanor.

The first tribe was called up to sing "California Girls" and came up to the stage with some trepidation. It's always fun to watch who holds the microphone and whether they share it and foster group singing or hog it and only put the mike in front of a teammate during the instrumental parts. The second tribe came up to sing "My Boyfriend's Back," including the do-over demanded a third of the way through. Tribes 3 and 4 did their thing and by then everyone was having fun. Doug emerged as the life of the party, dancing across the stage, playing the inflated sax with the wrong tribe, blocking the karaoke screen, disrupting any hint of serious competition. After all the tribes had gone at least once, everyone got their prize, a large button pin with the image of *Survivor* man that said "I Survived—Zercoe's Karaoke 2002."

Singing, or something like it, continued with couples, girls only, and the neighborhood guys singing their standard "Brandy." My mom and dad lip-synched Louis Prima and Keely Smith singing "That Old Black Magic." Both my parents were such hams. My dad was wearing a straw hat and miming playing a string bass. My mother actually thought Keely Smith's voice was her own and she was playfully in heaven. For just a second I could see them young, healthy, fun, and happy. Then I felt sad that I hardly ever saw this side of them. My dad by himself was a clown, yes, but together? Mom? *Enjoy the moment,* I told myself.

Inhibitions were falling by the time Mary's husband, our friend Brian, went to sit on a chaise lounge and missed it by three feet, hitting the lawn with a loud thud. Not quite sure what had happened, he said he was dizzy. After we made sure he was all right and seated comfortably, the singing continued. Later, he laughed off the ordeal, jokingly accusing the bartender of slipping something into his one drink. Cameron had been drafted to video the party, so later we saw that Brian had made several trips to the hut for refills before the spill.

As the sun was setting, before dinner and The Hidden Assets performance, the guys all got up and sang Steppenwolf's "Born to Be Wild" while wearing all manner of head attire—sombreros, grass hats, police hats, hats with dreadlocks, Indian headdresses, construction helmets. Doug continued dancing, singing, playing instruments. I wondered at the time where he was getting his energy and later discovered that he, Kim, and our neighbor Dennis had each chugged an eight-ounce glass of Belvedere vodka.

In a flash it was time for The Hidden Assets' big show.

The Hidden Assets were great friends, each of us possessing larger-than-life personalities. By this time, we had several of these performances at various parties under our belts. Lyn's husband, Bob, wearing a conquistador's helmet, heralded the upcoming performance of our group as he pranced across the deck carrying the three-foot-by-two-foot black felt sign, edged in lace, handmade by Jane, with *The Hidden Assets* craftily scripted in Elmer's glue and gold glitter.

Out through the door and onto the deck to a chorus of hoots and hollers came Mary, Jane, Lyn, Kelly, and me, dressed in our costumes of short skirts and large men's white shirts ready to sing "Man! I Feel Like a Woman!"

> The best thing about being a woman
> Is the prerogative to have a little fun
> Oh, oh, oh! Go totally crazy ..."

We were great! The husbands loved it and were especially excited when we stripped off our white shirts, revealing T-shirts, and did the cancan.

It was time for the intermission, and dinner, before things got too wild. Too late, someone was screaming *Fire*. There were actually two.

One of the real tiki torches had fallen over and was setting some of the landscaping on fire. At the same time, up around the decking of the pool, the tiki mask candle in one of the centerpieces had fallen over and lit one of the rental tables on fire after melting the orange plastic tablecloth. (We had to pay for the table later.) No big deal—all was well. It was now time for me to have my first drink, forgetting my stomach in all the excitement.

The servers had set up the dinner buffet, and while our guests were enjoying the fruits of Doug's culinary expertise, other guests rushed to form duos and quartets, attempt harmonies, and serenade the diners. Whenever there was a break in the music, Doug and the now inebriated Kim tried without much success to sing a song. They were so out of tune and slurred I had to put an end to it before the guests started leaving or heaving. This is when I noticed that under his safari vest and over his T-shirt, Doug was wearing a black strapless bra—and it didn't belong to me. I could only imagine what our son Brad, almost 12, was making of this bacchanal when he intermittently tore himself away from his computer game.

Once dinner was served, I could finally really relax and have fun. The singing continued. The Hidden Assets reprised a former number—"Stop! In the Name of Love"—complete with our feather boas. Then the Assets surprised me with their own routine dedicated to me, "How Sweet It is to Be Loved by You," the James Taylor version of the great song originated by Marvin Gaye. I was touched and humbled, and impressed by what a great dancer Mary was. She had so much soul. I felt loved.

The party was still in full swing when my mother decided to bypass the stairs to step onto the deck, missed, and gouged a chunk out of her shin. In the midst of all the revelry, Alane came to get me to take a look at Mom's leg. After assessing the wound, and not in the mood to tolerate any belligerence or martyrdom, I decided I would have to leave my party to take both parents to the emergency room. Everyone else was trashed, unable to drive. I ordered my parents to the car.

At the emergency room, Mom was visibly frightened and crying. The doctor told her she would need several stitches and a tetanus shot. At one point, she said in a tiny childlike voice, "The only time I've ever been in the hospital was when I had you kids."

I wish I could say I had empathy for her, but I didn't. I thought, *You big baby, stop your blubbering.* When she wailed at the tetanus shot, I wanted to kill her. As she was complaining about the scar she would have on her leg as the doctor was stitching her up, I thought, *You bitch, how could I have even imagined that you had any idea of what my life has been like.*

I felt sorry for Dad, standing helpless and far away from the child-like spectacle of my mother. The clock ticked away the remainder of my party while we waited to be discharged. I wondered if subconsciously she'd planned to once again make it all about her. I decided that the next day, limping or not, infected, even gangrenous, they were leaving. I was getting a car to take them back to the airport.

As I suspected, when we arrived back at home the party was pretty much over. Doug was passed out. Mom and Dad went to bed. Kim was in the tiki hut sucking face with the guy I thought was her "friend." The karaoke company was hauling away the equipment while Alane and Mary were cleaning up the remnants of the party in the kitchen. After a bit, I insisted on driving Mary home since I didn't think she would make it otherwise—she was insisting on walking home, almost a mile up a big hill, after midnight.

When we arrived at her house a few minutes later, I walked her to the door, pointing out a hose lying across our path. Despite my warning, she tripped over it and fell face first on the stone walk. She insisted she was OK and once I ascertained that there was no visible bleeding to attend to, I left her in her house and drove home. She was still chanting "I'm OK. I'm OK" as I pulled away.

The next day, while everyone was attending to their hangovers, Mom and Dad left in the black town car. I waved good-bye, feeling guilty but only as long as it took me to walk from the curb to the front door. Back inside the house I began making phone calls to invite people over for the traditional day-after party to eat the leftovers and watch the video of the event.

My out-of-town guests and The Hidden Assets, absent their husbands, came over. We were still waiting for Mary when the dog's barking alerted us that someone was coming up the front drive. It was Mary in a hospital gown, using a walker, sporting a shiner equal to a ten-round heavyweight boxing match. Several construction workers working on a remodel across the street were standing at the end of our front walk staring at the spectacle of this hospital patient coming to our house. Leave it to Mary to play down her real injuries; hanging out of the open back of her hospital gown was a very large naked plastic ass. I could see why the workers might have thought it was real from a distance.

At the end of the day, we all rated the party a great success but decided that in the future maybe we should have an ambulance and a fire truck rented and on standby. The next party, I decided, would be when I lived to the fifth anniversary, the next milestone, with even worse supporting statistics. I couldn't imagine. Kim would be graduated from college and working. Brad would be midway through high school. I would be so blessed to see that day. But for now, there was a today.

It took the whole summer to clean up the mess.

CHAPTER 24

THE RELUCTANT CONSCRIPT

JULY 2002–JUNE 2003

While passing the milestone of my 45th birthday we began to formulate plans with an architect for a house remodel. In August, Doug and Brad went out for a chartered deep sea fishing trip off the coast of Mexico, and I headed to Santa Barbara to spend a few days with Kim. She was thriving and involved in so many activities, especially ones that involved women's issues. I could see that she was hardly ever at the beach. I was so proud of her. One more year and she would be done with college.

Her apartment was half of a duplex fronting the ocean high on a bluff with her room in the upper loft overlooking the surf. The décor of the house was heavily varnished wood paneling similar to a ship's interior. It was quite a sanctuary from the *Animal House*–like ambiance of Del Playa, the party street of Isla Vista near the campus. During the day, Del Playa sparkled from the shards of green, brown, and clear broken glass while young males in boxer shorts chugged liquids on the street-facing balconies—not unlike Bourbon Street in New Orleans, except for the architecture. Pairs of sneakers dangled overhead from the utility lines and the humid coastal air carried the smells of rotting garbage, vomit, and the smoke from smoldering sofas.

At night, and especially on the weekend, the streets were like Mardi Gras—hordes of young, long-haired blonde females in short shorts or short skirts strutted back and forth, drinks in hand, between the shirtless well-muscled young men sporting surfing tans, all checking each other out. Giggling and hooting erupted frequently—the mating calls of *Homo americanus*. Couples paired up and left for doorways or darkened

corners. It was very different from when I was this age; everything
seemed so overt, hormones on overdrive.

After a dinner in town we went back to Kim's apartment to get caught
up on our lives and our sleep. But as the evening wore on the music of
the street became louder with the thumping of multiple subwoofers, the
pounding rhythm of rap, rapid-fire booms and crashes, sounds of shat-
tering glass.

The next day I was given a tour of the Women's Health Center where
Kim was spending many hours volunteering and doing peer counseling with female students. She was active in the university's Take Back
the Night campaign, which was making strides in campus safety and
facilitating sex crime reporting. She was also involved in WETT, the
Women's Ensemble Theatre Troupe, which was putting on *The Vagina
Monologues* on "V-Day." Kim's part involved depicting the various types
of female orgasms, complete with sound effects. *How did she know these
things?* I wondered. I left her in her college environs and returned home,
surprised by how little I really knew my child—who was no longer a
child but a young woman with her own identity, interests, and talents.

September was filled with return checkups with more doctors. My blood
tests were starting to reveal that I was consistently showing elevated
serum calcium levels. My oncologist thought I should consult with an
endocrinologist, another specialist, to evaluate the possibility of hyperparathyroidism, which could be caused by benign parathyroid adenomas. Was this next? This was supposed to be my off year.

Long before, I had noticed a pattern—all of the tumors were diagnosed in odd-numbered years—breast cancers in 1993 and 1995, funky
fibroid tumors in 1997 and 1999, and pancreatic cancer in 2001. It was
now 2002. I wanted to break the trend by not getting any more tumors,
not by getting another tumor in an even-numbered year.

The tests at the endocrinologist confirmed that I had a "mild" case
of hyperparathyroidism but that I didn't need to do anything about it
immediately, if ever; it all depended on symptoms. I didn't know what, if
any, symptoms I had, so I decided to dismiss the whole thing and focus
on living, moving forward.

Brad was doing much better in school. Dr. B. was really helping to
get him, and our family, back on track. Church choir and guitar lessons

continued. There was too much running around, and I was feeling run down. We continued planning our remodel, but I had fired the architect and was researching an alternate plan.

After the New Year I got a stomach ache that wouldn't go away. After a couple of weeks I called my oncologist, and she told me to get myself admitted to the emergency room in San Francisco. It sounded so easy, but arrangements had to be made, bills had to be paid, school applications had to be mailed or dropped off. Once that was done, I headed to the hospital, only to find that the ER was in full SARS contagion mode. Signs were up everywhere with instructions on hand washing, touching, coughing, sneezing. Some of the personnel were wearing masks and disposable gowns and booties over their clothes. When I saw a few people wearing goggles I wondered if coming to the hospital was more of a threat than the potential of recurring pancreatitis.

I was shown to a bed, and blood was taken. No, I didn't know that my abdomen was rigid, hard as a board. There were the usual questions—no, no, no, yes, no. The ER physician assigned to my case came in and told Doug and me that my amylase and lipase, the pancreatic enzymes, were through the roof. The blood level of amylase was close to 4000 and lipase over 1800 (compared to normal levels in the low hundreds and under 100, respectively). They started an IV with a Dilaudid painkiller drip. Soon I started to feel better. Again, I wondered, was I so disconnected from my body that I could live with all this pain? Was the fear of finding out what was causing it worse than actually experiencing the pain?

They wanted to admit me but I soon learned that I would be under the care of a doctor in the medical service on rotation in gastroenterology, not my own doctor. Since I had a GI doctor at another hospital, I wanted to go there. I told the ER doctor that I was leaving and would arrange to have myself admitted to Stanford the next morning. I had Vicodin at home for the pain, and I assured him that I wouldn't eat. The doctor and his staff looked at me with puzzlement. They said that with the enzyme levels as high as they were, the pancreatitis so severe, it would be dangerous for me to leave the hospital. Someone mentioned to Doug that it was likely that the pancreatic cancer had returned.

He was beside himself, but I knew that being there wasn't what I needed to do. I had to sign a release that said that I was knowingly leaving the hospital against medical advice. And then we left.

At Stanford, I received the usual treatment for pancreatitis—no water, no food, no ice chips, only an IV with painkillers until the symptoms subsided. In the meantime, I had limited testing that revealed that indeed my pancreas was inflamed and the pancreatic duct was dilated. Again the doctor and his entourage hinted that the cancer had more than likely returned. Within the week I was discharged and a follow-up appointment scheduled in a couple of weeks with Dr. H.W.T., the surgeon, after some outpatient tests, including a PET-CT.

Why was I getting pancreatitis? Did I have a recurrence? Was it my diet? Was it drinking alcohol on New Year's Eve? Were there microblockages in the ducts? The wheels started turning. I thought this was just a problem to be solved.

I knew I could easily remove any alcohol from my diet. I read somewhere that a high-fat diet was not good with hypercalcemia (high calcium) and would certainly cause the release of lipase from the pancreas. I decided that I could switch to a low-fat diet to help my pancreas. In fact, I soon became obsessed with my diet. I knew I didn't get pancreatitis if I didn't eat at all. I started to eat just vegetables, fruit, potatoes or rice, chicken, and fish.

After just a few days at home, my friends from church arranged another prayer circle—this time to pray for a miracle. It was imperative that this be done before the PET-CT so there would be nothing to see on the scan. My friends Lyn and Mary were there again. Doug came. There were also three other women, all of whom were extremely involved in the church.

We made a circle with seven metal folding chairs. We sat down and held hands. While we were led in general prayers by a woman named Martha, I closed my eyes and silently set my intention in prayers of petition that I would be cured of whatever was causing the pancreatitis. I offered prayers of gratitude for all the blessings in my life. While this was going on, the other people in the circle were praying fervently, and once again a few of them were transfixed and speaking in tongues. I soon found myself outside of my body leaving the room and walking up the center aisle of the church dappled in the soft golden afternoon sun. There were candles lit in addition to the paschal candle, which I thought was unusual since no one else was there. I laid myself on the floor before the altar, face down, arms spread. I raised my head and looked up. Somehow the altar disappeared and I was lying just before the large crucifix. I felt so humble. I gave my life to God and believed with all my heart and mind that I surrendered to God's will and that was that. I opened my eyes and realized that I was still in the Heart of Immaculate Mary room off the lobby of the church with everyone else, tears streaming down my face.

After this powerful shared experience, the tears and the hugs, Martha handed Doug a large rock with "Seek The Truth" engraved in it. I felt a weight lifted.

After the PET-CT but before my appointment with Dr. H.W.T., I had an idea. I knew from earlier in the year that I possibly had hyperparathyroidism. The parathyroid glands, located in the neck, regulate the levels of calcium in the body. In hyperparathyroidism the levels are not regulated properly and there is too much calcium in the blood. In addition to causing osteoporosis, kidney stones, and heart disease, hyperparathyroidism causes headaches, fatigue, bone pain, depression, irritability, trouble with sleep, fogginess, forgetfulness and a low sex drive. *Gee, I'd thought I was just dealing with cancer, chemo, surgery, my marriage and life!*

I pulled together all the blood test results I had for the previous ten months and plotted a graph using colored pencils—blue for results in the normal range for the parathyroid hormone, green for elevated, red for elevated calcium, and turquoise for normal. From the graph I could see that the parathyroid hormone went up out of normal range and then, soon after, the calcium level went up. Comparing the graph to entries in my journals, I learned that as the calcium level went up so did my malaise and symptoms of pancreatitis. But I could not identify anything that would cause the parathyroid hormone levels to go up in the first place.

I brought my chart with me to the appointment with the surgeon.

"It is very unusual to see pancreatitis post-Whipple surgery," he said. While almost jumping up and down like a 5-year-old saying Look, Look, I handed him my color-coded graph. He ordered an ultrasound of my parathyroid.

He called me later that week. "Well, Linda, it appears you may have an adenoma of the parathyroid, and this could be causing the fluctuations. I would like to order a sestamibi scan to take a better look."

A sestamibi scan is a nuclear scan of the parathyroid glands. I soon found out that I had not one but two parathyroid adenomas, one on each side. An adenoma of the parathyroid gland is benign, but is a tumor. Still, a benign tumor was so much better than a recurrence of pancreatic cancer, and for that I was relieved.

"This finding is very unusual," he told me at a subsequent appointment. "I'll order a consult with the best chap for this sort of thing. He's at UCSF."

I thought I'd found the cause of pancreatitis, which may have been the precursor to pancreatic cancer, with my primitive charting. No matter, that was just my ego. With an otherwise negative PET-CT and a positive sestamibi scan, I was sent to yet another specialist, an endocrinology oncological surgeon. While waiting for this consultation, I thought back to the many stomach aches I'd had in childhood. Could I have had intermittent hyperparathyroidism, intermittent hypercalcemia, and intermittent pancreatitis ever since then?

Surgery to remove the tumors was scheduled for the end of June. In the middle of that month we headed down to Santa Barbara for Kim's college graduation. Thanks to my new fat-restricted diet, I was now a size 2.

The first night we were there, we were invited to a special ceremony where Kim received a university service award. The dean of the school and several professors came over to greet us, singing the praises of Kim and how much she'd contributed to the school with her Women's Safety Committee work and volunteer hours. Another joyfully related how much she loved having Kim in her class. It seemed—not that I'd ever doubted it—that Kim had really blossomed.

The next day was sunny and hot. The commencement exercises were held outdoors, in full sun. I started crying as soon as we got out of the car. Doug and Brad asked me what was wrong.

"I don't know ... nothing ..." I said, and just started crying harder.

We found seats and waited while I kept wiping the tears away, blowing my nose using every manner and condition of paper product found in the depths of my purse.

The music started over the PA system, and the procession began. After half the seats were full, we could see Kim boasting a smile from a Christmas morning past and prancing in the procession sporting feather boas in all the colors of the rainbow.

What I released that day was twenty years of worry and hardship, and finally relief. I had lived to see the day that my daughter graduated with a college degree. I wondered whether I would live to see Brad do the same.

Within a week of the graduation, the parathyroid adenomas were removed. Other than waking up in the recovery room with a startle—suddenly returning from a free, expanded state and then being squeezed back into my body—the surgery was uneventful. Within a couple of weeks I started to feel like I had more energy and no longer felt the bone pain I hadn't realized I had.

I didn't have another occurrence of pancreatitis for many years.

Doug and I hired contractors to start a major remodel of our house beginning in September. At the meeting I was still wearing the post-surgical bandage on my throat. I have no idea what the contractors thought might have happened to my neck.

CHAPTER 25

RENOVATION

AUGUST 2003–DECEMBER 2004

At the end of the summer Kim moved to an apartment in San Francisco with a friend she had met while biking the coast of California in a cancer research fundraiser.

We rented a U-Haul and helped her move into a second-floor, two-bedroom walk-up over a donut shop in the outer Richmond district. We gave her much of our furniture (a mutual benefit) and filled a ten-by-twenty storage unit with as much of the rest of the contents of our house as we could before the remodel was to start.

The construction was scheduled to last from six to nine months and encompassed almost every room of our house—new energy-efficient casement windows replacing the old single panes, a new roof, a new kitchen, a remodeled master bath. Hardwood floors and new trim would be installed, walls moved, the ceilings raised. In other words, it would be a total mess.

Still recovering from the finding of yet more tumors, I was sent again to genetic counseling. There I was tested for more genetic syndromes, all of which were found to be negative. Since there were still no western medical answers about why this kept happening, I turned my focus back toward eastern and alternative medicine.

Through my acupuncturist I met Tricia, a marriage and family therapist. She also happened to be a certified hypnotherapist. She was very knowledgeable in indigenous and world spiritual practices. Her office was serene; in addition to earth tones décor she had feather decorations, rattles, and plenty of turquoise.

She asked me to make myself comfortable on the cushy velvet sofa and offered me a pillow, a chenille blanket, and an eye mask filled with lavender. After weeks of sessions where we got to know each other, she helped me through guided imagery to see the lake in my mind of calm and stillness, which I could access any time I wanted. She was always offering her gentle and mothering suggestions or giving little gifts of wisdom or homework for me to do.

For example, she would assign chants for balance, *ahh–hee-oh-hum-om.*

"These," she said, "are to balance all your elemental energies, to balance your male and female sides and connect you to the universe."

It all sounded interesting, I thought. I had no idea what she was talking about, but I vocalized the sounds regularly while going through my routine at the bathroom sink. She was a former Catholic, she explained, but now she was "spiritual." Her path in life exposed her to many different belief systems and truths.

She prepared a natal chart for me using the time and place of my birth. She did the same with a Mayan astrological tool. She discussed the Enneagram and personality types. Over and over she kept asking, "Can you imagine a life without cancer, without trauma?" I didn't understand what she meant. I understood the words but not the idea. I did learn from our guided imagery sessions, however, that I had a rich visual and creative imaginary life. I could conjure up images that were so full of depth, color, and texture that it was hard to imagine that they weren't real.

She said, "You are a manifestor."

"What's that?" I asked.

She explained that I was a creator and, as such, I was also able to create my reality. She told me it was important that I spend time setting my intentions and channeling my creations externally and in ways that I truly wanted. I believed I was already doing that. I had helped to create the plan for the remodel, worked with the architect, the kitchen and bath designer, was selecting materials, wood, tile, working with the cabinet makers, designing trim. I saw everything in my mind's eye and then hunted and gathered until I found exactly what I was looking for. Slowly, very slowly, the plan was executed. Later, I realized that my view of being a creator was extremely narrow.

We were living in three rooms of the house—which three varied depending on where the contractors were working. Our cooking was limited to a microwave in the garage and an electric frying pan in the laundry room. We ate out most of the time. The roof over our kitchen was removed and new scissor trusses were added to raise the ceiling. Even though our plans had been approved by our homeowners association, the day that the roof shingles were to be delivered we received a written notice that the association had contested our roof material and sent us a letter to cease and desist. We lived with a blue tarp on our roof for the entire winter while working with a lawyer and eventually an arbitrator. The temperature inside the house averaged about 50 degrees, and the pitter patter of rain sounded like continuous rifle fire.

In February, I went to see my father in North Carolina. He'd just been diagnosed with bladder cancer.

Dad had been dealing with kidney stones for years, so back pain and blood in his urine had not seemed unusual. The onset of heavier bleeding sent him back to the doctor, and he returned home with a diagnosis of cancer. He was scheduled to have surgery using cystoscopy and some scraping. This was similar to what my Aunt Marion had had done years before. I hated to do it, but I had to return home right before his surgery, since I had to be there for the final hearing that would deal once and for all with the issue of the roof.

I fell in love with Doug again as he presented our case before the homeowners board and the attorneys. He was eloquent and well prepared on every point. (It was interesting that while we were dealing with this issue and the never-ending skirmishes with the contractors during the past nine months we got along great—we were united.) We won the war with the board, with some arbitrated concessions. Our remodel proceeded.

My dad's operation was a success, and the cancer seemed to go into remission. Brad was accepted into De La Salle, an all-boys Catholic high school, for the next fall. Success at last. The three of us went to Hawaii while our oak floors were being finished.

While we were there, Alane called to tell me that Dad's cancer had returned. Even though we had been told they had gotten it all back in February, it appeared to be infiltrating the wall of the bladder and was now in his liver. She said my father was told he should consider getting chemotherapy but that he seemed reluctant. The chemotherapy wouldn't cure the cancer but might slow down the progress. His oncologist said he should evaluate the quality of his remaining life with and without chemotherapy.

What was I to do? I was almost five thousand miles away.

I called my father as soon as I got home. "So, what are you going to do, Dad?"

"I guess I'm going to do it," he said with resignation.

"It doesn't sound like you believe it will help," I said.

"I made the decision to have the chemotherapy for the family." He sounded defeated.

In the next few weeks he had two treatments. He had an allergic reaction to the chemotherapy and was having angina attacks. The oncologist said he would need to be admitted to the hospital for each of the remaining treatments to monitor his cardiac status. He was also scheduled for a scan of the bladder to see if there was any shrinkage in his tumors. I decided to go back to North Carolina in the next month.

When I saw Dad in July, he looked exhausted. He had suffered from the effects of scoliosis and kyphosis as long as I could remember. In fact, throughout my childhood I had spent hours kneading the knots in his twisted back with my hands, elbows, knees, and heels. He always sat in "his chair" with a ball pressed against some part of his back. In recent years many of his gifts from the family looked like implements of torture inspired by the Inquisition, all intended to relieve his back pain—balls with pointy acupressure knobs, some hook thing that looked like a shepherd's crook, massage rollers, shiatsu appliances and whatnot.

When Mom finally stopped hovering and went outside for a cigarette, Dad smiled. He was happy to see me. He spoke with bewilderment about his diagnosis and prognosis while heavily leaning on the sharp corner of the wall in his kitchen, rolling his body from side to side.

"What are you going to do?" he said. "I blew it."

It pained me to see him this way. For some reason he was blaming himself. I knew cancer was a tricky thing. How many times had I blamed myself?

"It's not your fault, Dad," I said.

I had never before seen him as someone so vulnerable, although I remembered he was somewhat passive when he'd had heart problems years before. I think what I realized at that moment was not so much that he was passive but that I *wasn't*. I was strong. I was a fighter. I was relentless. When I was a little girl, Dad was my hero. But now, more than anyone else, even Scarlett O'Hara, the heroine of my young adult years, I was the hero of my life.

I went with him to the oncologist for a checkup before his next treatment and listened as he got a download on what to expect. He didn't have any idea what questions to ask. This was something that was being done to him, and he was not going to be present. He treated the doctor not as an ally but as an omnipotent superior. Maybe this was a generational thing. I had never seen my father this submissive and powerless, but that night while lying in bed I realized this was exactly who he had always been.

In the eleven years of dealing with cancer, treatment, and surgeries, I had grown up. I no longer saw my dad through the eyes of a child. He was still an adult, but as powerless as a child. I worried that without his buying into the plan with his mind, body, and soul, it would be a miracle if he beat this. But even with his prognosis, I still had hope. I believed in the miracles.

Back at home, as the contractors slowly moved through the house, I followed behind with my eight- and sixteen-foot ladders, tarps, rollers, brushes, and pans. For the rest of the summer, I painted every single wall of that house, though I left the windows, doors, and trim for the pros. I selected colors like Warm Apple Crisp, Acorn, Wilmington Tan, Sandy Beige, Basil, Lenape Trail, and Custard. While I rolled away, day after day, room by room, I listened to the entire Led Zeppelin anthology over and over again, committing every lyric and guitar lick to memory. I listened to the music loud enough through my earphones to drown out the sounds of nail guns, slamming, cussing, and barroom renditions of ZZ Top sung by the contractors.

I felt good in spite of what was going on with my father. I was up early in the morning every day and then went up and down the ladders until dusk. Some days I would go out in search of materials, knobs, hardware, paint, window treatments, and furniture. My goal was to create a home of peace and Zen, eliminate the clutter, clean up, and cover every corner with freshness and light. I was rebuilding—this time with brick.

I realized that when Dave died, I'd rebuilt my house with straw. The house blew down when I got cancer. Then I rebuilt my house with wood

It repeatedly burned to the ground when I got cancer again and again. Now I was using brick, creating a more stable and durable structure to live in.

I was taking guitar lessons and actually learning Led Zeppelin songs. Playing and practicing the guitar was a total immersion into the present moment. I was becoming a better player but knew I would never have the time, at least for the time being, to be great. I had to take a break from singing in the church choir during the remodel but kept going to Bible study throughout.

In July, I went back to see my father. He had lost weight but didn't look any thinner. He had questions about reverse mortgages. I learned he didn't have a will. He didn't have an advanced medical directive. He had securities—paper certificates—in his name only. My mother didn't have power of attorney; nobody did. He was preparing to die. He knew he had to think about what would happen then.

It was difficult to discuss these things with my mother around, though. He wanted to talk about it, but my mother kept saying, "This is none of your business" and "Why do we need to talk about any of this now?" He wanted each of his children to tell him what stuff of his we wanted. Mom blew a gasket.

I could tell from his face and his breathing that Dad was in a lot of pain, but he never complained. My mother was never much for ever allowing her children to have any alone time with Dad. So when she would start drinking early in the evening, and finally passed out in the family room, I would sneak into their bedroom and lay down next to my father. He told me things I never knew about him. I listened to stories about his childhood, his brother, his mother, and his father. I heard how my mother and her family made his life complete. I listened to his worry about leaving my mother with a financial mess. He told me how proud he was of me and all his children. I heard about his career. Night after night he would talk and I would listen until the wee hours of the morning, friend to friend, human to human, heart to heart, father to daughter. By the time I left for home they had a banker, a broker, and a lawyer. My father met with the priest that I arranged to have come to the house. He made his confession and received the Sacrament of the Sick. We held a prayer circle.

I left without knowing whether I'd ever see my father again, but you get to a point in life when you feel like that each time you separate. I felt during the trip that I had been a Martha, the type of woman who is always doing, doing, task-oriented, taking care of business. Years later I realized that I had many moments of being Mary too, just being present, listening and loving.

Brad started high school in the fall. The contractors were still in the house but their numbers were dwindling, and some days no one came at all. It had now been a year. The whole house had been virtually destroyed and was now almost back together.

The house was like my life. While I painted, I thought how many times I had almost died to live, been destroyed to be born again. Did I have to almost hate my husband to learn how to love him? Did I almost destroy myself, bringing my life to the brink to learn to love myself? Could I accept myself as I was, imperfect, unable to paint over the cracks in my foundation, the dark spots bleeding through the paint, the imperfect human part?

The third week of September, Alane called me, crying hysterically. My father had been admitted to the hospital. That morning they'd had to call my brother to help my father who was propped up against the wall of the shower, unable to move. He dressed him and somehow walked him to the car after gathering up all the essential belongings that my father had prepacked. Once he got in the car, Dad was immediately paralyzed from the waist down. Later that morning they learned that his cancer had not only metastasized and replaced his liver but was now wrapped around his spine in several places and had eaten away the vertebrae.

After I made my flight arrangements, Alane phoned again and told me that my mother wouldn't leave the hospital; she and my brother were taking turns taking care of my mother. Dad was getting high doses of pain medication and radiation to relieve the extreme spinal pain.

A few hours later, Alane called a third time.

"I had a vision out of the blue," she sobbed. "Mike Williamson just spoke to me and told me that they were all so excited about Dad coming. They were getting everything ready. The equipment was almost done being assembled and wired. Mike told me he was so happy he was one of the people that was chosen and given the honor to welcome Dad."

"Who's Mike Williamson?" I asked.

"Don't you remember? When Dad had the store, Mike was the kid that Dad took under his wing and invited to come along on all his recording jobs," she cried.

I vaguely remembered.

"Remember he was decapitated in a car accident? Dad was broken up for weeks. Don't you remember?"

I remembered. "God, I haven't thought about that guy for more than thirty years!"

"Neither have I," said Alane.

I got chills all over my body. "Wow," I said.

"'Wow' is right."

"I don't think Dad is going to make it, Alane."

"I know."

Alane picked me up at the airport and brought me directly to the hospital. My mother had been there for two days straight. Dad wanted me there and for everyone else to go home and get some rest. Lying on his back in the bed, he had an IV, a nasal cannula for oxygen, and EKG leads all over his chest. His belly was covered in shiny skin that looked ready to crack and explode from the ascites caused by his failing liver. After everyone left, they came in to take him to radiology for a spinal radiation treatment. He told the transporters that he wouldn't go unless I could be with him the entire time. He was terrified.

On the way, the gurney hit every bump and banged into every door jamb it passed through. The transport people didn't care, not even after I told them that he had a broken back. I wanted to kill them. It almost seemed they were doing it on purpose. In radiology, I held Dad's hands as the tears rolled down his face from the pain of the trip. We waited in the cold, bustling hallway long after his IV pain medication ran out.

Back in his room afterwards, I wondered if the benefit of the radiation was worth the ordeal of getting there and back, being moved from the gurney onto the radiation table and back, handled roughly every step of the way.

When he was medicated and finally asleep, I went downstairs to get something to eat. When I returned, my mother was back, and my sister had brought my nephew. After they left, I could tell my dad was scared. I told him to relax and try to get some rest. I asked if I could read to him. I had brought my Bible and asked if he would like to hear the Psalms. He said he did. That seemed to do the trick. He finally fell asleep. While he slept he kept scratching his skin, and I noticed how long his nails were. My dad was a meticulous person. I went to his toiletry bags in the corner of the room. I was horrified to see baggies containing batteries of all sizes, a pocket knife, Band-Aids, radio cords, supplies for contingencies of every sort, bagged in a way that appeared obsessive. All of a sudden I realized that my father had a severe obsessive-compulsive disorder that had never been treated. Things about him started to make sense.

I never got a chance to trim his nails. He awoke in the predawn light having taken a turn for the worse. He was trying to take off the oxygen cannula and all the EKG leads. Nothing, it seemed, would calm him down. The alarms went off and nurses rushed in. They explained this behavior was due to the decreased oxygen to his brain. He kept picking at his skin.

"Can't we sedate him more heavily?" I asked. They called the doctor, and eventually he got more medication.

The priest came. Dad was out of it. He was still fidgety and restless and seemed to be constantly trying to get up, to hurl his body forward.

"What are you doing, Dad?" I asked.

"I see it," he said.

"What do you see, Dad?"

"I'm trying to get over the fence."

He must be hallucinating, I thought, or maybe he wasn't. He drifted in and out of consciousness.

Later in the day I realized that maybe the fence was the obstacle preventing him from letting go, to die. My mother returned. I told her what had developed.

"Ma, I really think you need to tell Dad it's OK. You will be fine. He can let go."

My mother looked at me, eyes filled with tears. But she did it.

For the rest of the afternoon, Dad held my hand on one side and Mom's on the other, saying over and over, "OK, OK, let's go. One, two, three ... Go."

It was like being in the delivery room and being told to push, except that Dad was trying get to someplace I couldn't see. It was so hard. It was breaking my heart. In between attempts he would collapse in exhaustion but still keep trying to pull everything off. Nurses kept coming into the room, responding to the alarms. Finally I asked a nurse to come out to the hall.

"What are you doing?"

"He keeps setting off the alarms," she said.

"Why can't you just leave him alone to die in peace?"

"Well, we didn't know that was the family's wishes. We don't have an order that says DNR or Do Not Resuscitate."

After discussing this with my mother, sister and brother, we all agreed that the nonsense had to stop. I informed the nurse.

Quickly, the leads were removed, the oxygen was taken away, his morphine was increased, and plans were made to transfer him to the oncology floor. By now I had been up for over thirty-six hours. I was exhausted from trying to help Dad "jump." I'd done all that I could do. I kissed him good-bye for what I knew would be the last time. Alane drove me back to her house, both of us in tears.

I couldn't believe I'd been so stupid, that I had allowed him to suffer so needlessly. I didn't know. Then I plunged into despair when I realized that I was the one who made them pull the proverbial plug—I'd killed my father.

Eventually, I fell asleep, only to be awakened by the phone in the middle of the night. Dad had finally made it to the other side.

He died on my brother's birthday, the day before my mother's birthday, two days after their forty-eighth wedding anniversary.

It took me a long time to realize that I was exactly what my father needed at the time and that everything had happened just the way that was necessary for everyone to accept his dying. For me, being with my father during his last day on earth helped me to see that dying isn't hard—he seemed to want to hurl himself there. He could see what was there. Dad's life was over, but he had helped me to realize that my life wasn't.

My mother came to California for a few weeks over the holidays later that year. This was the Christmas when, almost seven years since we got our first dog, I finally gave in and gave Doug the second papillon puppy he had wanted, an 8-week-old, one-and-a-half-pound female.

He cried in front of everyone, saying, "This is the best Christmas present I've ever received."

CHAPTER 26

LIVING IN THE PROMISED LAND

JANUARY 2005–OCTOBER 2006

With the remodel finally finished I could finally return to the land of the living. The first place I went was back to church. I rejoined the choir. While probably an alto, I felt more comfortable in the tenor section. I was the only female in a group of half a dozen men ranging in age from their forties to close to ninety. Learning the tenor part was hard as the harmony was almost always a fifth of an octave below the melody. I know I was barely heard except when I sang the wrong note, which was often.

My friend Lyn was the Bible study director and I'm pretty sure at this point was also the director of religious education, now working full time with her newly minted master's degree in pastoral ministries, post–empty nest. One day she asked me if I would be willing to be a group leader for the Bible study. As with most commitments I had to think about, one breath later I said yes. I thought this would force me to do the homework. It wasn't until much later that I realized I never questioned what was behind committing to an activity that forced me to do something I wasn't inclined to do naturally. But at this point I still wasn't deliberating before committing.

So every Wednesday morning I now had a reason to get dressed up, and I was at church yet again for the 9 a.m. leaders meeting. We prayed, discussed the business of Bible study, and then went over the entire lesson before we met with our groups. My group gathered in an ancillary building that was always cold, so we snuggled together on old sofas. Everyone there was on a quest—to learn more about the why of what we believed. We had great debates about the Baltimore Catechism, the elimination of limbo, plenary indulgences, the validity of purgatory, the abortion issue, and the latest priest sexual abuse scandal and concurrent cover-up, which seemed to occur weekly.

There were over a hundred women in the larger group. Many were mothers of sons who were in high school with Brad. It really was fun, and participating gave me a great sense of community. It was in the larger group that I learned the story about the chipped tea cup, the story of the starfish, the meaning of the four cardinal virtues (justice, fortitude, temperance and prudence), and the three theological virtues (faith, hope and charity). I learned of "The Lowly Road," where to heal the mind you need to forget; to heal the heart, forgive; the body, forgo; and to heal the spirit you need to surrender to God and do everything for God. Maybe these choices were what "free will" was all about.

We studied the Gospel of Mark, did our next study on the personal relationship with God, and then the mysteries of the Rosary. The overall group was close to having completed the whole Bible and beginning to debate how to start over.

I asked, "Have we ever done the Book of Job?"

In a thwack of unison I was told no. Then I heard individual comments. "It's too depressing." "People will quit." "No thanks, life is hard enough."

Well, I thought, you can't fight city hall—or the cry of the mob.

I finally used the gift certificate for painting classes that I had received from The Hidden Assets for my birthday a year before. Once a week for several weeks, I packed up my paints, brushes, and canvas and headed to class. I learned how to mix colors, set up a palette, and lay down paint.

I enjoyed the class but soon realized that painting was something that I would rather learn by doing and not in a class. So I set up my easel in the house and painted with a fury. My first painting was a fall landscape done in acrylic. The second painting was a copy of a *New Yorker* magazine cover of a man selling pumpkins. Upon completion, the picture turned out to be a portrait of my father. My first foray in oil painting was done on a four-by-three-foot canvas and depicted a scene in the Sea of Japan done mostly in shades of red. When I wasn't in church or working on things for church, I was covered in paint. I realized that, while I was painting, I thought of nothing else, including the guilt of being away from a mother who was drinking heavily and grieving.

As the house started filling with drying canvases, I switched from listening to music while painting to books or courses. Among a score of books, I listened to *Energetic Boundaries* by Karla McLaren and learned I didn't have healthy boundaries. I listened to Eckhart Tolle's *Realizing the Power of Now* and learned about Tolle's concept of the "pain-body" (accumulated emotional pain) and realized just how big mine was. I learned how my thoughts were reactive and that except for when I was singing, playing the guitar, or painting, I was never in the present moment, the "now." I listened to *Sacred Contracts* by Carolyn Myss and learned about archetypes and her tools to figure out your divine purpose.

The list of books on CD went on and on, and what I realized was that there were plenty of perspectives on looking at life and spiritual matters. All of these ideas were categorized as "new age," and the ideas presented were all on the order of heresy. The authors were probably classified as charlatans from a conservative Catholic-based perspective. Wasn't that what St. Paul warned of in the Bible? Yet, I could now blame my lack of boundaries for allowing me to sin and my trickster archetype for leading me down the wrong path, the one away from the pearly gates.

The spring college-visit trip for Brad to the East Coast was preceded and followed by two trips to visit my mother. She was overwhelmed; I heard it in almost every one of our daily telephone calls. When I was there, she constantly lamented that she didn't know what to do with all of Dad's stuff. She had two boats and a house to sell, other stuff to get rid of. I never saw my mother so incapable of taking even the tiniest of baby steps. All of a sudden she was incompetent, immobilized. I had to wonder whether grief had done this to her or if it came from drowning her sorrow in wine. It was hard to be patient since she was still so prickly. She couldn't make a decision but also wouldn't let me make one for her.

I set up a few containers on the floor one day and we started going through all the boxes from the garage that were stuffed with papers from Dad's high school days; Dad's days at Grumman; Dad's days of working on the lunar mission; his drawings, doodlings, blueprints; articles he found interesting; sheet music; magazines on jazz, boats, electronics; items from his father and mother. Everything smelled of mildew. In between sneezing and blowing my nose, I would present an item to my mother and we would negotiate whether it would go in Linda's box, my sisters' boxes, my brother's, the trash, or the "for sale" box. There wasn't a Mom box.

She didn't know what most of the stuff was, and apparently didn't share any interest in these parts of his life that he had cared enough about to save. She would begin to cry about how little she knew him after forty-eight years of marriage, then switch to raging anger about what a nerd he was, and then topple into despair, moaning about what a horrible wife she was. The process was exhausting, and I was heading toward a sinus infection.

Mom drank and drank and talked and talked and cried and cried, and I listened until I couldn't stand another minute. After a couple of 3 a.m. drinking, talking, crying nights that revealed nothing new, I said, "Mom, do you think you might be depressed?"

"No, I'm great. I'm just so angry."

"Mom, do you think it would help if we found a grief support group for you?"

"Why would I want to listen to anyone else's problems? I have my own. I'm too young to be a widow. Why would I want to spend time with all those old people?"

I quickly did the math in my head; she was 71. She forgot I'd been a widow at 26. I learned during those weeks that, inside, my mother was still a teenager. She wanted to kick up her heels, find someone new to wait on her, and fill up the hole. Instead she was buried alive in boxes of my father's stuff, a constant reminder of the real loss that she still denied.

I had already lived through this experience, and the thought of going into the deep with my mother was making me sick to my stomach. I tried encouragement.

"Mom, you will get through this, step by step, day by day. Maybe you can't move forward because you aren't ready to yet."

"Let's go out to look at houses." And that's what we did for the rest of the visit.

Brad was now a sophomore in high school, the time when someone typically receives the Sacrament of Confirmation, although only if they are ready. Funny, I was in fifth grade when I was confirmed, ready or not.

Brad asked all the right questions, including the one I couldn't answer for him. "Why should I bother getting confirmed?"

Indeed, I thought, why does anyone get baptized, receive communion, or any other sacrament for that matter? I told him that we were Catholics and as such we believed in the sacraments and the teachings of the Roman Catholic Church. It was a lame answer, I knew.

He enrolled but I'm sure he didn't know why. I hardly modeled the virtue of "prudence," or good judgment in making decisions, which was defined as right reason in action—gathering information and weighing the consequences.

In December, I was asked if I could teach a confirmation class that was already in session but short a teacher.

I said sure.

I thought that I could learn along with Brad and show commitment in action. Everybody thought it best that he wasn't in my class.

I would have twenty or so 15- to 18-year-olds who would probably not be happy to be there, and certainly not on a Sunday night. I thought about how to approach the class in a way that would engage them, impart the teachings of the Catholic Church, and prepare them to be "sealed" in the faith. I had a topical syllabus that I'd need to cover but had full creative freedom on how to cover it.

The fill-in matching worksheet on the attributes of God worked well; the lecture part of the lesson didn't. Working in groups was a success for the class on Jesus, but some of the kids almost wound up in a brawl during the class on morality. They loved the *"Jeopardy"* game I created on the books of the Bible, and disappeared from the church one by one as we walked the Stations of the Cross. They were heated up on the teachings of the Church on social justice, arguing sometimes with and sometimes without sound reason the concept of a just war. But then we were all happily surprised by all the good works done on behalf of humanity by the Church even in current times, since we normally weren't really aware of what the Church did.

Brad didn't like his class. They were using crayons, paper, glue, scissors, and stickers. I thought about having Brad join my class but knew it would make my job harder. I already had one problem kid: Carly, the 18-year-old who claimed she had to be confirmed or she would be kicked out of her house. She came in late, reeking of alcohol, and spent the class time texting, rolling her eyes, answering questions sarcastically. She was a beautiful girl, blonde, scantily clothed, and could have been a model. The boys in the class liked that she was there.

I didn't know until the end of the year that before class she and her brother were out in the parking lot getting high. When I made an attempt to befriend her, I was horrified to hear about her troubled life. When she asked me, I agreed to be her sponsor. *Yes, I could save her from hell and damnation.* Oh, the ego! I learned over the remainder of the year when meeting her for a soda or speaking with her on the phone that she was a beautiful person who had lost her way. Not surprisingly, she didn't make it to the mandatory weekend retreat in the Santa Cruz Mountains.

When I would come home on Sunday nights after Brad helped me clean up my classroom, I would find the master bedroom lit with candles or with a bath already drawn, sometimes with rose petals floating in the water. Maybe Doug was missing me with all the nights out of the house at church activities, but then again maybe he was happy seeing me occupied and seemingly happy with what I was doing. We were still getting along great since the pancreatic cancer and the remodel—four years, maybe a record.

Romantic evenings ended with me watching EWTN—the Eternal Word Television Network (Catholic cable television)—until the wee hours of the morning. I especially loved Father John Corapi, a repentant sinner and latecomer to the priesthood. He had programs that I had recorded on the VCR called "How to Make a Good Confession," "Immaculate Heart of Mary," "Surrender Is Not an Option," and a multipart series on the "Catechism of the Catholic Church." I was rapt. Doug would ask me, half asleep, "Would you please turn Father Crappy off, for God's sake!" I lowered the volume until I got my fill.

Early in the new year we helped my mother move into a newer home in a community with plenty of young couples with children and a few older homeowners. It was far away from civilization and, most important, big enough to fit all of her (and my father's) stuff. She soon decorated it beautifully, and then took to the shovel.

Day after day, sunburned and bruised, managing tools with her rheumatoid, crippled hands, she created an incredible garden out of the hard North Carolina clay. The garage was filled with Dad's stuff, which she had moved to a different house and still not dealt with. Soon she started complaining about the noise of all the little children in the neighborhood riding their bicycles and playing in the road, and about how she missed her old friends.

Shortly after returning home, my dentist found a cracked and abscessed tooth, in need of a root canal and crown. This was a warning—I was manifesting the stress in my life by grinding my teeth. I knew I wanted to live my life to the fullest, and that didn't consist of taking care of my mother.

A few weeks later, I was slicing rolls for the lunch platter I was preparing for the day laborers Doug had hired to help in the yard, and I sliced right through the nerve of my index finger. I could sense the abrupt loss of feeling, was bleeding profusely, and was about to faint when Doug heard, finally, my screams for help. He didn't think I needed to go to the hospital. I realized that if he pretended it wasn't true, then for him it wasn't. I could not even imagine how he prioritized. In the end, Brad wound up taking me to the emergency room, where I received temporary stitches. But then a few days later, as usual, Doug had to rearrange his schedule to accompany me while I had the surgical repair of the nerve.

The following Sunday, I walked down the church aisle with my bandaged hand resting on Carly's shoulder, my finger bandaged in bright white gauze, and even though it was my index finger, it still looked like I was flipping the bird at the world. Carly, with a tanning-bed tan, was dressed all in white, her pale blonde hair glowing like an aura of angelic light. Carly, Brad, and the rest of the candidates received the Sacrament of Confirmation from the bishop, regardless of attendance, whether they had gone on the mandatory retreat, whether they believed or not.

Then I spent four weeks in a ninety-degree hand splint, two weeks in a forty-five-degree splint and another two weeks in a straight splint. I knew from the moment I cut my finger that my guitar days were over, at least for a while. While I was still wearing the straight splint, Doug, Brad, and I went on a long-planned, two-week tour of Italy. Home again, with the splint on and off in varying degrees, Doug and I began preparations for celebrating my fifth anniversary of life after a diagnosis of pancreatic cancer. We did parties well together.

I was well into the planning stage for the "Stayin' Alive" disco party when a regular CT scan showed a lesion on my lung that would need to be watched. I was to be scheduled for a follow-up scan in the late summer. I tried to put it out of my mind.

At the party, I found it interesting that I was congratulated so many times. Was it for "surviving" for five years? What did I do? I had nothing to do with it. Did my actions change my fate? Maybe a little, but I still smoked. I believed it was grace, or luck, or just that my time here wasn't finished. I personally did not believe I deserved congratulations, praise, or reverence for waking up in the morning. But then I'd thrown a celebratory party, so what did I expect?

In September, Kim started graduate school, Brad started his junior year of high school, and I started another year as a Bible study group leader and a confirmation teacher.

In October Doug, Brad and I flew to New Jersey for Nancy's first wedding, at age 49. Two weeks later we flew back for Doug's younger brother's funeral. At age 38, he had finally succumbed to the brain cancer that first appeared at age 4, treated by over-radiation to the tune of fifty thousand rads and then a lifetime of growing new tumors. Doug and I invited some of his family for Thanksgiving and his mother to stay on through Christmas and New Year's.

Almost immediately after touching down in San Francisco after the funeral, I was told I would need to see a thoracic oncological surgeon for the 1 cm tumor at the bottom of my left lung, the one they had been watching, the one they suspected was lung cancer. I also had an arachnoid cyst in the left frontal region of my brain.

The next week I resigned as a leader in the Bible study, as a teacher of the confirmation class, and as a singer in the Sunday choir. I also stopped calling my mother.

PART 4

CHAPTER 27

THE CRUEL HOAX

OCTOBER 2006–MARCH 2007

OCTOBER 21, 2006

I met with the oncologist about the new lesion in my left lung. She explained that it could be something infectious like tuberculosis, which is seen in people like me with compromised immune systems. I asked her if all the other little spots are also time bombs? What about all the little spots on the liver?

I asked her a ridiculous question. "Am I ever safe to just live?"

I turned this latest news into immediate self-deprecation by announcing to the doctor and her nurse, "Well, aren't I just the poster child for an idiot? She survives bilateral breast cancer and pancreatic cancer and then dies from smoking! Just put a sign on my back that says 'IDIOT.' Maybe I am not humble enough, so now I should be humiliated."

Then Dr. T. kissed me on the forehead and said, "Let's just see what happens."

It is interesting to me that back in June I requested a CT of the chest since it was mysteriously not ordered as part of my routine follow-up since March 2005. Now, 1½ years later, here we are.

OCTOBER 24

Instead of compassion and support from some of my longtime friends, I am being criticized, judged, and admonished.

"Well, what did you expect? You smoked!" one of them said.

I smoked, therefore I deserved this! No mercy.

Maybe I should have known better, but in spite of all the claims of people who don't really know me and who think I'm strong—am I? What is it to be strong, to face the unknown, even though you really don't want to? Is strong not blowing your brains out when you are too weary to face any more? Is strong forcing yourself to function as a mother, spouse, and friend when you really don't want to get out of bed?

So now Linda the strong, Linda the inspiration, Linda the hero, is a fraud—nothing before even matters. She is really weak, imperfect, damaged goods, despicable. What a riot! I guess I'm just a hypocrite.

I remember when Christopher Reeve broke his neck jumping with that horse. Did people make a big deal that horse jumping was dangerous? No—he was a hero for surviving and being a spokesperson for spinal cord injuries. His wife Dana died of lung cancer. It was very important to know that she never smoked—so she was a victim, a hero? I don't understand what our society values. I surmise it is all right to be a victim of cancer—unless you had a hand in your fate. Since when were we all supposed to be so perfect? When did people begin to believe anyone was, is, or ever will be? We are all weak. We are all imperfect. We all live imperfectly, suffer and die.

OCTOBER 27

Still battling this addiction, but I am smoking less. I feel sad, scared and angry—really on the pity pot.

I caught a couple of minutes of the show *Mother Angelica* on EWTN. She was talking about someone dying of AIDS. She claimed their illness was caused by their "sin." However, if the person repented and was truly sorry for their sins then they would see Jesus and have eternal life. Her commentary sounds a little old school to me. Back to the eternal question—Why do we suffer?

Yesterday I was exhausted. I saw the Chinese MD/acupuncturist. She said I have too much phlegm. She said phlegm causes cysts.

I asked if I was born this way.

"No, it is from lifestyle—smoking, dairy products, too much sweets."

Is that over a lifetime? Does that go back to baby formula, my mother smoking when she was pregnant? Aren't we all influenced by the chemicals or exogenous materials from the moment of conception?

Were we even perfect at the moment of conception, or is there toxic DNA—genetic mutations, undesirable recessive genes to consider? I guess all we can do is the best we can with the hand we've been dealt and try to make good lifestyle choices.

But then how can you explain Dave's death, or anyone else that dies an accidental death? So, obviously, when someone is "perfectly" healthy, young, not toxic, not diseased, they can still can die. It all seems pretty random to me.

I guess you could conclude that living is the problem. Random events and circumstances, bodily chemical processes, things we do to ourselves, things that happen to us from our environment that are beyond our control. What's funny about all of this is that we wind up at exactly the same place—dead.

I suppose you really have to focus on all the clichés—the journey, rolling with the punches, how you play the game.

I think we need to focus on what we leave behind. What is our character? What kind of parent, spouse, friend, sister, etc., were we? How did our existence affect the community?

Obviously, if you are an athlete, movie star, CEO, philanthropist, artist, musician, architect, you will leave behind a legacy of fans, testimonials to your life's works. But what if you are nobody, did nothing notable, or, like my brother-in-law, never really had a chance to live? Surely the handicapped impact the lives of those they touch in ways we cannot calculate. Are they the angel sacrifices sent here for us to see the truth or to learn something different?

During the week before the surgery, I played out every scenario in my head. *What if this is nothing—a fungal infection or a bacterial infection? Well, in that case, I will be angry that I had to surrender to the sacrificial altar of a modern hospital operating room for nothing. What if it is cancer? If it is lung cancer—well, the culturally accepted answer is that you did this to yourself, and after the surgery you will be ostracized, whispered about, and punished by everyone who "loves" you for creating this problem in the first place.*

If it is any other kind of cancer ... well, let's take a stroll through the choices. If it is breast cancer in the lung—that wouldn't be a great prognosis—metastasis, chemo, advanced breast cancer, no hair, feeling like crap:

yack, yack, yack. If it's pancreatic cancer ... that's not a pretty picture either. Maybe it can be a metastasis from a yet-to-be-diagnosed cancer elsewhere in the body. None of these scenarios is a win.

Maybe while they are operating on the lung, I can have an embolism to the brain and wind up like Terri Schiavo, completely brain damaged, a vegetable. Do I even want to wake up and find out the answer anyway?

But then I thought of my children, the thought of leaving them behind to grieve and suffer. I knew then that I *was* responsible if I didn't fight to live. I had to live for Kim, for Brad, for Doug. I absolutely did not have to live for me.

Right before the day of surgery I found out that Brad had emailed all of his teachers at school using parts of an email Kim had already sent out to about five hundred friends and acquaintances. All of these emails were requesting prayers for their mother. My heart felt the horror that this situation must be creating for my children. I felt so sad for them.

The night before the surgery Kim came home for dinner. We were all going to the hospital in the morning together. I was still not in a great place mentally or spiritually, but the clock ticks away and before you know it, time is up. I knew what it felt like to be a dead man walking, knowing yourself to be innocent, but that it doesn't matter; your fate has been sealed.

The admission process was the usual clinical, personal connection–free pre-op assembly line. The surgical resident introduced himself and brought my consent form to be signed. The wrong lung had been identified for the surgery, in writing. Whoops, what do you expect with a 50:50 chance? He was nonchalantly apologetic. I hoped they would notice the ink mark Doug had drawn on my back that morning to mark the line below which they could cut that still would allow me to wear a backless dress. Better yet, maybe they would consult the films from the tests.

They injected the IV with Versed, and before you knew it I was whisked away. I remember asking Doug to tell the kids how much I loved them—and then I fell off the cliff.

Before coming home five days later, I learned they had removed a 1 cm large cell adenocarcinoma of the lung using a robot. It was lung cancer, but so small that it required no further treatment.

My mother-in-law arrived for the holidays six days after my surgery. We hoped the change of environment would ease her grief. She arrived with our nephew.

Doug spent my first week of my recovery at home chauffeuring our nephew around Northern California in search of surfable waves. When Doug was home, he was cooking and doing dishes for his mother, nephew, and a few days later, his sister and brother-in-law. His brother and his family also came for Thanksgiving dinner, which meant all the grandsons were together for the first time. The youngest was 14.

By then, however, Doug's mother had a horrible respiratory infection and a constant, rattling, wet cough.

At Thanksgiving dinner, Doug led a prayer of thanks and words of remembrance of his brother Joe, which was immediately followed by my mother-in-law's erupting into explosive crying and wailing, bereft and grieving. She abruptly left the table and sequestered herself in her room for the rest of the day. My sister-in-law dominated the Thanksgiving meal conversation; she was depressed, saying that she was not happy with her life. The rest of our guests spent their visit drinking wine and quarts of vodka and chain smoking in the backyard at every opportunity. Waking up in the morning to a bedroom that smelled like a bar from the seventies, I explained to my guests that I was trying not to smoke—since I had just been diagnosed with lung cancer—and asked if they could please move up the hill to the pool.

My mother-in-law told me, "You better not smoke or I will slap you—*cough, cough.*"

While the insanity of having all these guests was managed by my husband, for me the distraction and constant shock of glimpsing their lives helped to veil the utter despair and hopelessness I was feeling. I started smoking again, lung cancer diagnosis and all. How pathetic can you get?

The night Doug took the group to the Warriors game, Brad caught me smoking in the backyard. He stopped in his tracks on the walk behind the house, shoulders slumped, and looked as if someone had told him there was no such thing as hope. I felt so ashamed that I had really let him down. I asked him not to judge me and told him that I was very depressed. I told him that it was extremely hard to live with continually being slammed down and feeling like this was the way the rest of my life was going to be. I told him that the only reason that I could even get up in the morning was because of him. I was living for him.

I think he might have thought I was contemplating suicide at that point.

"I would rather have a sick mother than no mother," he said.

I told him that I was grieving and that in time I would feel better. He didn't know that I was only able to even get to this point—from wanting to die—thanks to the hours spent on the phone with Clara since the surgery, who was working tirelessly to talk me down from the ledge. She and I had concluded that Brad was the only thing worth living for at that point since Kim was already somewhat independent.

I was in so much anguish myself that I couldn't see the terror, despair, and turmoil this was creating for my teenage son. He just wanted a mother—and certainly not one that clung to him for life. To prove a point about my ability to quit smoking, he declared he was no longer going to eat chocolate. And he hasn't to this day.

Once Doug's siblings and their families left, his mother and nephew rented a car to continue to search for the waves, even though my mother-in-law was getting sicker. After almost two weeks of being at others' beck and call, Doug began to implode. He wasn't feeling well either and was annoyed that there was no one to take care of him. What did I expect—he should take care of me, attend to his grieving mother, his own grief, and be the ultimate host? I assessed his efforts as pretty good overall, although I was really on my own.

I escaped by hiding in my room, watching the first and second seasons of *Desperate Housewives* on DVD. Doug returned to work. Our nephew was about to leave and I suggested to Doug that his mother should leave as well. She was very sick, unable to fend for herself, coughing all over the house, and did anyone care that I just had surgery on my lung? Doug did not think it was kind to send his mother home in this condition. He felt bad about her grieving. As a compromise, I suggested that he should take her to the doctor.

So, before I was supposed to be driving, I wound up taking her to the doctor, to the hospital for X-rays, to the pharmacy for antibiotics. While we were at the doctor, I asked him to look at this area of my back that bulged when I breathed. It looked like a little balloon under my skin that inflated when I exhaled and deflated when I inhaled. He thought my ribs might be broken.

My mother-in-law and I went home to our respective beds until Doug came home. After her antibiotics started to do their job, at my insistence Doug bought his mother an airplane ticket. I agreed to tell her that I wasn't well enough for a visitor and she would need to leave.

She has not been back to California. I do not feel guilty.

DECEMBER 4, 2006

Monday I heard from Brian, the oncologist's nurse, that they wanted to collect all of my tumor pathology and have it looked at to determine–what, I don't know. The pathology is at three hospitals. There are four primary cancers, a rare hamartoma of the spleen, two symplastic leiomyomas, and two parathyroid adenomas.

I spent a good part of the day attempting to arrange to ship all of these specimens to UCSF for assessment, even though I'm sure that they will only be looking at the three adenocarcinomas. I don't understand why they wouldn't be looking at everything, since my body seems to grow more than one type of tumor. I'm sure that they are not looking for a cause but are probably trying to ascertain how the three adenocarcinomas are similar.

The upshot was that John Muir Hospital threw out all the pathology from my first breast cancer from back in 1993. They claimed they only store it for 10, maybe 12, years. Twenty-five percent of my malignant cancer history is now in the trash. What about research? Maybe they could offer the pathology to the patient before they throw it out. Someone should start a business for this. I am living in the age of cavemen.

The day after Christmas, Doug, Kim, Brad, and I went on a weeklong cruise to Mexico. My emotions were out to sea, calm, smooth, smelly, misty, murky, stormy, violent, and dark, cycling over and over, sometimes within minutes. After returning home for a couple of weeks, I got back on a plane and spent most of January at a friend's condo in Kauai by myself. I had to take the time to reflect and process the latest cancer diagnosis, analyze the questionable support from long-term friends, consider the reactions of my family, and most important, consider how I felt about all of this. Even though I didn't require further treatment, it was another cancerous tumor, another type of cancer, and another surgery.

Doug was not happy about my leaving him at this busy time of the year. I didn't care. I knew if I didn't do something to change the tide of my despair, I was heading straight for the iceberg that sank the Titanic. I was a survivor. I needed to do this, and they would survive my temporary absence.

On Kauai, I drove the Kuhio Highway through Hanalei and hit all the beaches on the way to Haena State Park, the literal end of the road. Slathered in sunscreen and wearing a hat, I carried my chair, umbrella, books, water, and snacks down to the beach. The weather was beautiful, not too hot, too cold, or too humid. Every day I sat and stared out at the clear, turquoise-blue ocean. I watched the sun move across the sky. I watched the waves crashing again and again, the tide coming in and then going out. I watched the birds along the shoreline looking for food and heard the occasional sounds of someone frolicking in the surf. The whole process was so cleansing, so harmonic.

It was while I was zoned out to the white noise of the surf that I had a revelation, though not necessarily a good one. I was thinking about how I felt about being abandoned by some of my friends during the lead up to and after the lung cancer diagnosis and surgery. I thought about Mother Angelica and the guy with AIDS. I thought about sin. I thought about the story of Job.

I reviewed the Collegeville Bible Commentary I'd brought on the trip, some light reading. Job, after losing his family and all his possessions, still did not curse God.

> So Satan said to God, "Skin for skin! All that a man has will he
> give for his life. But now put forth your hand and touch his bone
> and his flesh, and surely he will blaspheme you to your face." And
> the Lord said to Satan, "He is in your power; only spare his life."
> So Satan went forth from the presence of the Lord and smote
> Job with severe boils from the soles of his feet to the crown of his
> head.

To make a long story shorter, Job covered his boil-infested body with ashes and sat as a homeless man and began lamenting, even cursing the day he was born and the night of his conception. He questioned why this horrible thing happened to him. He wanted to die. Three of his friends heard of his plight and went to give comfort and consolation. They started off quiet and listening, but after a few days of hearing his lamentations, they all began to verbally assault him relentlessly. They told him that all this misfortune had happened to him because of his sin, his shortcomings, and his ignorance of God. A fourth friend joined in the put-downs, telling Job that man cannot fathom God's motives.

I started crying. Lung cancer is associated with so much shame, judgment and blame. This diagnosis wasn't supported by ribbons, walks, and store promotions. With the diagnosis of lung cancer, I realized that I was harder on myself than anyone else could ever have been. While the sun began to set I had an epiphany, that I was very judgmental and hard on myself. Therefore, why wouldn't I see everyone else in my life as being the same?

In the days that followed, I continued to ponder the story of why does a good man suffer? I was good, a good wife, a good mother, a good daughter, a good friend, a good person. There weren't many things I had done in my life that I would be ashamed of—shoplifting, lying, acting out in junior high, things of that sort. Surprisingly, smoking wasn't one of them. But then it struck me like a brick to the head, maybe the whole premise of the story was screwed up. Why would God play a cosmic game with Satan over the faith of a man? Are we all just playthings? Does God have an ego? Why would God care about Job's faith? Does God *need* to be worshipped?

My mind started spinning. I had to force myself to pause and remember to breathe. I was getting very angry. I rationalized that the Book of Job was a story and, as such, it could not be a literal truth—because if it was, then life was nothing but a cruel hoax. What was the point of all of it? It seemed to me that then we would all be doomed from the beginning. Then it would mean that the Church, while providing tradition, ritual, community, history, the teachings of morals, and the virtues of society, was also part of the hoax. If you don't believe what the Church teaches, you are damned.

I was really having a hard time with all of this. Wasn't it OK to be human? Isn't that what God created? The idea of temptation and the fall from grace seemed so antithetical to the notion of a loving God. Why would God create man only for us to be damned, weak, have to struggle and suffer on the eternal wheel of life for all of creation. Is all of this just another myth to help explain what we cannot understand?

Then I thought, *The magnificence of creation is here to put everything into perspective. Yet we have pride, ego, we suffer, we transform in the pit of hell or the cauldron, and then we relapse into pride. And then the cycle begins again and repeats again and again until we get it. But then, aren't we created as humans, and isn't this is part of being human? As humans, don't we house the divine spirit within us? Is all of creation deemed wondrous except for us?*

I thought that perhaps this *is* all a game. Maybe this life is all supposed to be fun, a great mystery to be solved. Maybe the *only* point to all of this is to laugh at it all, find the good in everything, and just love. The God puppet was on one shoulder debating with the Satan puppet on the other shoulder, and they both wore my face. I wanted to drown them.

I woke up at dusk. The circuits in my brain were fried. As I stumbled back to the car, I remembered that I had to write a note to remind myself—Do Not Take Life So Seriously. *Ha, yeah right,* I thought, as I emptied my bag on the ground to find my keys.

While I was in Hawaii, Brad's robotic parts kit arrived and he went to pick it up at the designated drop-off site. Brad and a few like-minded friends had six weeks to build a robot for the 2007 FIRST Robotics— Silicon Valley Regional competition.

FIRST is an acronym for "For Inspiration and Recognition of Science and Technology." The program had sounded like a win-win when Brad and I discussed starting the club and team early in the previous fall. At the end of the six-week build period, the robot needed to be shipped to the competition in accordance with a chapter's worth of rules and guidelines, regardless of its state of completion. Once the robot was shipped, I had a few weeks to recover from the months of coaching (organizing), mentoring (nagging about sponsorship), planning logistics not related to building (being ignored), and fighting with my son. Through all the aggravation, I could see this was Brad in his element, building, creating. Quite frankly, he didn't know what the heck I was talking about in organizing and starting the business of the club. Brad made it clear with a look of *Really, Mom?* that organization and preparation was not what this was about. And he was right—I knew *I* wouldn't have been able to build a robot if there was a gun to my head.

In March, ready or not, the matches were called up one by one, three teams on the red alliance and three on the blue alliance. The referees were introduced—volunteers from Google, NASA's Jet Propulsion Lab, San Jose State University; mechanical engineers; electrical engineers; rocket scientists; and experts from the who's who of Silicon Valley technology companies. An experienced announcer detailed each two-and-a-half-minute match play by play, as if it were a gladiator tournament.

Each team's robot had to be controlled remotely using a joystick. It had to pick up an inner tube and hang it on a large rack of three rows. Each row had eight hanging posts suspended by movable chains. Hanging the tubes was to be done within the framework of a three-team alliance competing against the other three-team alliance. While doing this they had to employ strategies to maximize points earned for each match. Scoring was based on the number of tubes hung, more for tubes hung in a row and their height on the rack, as well as bonus points for an automation sequence, and, finally, where on the field the robots ended up when the final bell rang and the power was cut off.

The master of ceremonies was a man named Mark who worked at NASA as some sort of aerospace engineer and sported royal blue hair. As the matches were set up, he announced each team, athletically ran their flags around the field wearing a cape, then a hula skirt, then a large police hat, a jujitsu outfit, and a NASCAR jacket, showing us all how much fun he was having. He was very funny.

"Let's break the law—the law of technology!"

"Let's get these buggies rolling!"

"This is why we do *the math*!!!"

"Here's to the Best of the Best!"

He definitely had a flair for the dramatic.

In the early matches very few inner tubes were hung. Brad's team, The Spartonics, had a problem with the power supply to their robot and it sat paralyzed for one entire match. In the subsequent match, Spartacus, their robot, was intentionally rammed by another robot and critically wounded, leaving the arena at the end for emergency surgery. The team seemed to take it all in stride, as if this was expected and was just an opportunity for improving their robot.

Later, I held my breath while Spartacus picked up and then dropped the inner tube, finally picked it up, held on to it, and tried to center it on the post, which was moving back and forth. I held my breath some more while the robot's arm tried to disengage from the tube and leave it on the post while the rack was rammed, and the robot was tussled about by the other robots. In another match, someone threw an inner tube and horseshoed Spartacus's alliance flag, disqualifying the team in the match unless it was removed by another alliance robot. No one came to their aid as the rapid, eight-count bongo drum played, followed by the robotic female voice that gave warning of the last thirty seconds of the match, "B-e-g-i-n ... t-e-r-m-i-n-a-t-i-o-n ... s-e-q-u-e-n-c-e."

By the middle of the tournament, robots had been improved, perfected. On the rack tubes were hung on the posts six across, three vertically, and evidence of alliance strategizing started to emerge. Some robots were clearly designated as offense and others played defense to prevent the opposing alliance from scoring. There was wedging, ramming, entanglements in the rack, and the complete overturn of one robot, which caused a yellow flag to be thrown down by the referee indicating "not playing well with others." The referees huddled after the match for a good long time while inspecting the carnage, submitted their ruling, and then the penalties were announced.

Spartacus began scoring consistently once its "new" pneumatic arm was perfected in a series of surgeries performed in the pit between the team's assigned matches. Brad and the Spartonics would wheel the robot on a Radio Flyer wagon back and forth from the pit to the field, oblivious of the banners, team spirit chants, and team mascots, which included a person dressed as a hat, a wolf made of metal diamond-plate, and a spaceman. Nor did they hear the incredible soundtrack, mixed by a live DJ, playing at stadium volume between the matches. I finally understood the mentality of the sports mom. I felt like I was back in high school myself but doing something great instead of waitressing at the coffee shop on the weekends or working at the puzzle factory after my dad's store closed.

The matches continued the next day. The winning alliance would advance to the national competition later in the spring. The increasing ability to accrue bonus points ratcheted the scores higher and higher. The thrills became greater, the cheers, louder as the stadium filled to capacity. The stands looked like a multicolored checkered flag with the large blocks of seats occupied by each team's parents and other fans dressed in team colors. At our peak, the Spartonics cheering section comprised maybe six seats of unmatched outfits, and we didn't have the color-coordinated sticks either.

I noticed one young woman wearing a T-shirt that said "I ♥ NERDS!" I too loved nerds. I *was* a nerd. In between the matches there was team dancing and performances, one that included twenty or so girls from Hawaii doing an aerobic Irish jig that would rival a cardiac stress test, accompanied by some fun music.

At the end of the day, Brad's team wasn't in the top-eight seed. They weren't picked in the first or second round of alliance building. However, they were ranked high enough to be a second alternate, just in case two robots bit the dust on the way to finals. They waited in the wings as the best Super Bowl *ever* was played out in the San Jose State Arena. It was so exciting to see a thrilling competition of the mind, with science, math, technology, and strategy played out—robot fashion.

Brad's team did great for their first time out, on a shoestring budget, with little or no help and minimal classmate support. I was so proud of him and so happy for him. Being involved in FIRST Robotics with my son was one of the best times I ever had in my life. Seeing him shine, doing something he loved, having it be about him, was worth it all. And I felt happy, like a kid myself, but also humbled and grateful to have lived to see it.

This experience was also just like the game of life, riddled with the drama of ups and downs, the proverbial thrill of victory and agony of defeat. Although the agony wasn't so bad if you took it in stride and saw *not* winning as an opportunity to refine yourself, the player of the game. The drama of the game *was* the point. Brad seemed to get this already.

CHAPTER 28

REPROCESSING

FEBRUARY–OCTOBER 2007

Since the lead-up to the most recent surgery and cancer diagnosis, I knew I was spiritual, but I could no longer subscribe to organized religion and the dogma of the Catholic Church. I just couldn't believe that I was that bad, had sinned that much, or deserved any of this. I didn't think these things were about punishment; otherwise, I was chained to the wheel in hell. I no longer believed that I needed to be redeemed just because I was born a human being. It didn't make sense to me that everything created was perfect and good, except us.

Early in the year, I hosted my book club at my house for the discussion of *Eat, Pray, Love* by Elizabeth Gilbert. Everyone in the group wished they could take a year off to find themselves, redefine themselves, travel, or just plain get away.

As hostess, I said, "Let's go around the group and tell one word that you would use to define yourself." There was a teacher, a helper, an artist, a mother. There was a different word for each of the women in the group.

"I am a seeker," I said.

FEBRUARY 27, 2007

The weather has been cold and raining every day, sometimes with hail. There has been snow on Mt. Diablo twice this week. Naturally, the dogs do not want to go outside and get their paws wet. I smudged the house with smoldering sage this week to get rid of all the toxic and negative energy. I have been collecting crystals for creativity, healing, and abundance. I have started on my yearlong picture project. I want to organize the photos, transfer the videotapes to DVDs, and transfer the slides to digital. I want to remember the good times and see my life as a flowing river rather than functioning between blasts from within a fox hole.

Yesterday I met Kim in the city. I took her shopping for clothes for her birthday. It's hard to believe she will be 26. She's enjoying graduate school and her boyfriend. But she's still not feeling that well physically or mentally. She sees a therapist whom she really likes. She also sees a nutritionist and an energy worker.

Kim told me that she has been told that she has "adrenal burn-out" and is dealing with a lot of "mom issues," meaning me. She said something about some archetypal contract she made. She is also working on her issue of letting go and the feeling that she is responsible for this or that. She has had such a heavy load in life. I want her to be happy, healthy, and fulfilled. But her journey is hers to walk.

MARCH 20

I'm angry with Brad. Tonight before my doctor appointment, I shared that I was nervous and trying not to focus on my appointment and the outcome. He told me that I just wanted pity.

"Oh! Here we go—just cry me a river."

"I thought you were old enough to share this with," I responded. "And by the way what happened to compassion and empathy?"

"That is the same thing as pity," he said.

MARCH 22

Today is Nancy's 50th birthday. I've known her since we were 14. We are still 14 inside. I had my oncology appointment yesterday. The PET CT was good—nothing new going on. I'm not even feeling relieved or happy. I'm thankful, yes, but for some strange reason, I feel irritable. I'm still depressed. My oncologist thinks I might need an antidepressant (I'm already on one) and therapy (again). She added, "By the way, why wouldn't you be depressed?"

I told her, "I feel like a POW in a torture camp, in a cage, waiting, anxious for the unseen door that squeaks open. I can hear the footsteps, my skin is crawling. Are they going to stop at my cell to beat the crap out of me, or does this mean this is just the end?"

Kim and I went to lunch at the Cliff House. When I got home I read the reports. Apparently the lung tumor tested positive for EGFR, epidermal growth factor. I don't understand the significance of this. The report also noted that there is a splenule located adjacent to the spleen bed. I need to follow up on this, since the spleen was removed six years ago.

APRIL 21

I started reading a book, *Your Body Speaks Your Mind: Decoding the Emotional, Psychological, and Spiritual Messages That Underlie Illness,* by Deb Shapiro. I was reading chapter 2 when I started having an anxiety attack.

The text posed the question whether illness was a time when you can feel special, allow yourself to rest and be nurtured? I asked myself, Has my disease made me special; extraordinary disease and history equals extraordinarily special? Do I feel special without defining myself externally or by cancer? Why not? Aren't I just special because I am? This is what I need to work on to heal. I don't need to be anything, a great anything, always, never, whatever. I need to accept myself as no one has ever done before and that's that! This is my mission—unconditional love and acceptance of me.

GOOD LUCK TO ME!

APRIL 30

I listened to a book on CD this weekend called *The Wisdom of Your Cells: How Your Beliefs Control Your Biology,* by Bruce Lipton, PhD. It was fascinating. He is a biologist that has studied cells. His theory is that the cellular membrane controls the cell, and it is influenced by the environment and how *we perceive* the environment. This study of the cellular membrane revealed that the membrane is like an organic computer chip. It is the "brain" of the cell. Messages from the environment registered by the cellular membrane could turn the genes on and off.

This book was also the first time I heard of the field called epigenetics. Epigenetics could mean that you could manipulate the environment of the cell. Even genetic mutations could be overcome by switching the expression of the gene on or off. This means that your behavior and environment actually change your genes, which could be good or bad for you.

He also spent a lot of time talking about how threats and perceived threats influence our immune systems and thereby influence the health of the cells. Chronic stress creates a less than optimal condition in the environment of the cell when cortisol is released from the adrenals in the "fight or flight" response. This puts the body in survival rather than thriving mode. This response is automatic. The only thing we can change is our belief about the threat. These beliefs are usually recorded to our "hard drives" (our subconscious minds) before we are six years old. How do you change beliefs you don't even know you have?

In early May of 2007 I telephoned Bill, a therapist and an expert in the use of EMDR (eye movement desensitization and reprocessing) for treating post-traumatic stress disorder, or PTSD. I had learned that EMDR could help identify repressed traumatic memories and triggers that create the stress response throughout life. Put simply, the technique occupies your conscious mind to access memories—even ones that are preverbal. Then, through a series of steps, you can rewrite your sub-conscious mind. I scheduled an appointment. Bill was the seventeenth therapist that I was meeting on the path of recovery since 1994.

When I arrived for the first appointment, Bill opened the door, intro-duced himself, shook my hand and invited me in. His office was hot and stuffy.

"Is it all right if I video record our sessions?"

He said the tapes would be for me to review after our sessions. I said sure, thinking I would probably never watch them. Then he asked me why I came to see him.

"I am specifically interested in the EMDR, the eye movement desen-sitization and reprocessing."

I told him about reading the Lipton book. He said he hadn't heard of it.

"I want to get to the bottom of why I keep getting sick."

He responded with a skeptical eyebrow and in between asking ques-tions soon began to furiously take notes in a red spiral notebook.

For the next hour, I downloaded the highlights of my life thus far. It was like a tsunami. I think the guy took a solid six to eight pages of notes while occasionally wiping his brow with a pressed white handkerchief. He said something about there being "a lot of low-hanging fruit."

He gave me a homework assignment to journal events that bothered me or got me upset, "triggers," and how I felt about these things. At the end of the hour his telephone rang, he put the caller on hold, and we set up our next meeting. I felt exhausted.

In the next couple of meetings, I learned that EMDR would bypass a great deal of talk therapy and that it could "cure" things that always bothered me. If it was successful, I would cease to notice my triggers. It sounded great to me.

Bill asked me questions about my children, my husband, my illnesses and surgeries. He wanted to know more about my family, my parents, my sisters and brother. In the third session, he asked me for the first time if I was sure that I wasn't molested by my father when I was growing up. I was taken aback by that.

"My father," I mused "wouldn't have harmed a fly." He asked me to make a list of the "ten worst things that ever happened." Whoa, that would be a challenge. How could I limit the list to ten? It seemed impossible. We would discuss this at the next visit.

During the week, after much consideration, I began my list. It came to the point that I had to think in terms of *yes, this was bad ... but not as bad as....* Eventually, I came up with my "worst things" list. And honestly, even though each one of these was bad, I had survived, hadn't I?

Linda's 10 Worst Things:
Dave's death
Waking up during surgery
Waking up in the recovery room without medication
    for pain after the Whipple and no one listening
The Whipple
Losing both my breasts
Diagnosis of cancer each and every time
Wanting to die
Almost dying
Not feeling loved
Not being heard

At our next appointment, Bill looked over the list, did some professional prefrontal cortex machinations and asked, "So what is your earliest memory?"

I thought to myself, *What are you talking about? Look at the list! Why did I bother to even make the list?* Perplexed, I closed my eyes and thought back—Linda in the playpen, Mom on the phone, silver and turquoise kitchen, Mom ironing, talking to someone else, she's laughing on the phone. Next memory—Linda in the playpen, Mom on the phone. In fact, I felt like I was always in the playpen, trapped, jailed.

I remembered something! I told Bill that when my children didn't walk until they were 15 months old, my mother had told me, "You were toilet trained, walking, and singing "Mary Had a Little Lamb" at your first birthday."

"Wow!" Bill said, "that means that by one year you were already trying hard to win your mother's love and approval." That sent me reeling. I felt so much rage toward my mother.

"How does that make you feel?"

"Angry," I replied.

"On a scale of one to ten, how would you rate that?"

"Eight to ten."

Using a metallic wand that looked like an old TV antenna with a ball at the end, he instructed me to follow the ball with my eyes as it moved back and forth. As he distracted my conscious mind, he asked me a series of questions. Slowly guiding me through these earliest memories with questions, he instructed me to focus on my feelings. We paused after each set to check in with what I was thinking and feeling and assign a number on the feeling scale. The more I dug, the more anger I felt.

The next week, Bill had me beating the sofa with a tennis racket, then stepping on a rope attached to a bar trying to dislodge the bar from the rope until I almost broke a blood vessel in my eye. I felt like a jerk, but it felt good. I wanted to kill her (my mother), and that feeling wasn't coming off the top of the rating scale. It was hovering at around a nine. My hate was so intense that sometimes we would have to digress onto something else. He told me that I probably had these feelings when I was little but that I had to suppress them to survive. He postulated that maybe I felt as a child that I was a monster and compensated by having to be a superhero just to live.

"Mmm," I said. I'd have to give that some thought.

After a few months of seeing Bill, I had to switch my appointment time. My slot was following a woman who came out of her therapy appointment looking like she had been reliving a weeklong gang rape and Bill was glazed over for the first quarter of our session.

I now had the first appointment of the day. Soon, I began noticing that Bill was developing a trend of showing up five to ten minutes late for our appointments. Interestingly, while I was waiting I would get nervous and fidgety, obsessing about how he wasn't going to show up. I had to tell myself that it wasn't personal; it didn't mean *See, you really don't matter,* the way I automatically thought. Starting to feel like I was "owning" my power, I brought up his lateness, telling him in a nice way that I thought it was disrespectful and unprofessional. He apologized and showed up on time for the next appointment.

He asked me where my father was and what he did during my childhood.

"Either he was working two jobs, starting a business, losing a business, or just plain checked out. He wasn't around."

"How does that make you feel?" And for the first time, I realized how angry I was at him too. Why didn't he protect us from her? Why wasn't he around more if he knew how she was? Didn't he care? Maybe he was trying to stay away from her. *What a coward,* I thought. Maybe he didn't know everything. In my thoughts I was defending him, excusing him, but also wondering why he wasn't the parent. My feelings vacillated between compassion and anger. I thought it was all crazy.

Bill asked me if I had any other medical history other than what I had already described.

"Yes, when I was four years old I had surgery to remove two moles, one on my shoulder and one on my back."

Up to this point, this was just some benign statement I had transcribed onto innumerable patient history forms.

"Let's talk about what happened."

He handed me a double buzzer apparatus that alternated a *zzzzz* in each fist, again with the purpose of distracting the conscious mind, allowing better access to the subconscious and repressed memories.

"On a scale of one to ten, how do you feel right now?"

Whoa, I thought, *I was a joke. When the stitches were about to be removed my mother did nothing to comfort me. She not only didn't care, but she was also making fun of me. I was less than a nothing. I hated her. Oh! How I hated her. Why did I have to have this surgery—to remove the remote chance of getting cancer someday? For God's sake, I was 4 years old. What was she thinking?*

As usual at the end of the hour, the telephone rang.

"Hold on, please."

I gave him my check, agreed to meet the same time next week, and stumbled out of there like I'd been binge drinking. I made it to my car and just sat there, so sad, tears streaming down my face along with my makeup.

Eventually, I made it home. And then it hit me. I thought, wasn't it ironic that the mole removal was ostensibly done to prevent me from getting cancer, but each time I really did get cancer the aftermath was always the same—not getting the love I needed, not feeling special, feeling pathetic, really. On top of that, each time the likelihood of surviving the disease was decreasing but the outcome was exactly the same. This was the pattern. *Whoa! This getting sick has got to stop now!* I thought.

It scared me a bit to think of the possibility that I had created all of this on some level, a subconscious level, looking to resolve some old shit. I felt like I had struck gold. At least now I might be able to understand how to fix the pattern. If I could fix the pattern, getting the love I needed from myself, feeling special just because I am, then—abracadabra—I'd stop getting tumors! My god, I was mighty and powerful in a very self-destructive way.

At the next visit with Bill, who was late again, I shared this revelation. He seemed dismissive of my theory. He wanted to get back to the memory of the car ride to the doctor and being ignored.

This time he wanted me to imagine being the mother to myself. I couldn't do it. He then asked me to imagine that it was one of my children. Would I have been able to comfort my child?

"Of, course," I said.

Then, using EMDR, we went back to the car, where I had Uncle Joey drive and I sat in the back with my child, holding her the whole way, offering words of comfort. I didn't know why I couldn't do this for "little Linda." I was blocked.

For the next several weeks, we revisited the appointment with the doctor who removed the stitches. I don't know if it was stubbornness on my part, but I just could not get off eight to ten on the scale of rage with my mother. Bill postulated that I turned this rage inward and somehow embodied that I was bad. He referred to my feelings as a "toxic cesspool."

Soon I began to have physical manifestations with the memory of rage at my mother during the EMDR—a sudden intense headache, eyeball pain, neck pain, loss of power directly affecting my solar plexus with a sensation of a ball in the gut. In my mind's eye, my rage focused my power—I imagined sending out a ball of death to my mother but it was never released. As instructed, I went through the exercise of biting her, chewing her up, and spitting her out. Then I felt sad, especially that I had disappointed my father. Bill told me I had internalized a pattern of being angry rather than hurt. I learned that rage didn't help. Killing my mother didn't make me feel better. But I sure did have passion.

In between visits with Bill, I decided to give my mother a call and ask her in an as matter-of-fact a way as possible to tell me what she remembered about this surgery. As I expected, she immediately got defensive. She said she did it "because the doctor said I should have it done."

"Why did you decide to do this when I was 4 years old?"

"I think it was because we were living with Grandma but were about to move. I thought this would be a good time, since Grandma could watch your sisters."

She was 26 at the time and the mother of 4-, 3- and 1-year-olds. She wasn't thinking about any untoward outcomes. It was interesting to observe that for the rest of my childhood, she didn't bring me or my siblings to the doctor for anything unless it was close to a life-threatening emergency—hence the rest of the trauma and corresponding anger. To this day she goes to the doctor only kicking and screaming, to the detriment of her own health.

At the next session with Bill, I told him about barricading the bedroom door as child.

"Are you sure you weren't sexually molested?"

"I locked the door because you never knew when Mom would burst in yelling, screaming, hitting or pulling your hair."

He told me my mother was mentally ill. From all that I had told him thus far, my childhood was far from normal. He thought that I was emotionally and physically abused. He told me my diagnosis was complex post-traumatic stress disorder.

One day I noticed a large budding amaryllis bulb in Bill's office, replacing a dead sprig of something. That was the day he fell asleep while I was talking. I felt offended, hurt, betrayed. He didn't seem too upset and was very matter-of-fact about the whole thing. I rationalized that the room was hot, as usual. I thought maybe he was sick, on some medication, didn't sleep well the night before. I called him during the week. I thought he owed me an apology and some explanation for his lapse. Reluctantly, he finally apologized, but offered no explanation. It didn't help me feel any better.

I overlooked all of this behavior though. I supposed my reaction was another by-product of my childhood. We continued working together, doing EMDR for other incidents of trauma, learning how much junk I was holding inside. We were still trying to work through the stitch removal incident, slowly making progress on mothering my inner child, when at the end of our session he told me to visualize putting my feelings toward my mother in a box on the shelf. Instead, I visualized throwing her into a putrid New York City dumpster and then frantically winding a cable around it multiple times. Then, heroically maneuvering the dumpster using a crane, I hurled it into the Hudson River. While this was going on, I was giggling, ecstatic in fact—never in my life had I had such an extreme feeling of joy. It was a bit frightening. I felt a little crazy. I felt such relief. I felt free for the first time. Maybe I finally tipped over.

We never really had an opportunity to find out what that was all about since Bill fell asleep again at the next meeting. I was stunned.

"We are done here."

He wanted to continue our sessions, but I didn't think I could trust him anymore. I asked myself, *How is this therapeutic?*

Someday I will know whether I am the one who creates the pattern by choosing to see only proof that nobody really cares. But I learned from seeing Bill that *I* care about me. Maybe I don't need to self-destruct anymore. I'm learning to hurl the dumpster again and again until it's gone forever. I want to feel the glee, giggling and free.

I definitely hurled the videos of our sessions in the dumpster.

CHAPTER 29

SEARCHING FOR THE *OM*
IN -OMAS

MAY 2007–OCTOBER 2008

MAY 16, 2007

I had an appointment with the head of genetic counseling at UCSF.
It seemed to me she was curious about how I am dealing with all
of this. The bottom line is I am still here. However, I feel like a POW,
on a constant state of alert, overly vigilant, looking to make sense of
insanity, trying to hold on to hope.

She seems to think I have a genetic syndrome (of course). She
wants to do BRCA analysis rearrangement testing (BART, for short), an
updated and expanded test for BRCA 1 and 2, for $995. My thoughts
are that they should pay for this test for their possible research article
if the results are positive. I would rather spend my money on a trip.

Having a genetic syndrome creates a feeling of doom for me.
It doesn't make sense. Why haven't I had more tumors if I have an
inherited mutation in my DNA? Nothing seems to have changed much
since my last visit in 2001.

Nixon launched the "war on cancer" when I was a child. This
country can rally around terrorist bombings. What about the terrorism
of cancer, the internal bombs, the WMD of the disease that affects
millions of people? So many people are living with suicide bombers
lurking around every corner. As this population of baby boomers ages,
will anyone correlate this disease to an avian flu pandemic or anything
else? We can spend billions of dollars to fund killing one another. Why

isn't there more funding when the war is inside the bodies of so many of us?

I get so enraged, I need to scream. When is this to be considered an epidemic, possibly a pandemic? It won't be, due to apathy, indifference—too painful to think about, we all die from something. Someday the light will go on—it will be simple. No more mutilation, poison, frying. DO IT NOW! In 20 years it will be too late for the majority of this population.

JUNE 7

The genetic counselor called. She said their genetic group met and now they think I might have a p53 germline mutation. She would like me to reconsider the BART. Come on. I don't believe any of it.

I turned 50 in July. I was excited to still be alive and grateful for an incredible life. There were many birthday celebrations. Doug and I were planning a trip to Japan as my gift in November. I was finally getting over the last cancer diagnosis.

JULY 28

Wouldn't it be funny after 50 years of living to finally begin to learn to live, to no longer be an extreme tide of reactions, rising up to a tsunami or being flat and splattered. Oh, to be an oak tree, strong, rooted, grounded to the earth, rustling with the winds but not toppled. I'd lose my leaves in the fall and rest in the winter, leaf out in the spring, be energized in the summer. I'd be a place of rest and refuge for the birds, home to the squirrels, nourishment for the planet, filtering the air, providing shade, warmth and beauty. My soul would be at peace knowing who I am.

Be the tree, unwavering, knowing the cycles, accepting all as it is.

AUGUST 13

I finished reading *Man's Search for Ultimate Meaning* by Viktor E. Frankl. I want to quote what I found to be the profound passage:

> The fact remains that not everything can be explained in meaningful terms. But what now can be explained is at least the reason why this is *necessarily* impossible. At least it is impossible on merely intellectual grounds. An irrational rest is left. But

what is "unknowable" need not be unbelievable. In fact, where knowledge gives up, the torch is passed on to faith. True, it is not possible to find out intellectually whether everything is ultimately meaningless or whether there is ultimately meaning behind everything. But if we cannot answer the question intellectually we may well do so existentially. Where an intellectual cognition fails an existential decision is due. Vis-à-vis the fact that it is equally conceivable that everything is absolutely meaningful and that everything is absolutely meaningless, in other words, that the scales are equally high. We must throw the weight of our own being into one of the scales.

And there is the answer. *We need to have blind faith to believe that everything is meaningful*—not just some things, like we get to choose what is or isn't meaningful. Everything is meaningful if you have faith. Nothing is meaningful if you don't. And if you don't, how do you survive? You believe in luck or science with no God.

If I didn't believe in God or in something greater than myself and the ultimate meaningfulness of every person, instant, place, event, good and bad, that drives my sense of purpose when having to face life-changing events, life-threatening illness, living with a chronic disease, losing body parts, putting faith in health care to allow 17 surgeries, knowing I will be OK no matter what, I would have died a long time ago.

My faith in something more gives me the courage, fortitude, a fighting spirit and hope to look forward to what comes next. Without this faith, I wouldn't be able to take my next breath. I think this and this alone—faith, grace and grit—is the only reason why I'm still here and have not broken and gone completely insane.

In the spirit of continually learning to improve our relationship, in the heat of late August Doug and I headed out for another weekend retreat. This time it was at the Tassajara Zen Center for a course called Taming the Jackal: A Retreat for Nurturing Relationships, a "nonviolent communication" workshop that taught the tools pioneered by Marshall Rosenberg.

For hours we drove in the truck to the Zen Center, famous for its curative hot sulfur springs in the Los Padres National Forest, two hours southeast of Carmel. After passing the turnoff several times, we finally found the dirt road that, according to the printout of the driving instructions, was sixteen miles long with no signs indicating whether we were getting anywhere.

Doug drove like he was breaking a horse while I was bounced around, almost cracking a molar, and hanging on to the handle above the door like a monkey as we left a large, brown cloud of dust in our wake. Driving over large rocks while skirting the edge of a cliff, I bit my tongue, refusing to yell or scream. I confirmed my determination to keep silent when I squinted at the odometer and saw we were going only fifteen miles per hour. Finally, we arrived at the bottom of the gulch and opened the doors. Once the cloud of dust settled, we were hit with the eau-de-stink from the sulfur springs. As I was adjusting to the aroma, I spent about ten minutes unclenching all my muscles. I had to use my left hand to straighten out my right fingers from their hook shape.

It was a good thing Doug was enthusiastic about going on this retreat, I thought, as I struggled to wheel my luggage from the parking lot to registration and past the Buddhist temple to our rustic room with no electricity and rationed cold water. I was sweating buckets, wiping the layer of grime from my face, when I looked over at Doug, who was already flopped on the mattress grinning from ear to ear.

For three and a half days, we braved the heat, the mosquitoes, and the fart-like stink that faded and wafted. The food was gourmet vegan and was actually very good, though I was constipated even on that diet.

The workshop was held in a yurt—no air conditioning, of course. It was about learning a communication technique that uses empathy and connects with the heart and what is alive in the other person. I learned from the lectures that my language was considered judgmental due to my habit of using qualifiers and adjectives to describe anything that was subjective. The step-by-step process forced me to get in touch with my feelings. I learned that my feelings were a limitless ocean of hurt and sadness.

Doug seemed to have a very hard time connecting to his feelings. He stated in a very goal-oriented way, "I really want to learn how to do this!"

Before the end of the weekend, I could hear an argument erupting from the other side of the yurt. Doug's group was chastising him for talking about how he felt when his "wife yells from across the house" (calling the family for dinner, to answer the telephone, things of that sort). The more vocal people in his group, which included a couple of therapists, told him to "get over it." The teacher had to get involved and use Doug's "feelings" around this topic as an instructional tool for the group.

Doug seemed hurt when he told me about the incident later. "This is something I need to work on," he said.

I didn't tell him that I didn't need fifty-nine bloody mosquito bites and bad body odor to figure that one out. I did, however, feel empathy for him instead of the usual anger. I gave him a hug.

I learned more about my need for safety. I learned that beating myself up, "self-jackaling" in the workshop's parlance, is about expecting too much of myself and feeling bad for even having any feelings or needs. I also learned that the way I communicated brought me exactly what I didn't want. I decided that in the future I was going to plan on doing many more activities around self-discovery and healing.

We ascended and then descended the mountains to return home, back through the dust cloud and rocks, seemingly a little closer. We tried for about a week to implement the techniques of mirroring back what each of us was saying, going through the checklist until we each felt heard.

Then Doug said, "This way of talking doesn't seem natural to me."

I knew that I could continue only to work on changing myself. I signed up to attend another workshop in the fall on "self-jackaling," or self-nurturing, but a week before the retreat I got a call saying that the workshop was cancelled since I was the only person who had enrolled.

Brad started his senior year of high school, and in November Doug and I went to Japan for two weeks for my 50th birthday gift. The focus of the trip was on the landscape, particularly all the different species of maple trees dressed out in all the fall colors.

We also spent considerable time investigating some of the artisanal crafts of Japan, from sake to Japanese woodblock prints. We met with the artist who made the prints and learned how they were made. We went to learn about the artistry in making rice paper. We went to botanical gardens where everything was art, the art of perfection, even in the way the gravel was raked. Everything was so clean and there was such order to even the tiniest detail.

We toured Buddhist monasteries, and attended a tea ceremony with an abbot at one of them. One of my favorite experiences was our visit to the Japanese watercolor shop, which sold not art prints but paint and brushes. The woman who ran the shop didn't speak English, but somehow we managed to learn all about the full array and nuanced spectrum of the powdered pigments she sold, the different animal hairs used for the brushes, and the varieties of scroll papers.

We walked out of there with watercolor pots of paint in every available color, a selection of brushes rolled in a bamboo mat, and a neat stack of rice paper. Everything was carefully wrapped in tissue, then in brown paper, tied with twine, and then stamped with the shop information. Both of us were delighted—we practically skipped down the street. I was excited about my new artist "toys"; Doug was happy to see me happy. The woman waved until we were out of sight, also delighted by our large purchase. The entire country was an oasis from a life of chaos. Everything made sense, despite our inability to read signs or understand the language!

JANUARY 21, 2008

I am the luckiest woman in the world to have been born in 1957. Yesterday I had my car serviced and was given a loaner with XM Satellite Radio, a commercial-free subscription radio service that has been around for a few years. It has channels for just the 1940s, the '50s, '60s, '70s, '80s and '90s, and many other specialty channels.

I had so much fun listening to all these types of music. If I was born at any other time, I don't think I would have so thoroughly enjoyed all these different decades. I was so happy driving around doing errands and I purposefully took the long way around just to listen to the music. I spent $10 on gas before returning the car. I love music and singing; they are like a happy drug. In the afternoon, I put on some CDs at home and just danced for an hour. What a high—better than any drug I can imagine.

Music helps me to feel mentally better. I see my life as a soundtrack, so varied and complex. Music is like the recording of life, ongoing no matter what happens. The overriding current of music depicts all of the human emotions—joy, love, love lost, blues, fun, sadness. It is the poetry of the human experience, touching each of us in such a special way. Thank God for these artists, their gifts and talents, and the technology and ears to enjoy it.

I finally decided that I was going to realize the fantasy and build my own karaoke system. Using the Internet, searching night after night, I decided which equipment to buy. I shopped for the best prices and bid for equipment on eBay and then paced day after day with the anxiety of waiting for someone to give birth. I was crushed when I lost the bid and jumped for joy when I won. As the boxes of speakers, amplifier, microphones, cables, and assorted items I required began arriving, I started bidding on libraries of used karaoke CDGs that contained the music and graphic words for the screen. It didn't take long for Doug to notice that something was going on.

"What are you doing?"

"I'm building my own karaoke system!"

"Why?"

"Because I want to," I answered, sounding more like a defiant child than an adult. "And because singing makes me feel better."

"Seems like you are spending a lot of money."

"Would you rather we spend it on hospital bills or more therapy?"

I abandoned painting, the picture project, and everything else for a while, and worked day and night until I had installed and created a music book by title and by artist for more than four thousand songs, using special software. Then I started singing. Doug and Brad thought I was crazy. And I was—crazy about having fun.

At the end of April I went to the Chopra Center for a workshop called Emotional Healing. It was near the ocean, in Carlsbad, California, where the sky was turquoise blue. The air was clean, sparkling with the good ions. In a candlelit room, a beautiful woman named Amanda sang a chant in Sanskrit looking right into my eyes. She had a lovely voice, and I could sense her outpouring of love.

I was given my unique mediation mantra as if it were a large precious jewel. I met thirty or so people from all over the world, each with a story, each wounded and recovering from something. I learned how to meditate, and we meditated twice a day for thirty minutes. The meditation teacher also taught us about the doshas, the constitution each of us is born with—vata, pitta, and kapha. The doshas are derived from the five elements. Vata is space and air. Pitta is fire and water. Kapha is water and earth. Each of these doshas is associated with specific attributes that are natural tendencies, both psychological and physical, of the individual. When the doshas are out of balance in a person, symptoms emerge. I was mostly a vata with some pitta, based on the quick-and-dirty assessment criteria. The topic of the doshas was entirely new to me. This was my introduction into the ancient field of Ayurvedic medicine. I knew it would take years of study to really understand this field.

I learned about agni, the internal fire. When it is strong, it converts poison into nectar. Weak agni converts nectar into poison (ama). We learned about emotional ama. We learned about the philosophy of yoga and practiced the "Seven Spiritual Laws of Yoga" every day. Individually and with partners we did many exercises that focused on our beliefs and went through a step-by-step process that started with identifying feelings and worked toward eventually releasing the emotion.

I sat rapt, and for once not crying, in a darkened room decorated in the beautiful and exotic fashion of India. I was amazed by the presentation of a completely different approach to perceiving and living life. I learned that I had a really hard time even recognizing how I felt. I thought others were responsible for how I felt—on those occasions when I *did* feel. And this was not true. Just as I wasn't responsible for my mother's life, I *was* responsible for mine. I learned that everyone we encounter is a mirror of ourselves. Also we possess all the qualities we see in others that we admire as well as those we dislike.

Toward the end of retreat, I selected three large rocks on the beach. As a group, we held a ceremony around a bonfire. Then one by one we each peeled off toward the ocean. I put the story of my mother into one rock and then, with forgiveness and love, threw it into the ocean. My second rock was letting go of all the issues around Dave's death once and for all. The third rock was about forgiving Doug, letting go of blame, and thanking him for being the person who was intricately involved in teaching me how I needed to love myself and others. I left the retreat feeling fifty pounds lighter and signed up for the 200-hour yoga teacher training, which had two other Chopra seminars as prerequisites.

The first prerequisite, Seduction of the Spirit, was held in Ireland. More than five hundred people from all over the world attended, requiring seven translators. The week included twice daily yoga, meditation,

Ayurvedic-based vegetarian meals, and nightly activities. I loved it. I felt energized, physically great and emotionally connected to everyone there—seekers on a similar quest to mine. The concepts I learned changed my life, giving me a new understanding of the intersection of spirituality and science, and consciousness and reality. I was blown away with new insights into who we are, who I was. The experience was incredible.

One evening, the activity centered on Deepak Chopra's nonprofit called The Alliance for the New Humanity. We heard the poetry of John O'Donohue, listened to a Celtic singer and harpist, and heard presenters from Ireland tell stories of how, in spite of hardships and obstacles, each was doing something to make the world a better place. After that we broke up into groups of thirty people and one by one went around the circle answering the question "If you could do one thing to change the world, what would you do?"

I didn't have to think for more than a second. My answer was that I would do something about cancer, raise awareness, help to find the cause and the cure. Not too big a dream. What really surprised me, however, was that each of the people in the large circle had a different thing they would want to do to change the world. The point of all of this was that if like-minded people could connect through an alliance, critical mass could build momentum to actually change the world. It was exhilarating to imagine going global and that each person could really make a difference—that *I* could make a difference.

What I also realized on that trip was how grateful I was for Doug. Because of his support and hard work, I was able to have such an experience. I had the freedom to search for answers, even trot around the globe, in my quest for healing and learning who I was and what I wanted. I realized that we couldn't be on the same wavelength or growing in the same way. He went to work and held down the fort while I had all of these amazing experiences. I could have never have done these things otherwise. My perspective was changing.

Brad graduated from high school that year, and I lived to see it, albeit through the usual rivers of tears and relief.

The same month I thought it was strange that Clara, who never went away, would be calling from a PTA conference in Long Beach.

"Linda, Don is home and having a really hard time with constipation."

The situation was so weird. Don and I were very close, but not on the level of discussing bowel habits. Apparently, in Clara's absence and Don's desperation, I had graduated.

"Don't worry, Clara, I'll go to the store and pick up a few things that I think will help, and drop by and see him."

When I arrived at their house, Don answered the door in his robe, T-shirt and sweatpants. His six-foot-three figure was contorted a bit, for what reason, I didn't know. His usual joviality was still evident as he hobbled to the sofa in their family room and I followed behind him, but I could tell something was really wrong. As he sat down gingerly, a faint, guarded wince was evident on his face.

"My back," he said, "it's been driving me nuts since the trip to Hong Kong in January. You know those horrible plane seats."

"Yes, I know," I said and paused for a few seconds. "Well, you seem really uncomfortable. What are you doing about it?"

"I went to see an orthopedic doctor. I have an appointment for an MRI in a few weeks."

Feeling bold seeing him in such bad shape, I said, "Why are you waiting, suffering in the meantime? Call him back and demand that they do it sooner, or go to the emergency room." I felt like I was overstepping my bounds, but bowels were the stuff of families.

After Clara returned home, they called an ambulance. Within a couple of weeks Don, who hadn't smoked in more than 25 years, had been diagnosed with stage 4 lung cancer with metastasis to his lymph nodes and the sacral region of his back. The cancer had almost completely eaten through his spine. He really could no longer walk.

I started a Caring Bridge website to update friends and family and allow them to post messages to Don and Clara. Don was in the hospital for more than three weeks while they tried to get his pain under control, gave him ten spinal radiation treatments, surgically placed a port for chemotherapy, started chemo, and fitted him for a brace and corset to stabilize his spine when he could get out of bed.

After talking with Clara and hearing about the ups or downs of the day, I would write an entry for the website. Then I would pick an artist or a letter of the alphabet or scroll through the karaoke menu for songs of loss, anger, or hope, depending on my mood, and start singing. I sang until I felt better or had to go to the bathroom or start dinner or take the dogs out—but usually after just one more song. This was a great survival tool that forced me to be in the moment. For just a little while I wasn't in anguish, worried, triggered.

Don never lost his wit, his graciousness, his cynical, loveable sense of humor while he was in the hospital, even when his pain was a ten on the pain-o-meter. He was given a tall-man size bed, complete with a state-of-the-art Gore-Tex mattress cover that would prevent pressure sores. Then he was upgraded to a "king suite" room on the oncology floor. The radiology staff all signed a card and presented it to him when he finished the tenth radiation treatment.

When the "king" returned to his castle, I raced my car up the street and beat the ambulance to the house, arriving in time to open the door for them. Clara was at the pharmacy filling his prescriptions. He was wheeled in on a gurney and chuckled when I said, "You look like Hannibal Lecter!"

In between trips via ambulance for chemotherapy and progress MRIs and CT scans, Don held court from his La-Z-Boy recliner for the family members and friends who streamed through the house day after day. Clara was losing weight as she worked nonstop—bathing Don, cooking what he would eat, arranging for his comfort, and hosting their visitors. I listened, researched, visited, meditated and offered advice. I picked up this or that, updated the website, waited and sang.

One late summer afternoon, I sat with Don so Clara could get out of the house. He and I both sat in recliners looking out at the vista of open space viewable from their back deck. The lanai was covered in wisteria well past its bloom but with thick foliage that filtered the sun. It was so peaceful. I wasn't sure if Don wanted to talk about anything so I just stayed quiet, listening to the sounds of birds and leaves rustling as the warm soft puffs of breeze caressed my face.

I read while he dozed. Then Don woke up and cleared his throat. "How have you gone through this so many times?"

"Day by day."

I had recently compiled all of his reports from scans—I was the appointed medical interpreter—and made a spreadsheet to track his progress by date over time. Don and Clara knew that I was doing this. I couldn't tell them that over a very short time the tumors were increasing in quantity, more than three steps backward for every step forward. The prognosis did not look good. Looking over at Don, I could sense that he knew.

"Are you scared?" I asked him.

He didn't answer. I thought maybe I crossed the line. We talked about how life doesn't seem to make sense. He talked about Clara, stories about his daughters. Then he was tired again.

I shut my book and thought about Don the man, in relation to me, always accepting, a fan, on my team, such a great sport at all the parties. Don, the guy who'd just retired, was taking classes to learn French, who was learning how to vacuum the house while singing a little jingle in his deep baritone voice. Don and Clara together were the best example of a good marriage I had ever seen, at least from the outside. Don was at ease with himself and the world. I thought about Don the cancer patient, gracious, jovial, always appearing to take life as it came, never raising his fist to the sky. And the medical community seemed to respond well to his personality and temperament. Clara's manner, too, was no minor consideration in the ripples of love that came back to them.

In the fall, Don entered hospice. I visited the day before he died. This time, at the bedside of someone I loved who was dying, I spoke. "You are one of the greatest men I have ever known. I love you."

He mouthed the word *wow*, and tears streamed down his face.

Clara became a widow, and the dark infinite cloud enveloped her. At 61, she believed the best of her life was over. Her two daughters, other family, many friends, and I would do our best to get her through her grief. Life would go on, but for Clara it was her turn to wear the black veil that mutes the world. I hoped it wouldn't take too long for it to be lifted.

It was the type of day that wraps itself around you and warms you to the core like a hot bath. It had been filled with activities for the orientation for the new students and parents at the University of Virginia. Brad had been accepted at several colleges, and had chosen to attend my alma mater. Although I was afraid to even ask why he had done that, I was honored and excited. Overwhelmed by the barrage of information presented at a seminar on all things pertinent to parents and students—security, financial matters, disaster planning—I sat admiring the beautiful hand-painted murals that spanned the walls of the amphitheater in Old Cabell Hall.

I had studied the history of jazz in this amphitheater more than twenty years before, and could remember the stage, the seats, maybe the columns, but I never knew these richly colored beautiful murals were even there. The entire weekend had been surreal. Walking again along the historic pathways I'd traveled more than two decades before, deeply inhaling the smell of the boxwoods, awash in all the greenery, I felt so many emotions, among them a deep sense of nostalgia. Who could have possibly imagined what life would bring my way after graduation.

Doug, Brad and I sat on the steps outside Old Cabell Hall taking a break. Without realizing it, I had tears streaming down my face. Brad noticed. "What's wrong, Mom?"

I was thinking about how life comes full circle and choked up about Brad going to the UVA. I was so grateful.

"I hope you have a great experience here, Brad, and are able to take advantage of all this school has to offer." He put his arm around me and gave me a squeeze. Doug looked at me with eyes that I knew said *I love you.*

CHAPTER 30

THE WORST THAT CAN HAPPEN—ALMOST

DECEMBER 2009–JULY 2010

On a cold, wet and gray December day in 2009, Clara, still raw just a little over a year since Don's death, met me for lunch at our favorite Greek café, Daphne's. Over a grilled chicken pita sandwich with tzatziki sauce, rice and a salad, Clara updated me on her anxiety over her daughter's upcoming cervical biopsy.

After several abnormal Pap smears, her doctor wanted to take more tissue to determine whether her condition was more serious. This procedure was scheduled for the following week. Her daughter, like mine, was only 28 years old. I felt very connected to her suffering. We held hands across the table, sitting in a high-backed upholstered booth, just like countless other times, sharing our meal and our lives, oblivious to other diners through the lunch rush and into the early dinner crowd.

My daughter was finishing her graduate degree. More than a year earlier, when Kim had been juggling a waitressing job, an unpaid internship and her full-time studies she wasn't feeling well. Thinking it was caused by stress, I asked Doug if we could help her out financially until the end of her classes so she could focus on her studies and have some time for balance. Doug agreed, and Kim had gladly accepted our support until the end of the year, which was now just a few weeks away.

Kim had been pulling away during the last few months, calling maybe once every two weeks, communicating pertinent information mostly by text message. I understood why this had to be at her age. I had learned, to my dismay, in a joint therapy session a couple of years earlier that she never had really detached during her teens or early twenties, fearful that if she did and I died, then she couldn't live with herself. After that, I explicitly gave her permission to focus on herself, hate me if she had to. She didn't understand that I would still survive without her constant worry and her overdeveloped sense of responsibility for me.

So detaching, I realized, was exactly what she was now doing. Still, I felt a hole in my heart. We had always been so close. Now, although it was necessary for her development, the process itself seemed so extreme. Our infrequent encounters were difficult. She was short with me, snippy, jumping down my throat at every opportunity, but they would always end with her flipping the switch to sweet, asking, "When are you making the deposit, Mom?"

Now, though, our financial support was about to end, as we'd agreed. As I intermittently blotted the moisture welling up under my glasses with a Daphne's napkin, I said to Clara, "And Kim is going to New York at the end of December—so when exactly is she looking for a job?" I gazed out the window where it was pouring tears from the heavens. I realized that I absolutely had to let go. Kim needed to become self-supporting; I would have to learn to say no. I went home resolved to do just that.

A few days later, Kim phoned to tell me that she had seen the gynecologist earlier that day. She'd gone for a colon cleanse the previous week, and the hydrocolonic therapist had felt a hardness in Kim's belly that wasn't poop and thought she might have a fibroid. The gynecologist said she didn't know exactly what it was and scheduled her for an ultrasound in a couple of days.

Kim was obviously upset and unnecessarily defensive about the expense of having a colon cleanse. I knew she was exhausted from having given the oral presentation of her master's degree thesis the day before. I stood looking out onto the green lawn through the leaded glass front window, processing all this data. Upon hearing my daughter's sobs, I immediately thought in horror, *Oh my God, she has terrible student health care insurance, the catastrophic kind! Will she even be covered, since she is technically finished with school?* Practical as ever, I asked her about the insurance.

She was angry. "Obviously, you don't care about what I'm saying. You are worried about things that don't matter."

It wasn't true, but even though I intuitively didn't have a good feeling about the situation medically or financially, I dropped it. I wasn't going to go "there" yet. Then to punish me, she told me she wouldn't be going to the Lady Gaga concert with me, as we'd planned. Once again, I let her down.

Two days later, the ultrasound showed a large mass with a blood supply that "looked like Medusa's head," Kim said.

They scheduled her immediately for a CT scan, that afternoon, in fact. I dropped everything and met her at the hospital. Driving in the car to San Francisco, I had a premonition that this could be very bad. According to her gynecologist, it was unclear where this large mass with an intricate blood supply was arising from, but it was probably not her uterus. I had to work hard on staying positive and calm.

When I arrived at the hospital, Kim was pale, with big black circles under her eyes. This scene had played out so many times before in our lives, but now the roles were reversed. I could see Kim the adult—competent and efficient, though visibly frightened—but I could also see Kim the child, holding back the tears while trying to be strong, a vision of getting a childhood vaccine, only worse.

After the CT scan report the gynecologist scheduled an appointment with a GI surgeon for Friday. I forced myself to default to technical issues; the emotional issues would have to wait for later. The guardian, warrior, scientist, left-brain thinker was back.

The CT scan recommended surgery to diagnose the origin of the mass. The report's "impressions" section presented three possible scenarios—all horrifying, but I kept that knowledge to myself. I called my doctor to help us find the appropriate doctor for Kim at my hospital, but she couldn't help since she didn't know where the mass was arising from. Different surgeons would handle GI issues, gynecological issues, and bladder issues.

On Friday, the clerk at the GI surgeon's office asked, "Do you want to put the charges for this visit through your insurance or would you rather pay cash"?

"What's the difference?"

"The cash price is less since we don't have to process the insurance, especially if you haven't met your out-of-network deductible or have a large insurance co-pay."

I gave them my credit card. I sat down musing about the implications of this new "care for cash" model.

The surgeon was a friendly young Asian man complete with his requisite white lab coat. He showed us on the film that this mass appeared "urachal" in origin. We learned that the urachus is a canal in the fetus that drains the bladder of urine and joins and runs within the umbilical cord. Kim apparently still had a fibrous remnant of this canal, which usually disappears shortly after birth.

"This is so symbolic, that even in this I am still attached to my mother," Kim noted to the doctor, looking at me in a way that I could only interpret as blame.

I followed her into the exam room. When she lay down on the examination table with her pants pulled down to her hip bones, under the young skin between her naval and pubis was a large protruding lump that looked as if an alien was ready to burst out. It didn't look like a pregnancy; it was too narrow.

"See, Mom, I've been telling you that I didn't feel well."

The doctor recommended surgery and thought she should probably see a urological surgeon, since this site was most closely related to the bladder. He would try to get a consult with the best person at my hospital as soon as possible.

Kim asked all the right questions. "Do you think this is a cyst? A tumor?"

I wondered how she even knew what to ask? I could see by the look on her face that her brain was calculating like a super computer, analyzing the doctor's responses, running probability statistics. When I asked a question, she looked at me, rolled her eyes, and turned her attention back to the doctor.

Later that day she was called by an assistant of the urinary oncology surgeon at UCSF, was informed that she had an appointment for the following Monday, and was scheduled for surgery to remove the mass two days later, one week after the ultrasound.

The description of the surgery was frightening. The surgical possibilities included bladder removal, hysterectomy, bowel resection, the loss of her navel, mesh to replace abdominal muscle removal—enough scenarios to make me want to throw up, but not in front of Kim. My daughter's abdomen would forever be marred with a big scar. *This thing seems to be growing so fast,* I thought, *what if it ruptures before surgery and she hemorrhages to death? What if she has cancer? What if she dies?*

I held my breath when I wasn't sobbing with anxiety and anticipatory grief. At night I sat outside on my back deck, chain smoking while talking on the telephone with Clara, going through each day's events, hurling myself back and forth in the rocker until, spent and exhausted, I collapsed into bed.

Doug, as practical as ever, kept saying, "We don't know anything yet."

I was disgusted to learn that after all these years I hadn't learned anything. In the avalanche that was still in process, it became obvious that meditation, being in the present moment, witnessing the turbulence of my mind and emotions were skills that I hadn't integrated enough in practice to have any sound footing. Suffering for what hasn't happened yet, pretending to be all right, supporting my daughter with words of encouragement—as well as hysterically weeping and rocking back and forth when I was alone—were still my "go to" place. At least this time there were tears, one improvement.

On the day of the operation we sat for six and a half hours in the glass-walled surgical waiting room. We repeatedly looked at each other, Doug, Brad, and me, not saying much, and eventually avoided looking into each other's eyes for fear of starting each other crying. We were occasionally distracted by the twenty or so family members of another surgical patient who were taking up more than half of the chairs in the waiting room, arguing in Spanish, arm wrestling, playing musical chairs. At around 10:30 p.m. the surgeon came down, dressed and on his way home. You could just tell he was a father even before he told us he was on the way to the airport to pick up his daughter for the holiday. The next day was Christmas Eve.

Searching his face for clues, I could see he was tired but warm and kind. He asked us to follow him to a more private place, causing my heart to pound. We followed him down the hall like ducklings and formed a huddle to the side but in the hall.

"The surgery went well," he stated. "Kim's reproductive organs and intestines looked fine and she didn't need the abdominal wall reconstruction. We removed a large mass." With his hands he showed us something big and oval-shaped, the size of a mango. He continued, "The mass was resting on the top of her bladder, so we had to remove the dome of her bladder to be safe." I knew what that meant. "But that will heal, and she shouldn't notice any difference in her bladder," he concluded.

"Did she get to keep her navel?" I asked.

"Yes." He continued, "It will take some time for the pathology to be completed with the holidays upon us, but initial findings were that we could see some spindle-shaped sarcoma cells."

"So this is cancer?" I asked.

"Let's just wait and see what the pathology report says."

I started to cry. I knew what he'd said. I knew how this works. In the hall outside of the waiting room I heard that my daughter had cancer; my husband heard that they don't know what it is yet; my son heard that the surgery went well, she is fine.

Three weeks later, Kim was diagnosed with an 11-by-8-by-5 centimeter leiomyosarcoma of the urachus, stage III cancer. By the time we heard this news, Kim was already starting to feel much better. "Well, they got it all out," she said. She thought it was over. I suggested, my heart wincing, that she might want to keep an open mind, since she hadn't yet seen the oncologist.

She ripped my head off. "No one said anything about seeing an oncologist!"

By the time we met with the oncologist, we had both done our homework on the diagnosis. The information, as we read it, wasn't good. Kim's reaction was to become afraid that she was going to die. I told her that she could be the good statistic.

"Why don't we stop researching this and just take one step at a time?" I suggested.

Together we went to the oncology appointment at UCSF. I already knew this oncologist as I'd met with him after my lung cancer diagnosis. My memory was that he was a kind, jolly sort, short, balding, French, I think. He was a straight shooter and did his homework. When he entered the room he was noticeably frazzled. He remembered me. When I had seen him three years earlier, he'd said, "You have nerves of steel" and "You ask a lot of questions that I can't answer."

The oncologist recommended aggressive chemotherapy treatment, one week in the hospital, two weeks outpatient, one week off, every month for six months, no radiation. He was a lung cancer specialist as well as the head of the sarcoma center. In fact, he *was* the sarcoma center.

I was verbally smacked down by Kim every time I asked a question. I wanted to walk out, this was hard enough, but then as Kim had been saying, this wasn't about me. It soon became clear that I couldn't do anything right, say anything right. Kim didn't want to know what I knew from experience. She soon let me know in no uncertain terms that she wasn't me, didn't want my life, this was her experience. I was now the support person, the unwanted caregiver. This was my daughter, grown up, multidegreed, frightened for her life, lashing out.

After that appointment, I thought we should get a second opinion on the treatment for her. I knew that her type of cancer was hard to treat. I wanted the recommendation of someone on the leading edge of this type of cancer, either at MD Anderson or at Memorial Sloan-Kettering. Kim accused me of trying to undermine her trust in her doctor. I told her, "I'm alive because I don't put blind trust into the opinions of doctors."

"I'm not you," she reminded me, again.

Kim was told that because of the aggressiveness of the treatment she might never be able to conceive a child. The chemotherapy would kill most of her eggs and potentially damage the rest, and might cause her ovaries to stop functioning altogether. After meeting with a fertility doctor, Kim wrestled with whether she should go through fertility treatments and harvest her eggs, and then either freeze the harvested eggs or create fertilized embryos, which would require finding a sperm donor. To me, all of this was overwhelming, even on top of all the other things that were overwhelming. It was another big issue Kim had to address as a young adult diagnosed with cancer.

She applied for and received a grant from the Lance Armstrong Foundation to cover the cost of the hormone injections—somewhere in the neighborhood of $8,000. That didn't cover the other medical procedures.

I said nothing about the options and told her when asked, "Trust your gut." I was heartbroken that she even had to deal with this issue. Let's not even talk about being a grandmother. I just wanted my daughter to live and have a long, healthy, happy life. I learned that she wasn't sure if she ever wanted to be a mother. Ultimately, she decided that she didn't want to delay her treatment; she said if she changed her mind about having children, she'd look at her options then.

In early February, we flew to New York to meet with a top specialist at Sloan-Kettering for a second opinion on treatment protocols. On the morning of the appointment, arm in arm, we walked together around the corner from our hotel to the clinic in the gray, blistering cold, noticing light snow flurries. The inside of the building was beautiful, so Zen, with calming water fountains, soft earth tones, soft lighting, soft light music—or maybe I was just wishfully imagining it as being like going to the spa. *Yeah right,* I thought.

We were escorted to the infusion center waiting room where we could help ourselves to coffee, tea or juice. There were so many people there, especially so many young adults with cancer, couples huddled in whispered embraces. On either side of the waiting room, the brass sign over the double doors heralded "Infusion Pavilion." The décor attempted to create an atmosphere that said even if you had cancer and your life sucked at this moment, at least you were doing it in style. You certainly felt from the care that went into the planning, execution and effect of the space, that you were special.

I summed it up to Kim. "Well, this *is* New York."

When Kim's name was called, we crossed the threshold of the pavilion onto linoleum tile floors accompanied by typical hospital walls and lighting, and then entered the even-more-clinical clinical exam room. First we met a leiomyosarcoma fellow, a researcher who specialized in this type of cancer. She was about Kim's age, asked questions quietly, and gave answers in a nurturing way. While she was examining Kim I noticed that under her lab coat she was dressed in a way that demonstrated the low priority of appearances. This sharply contrasted with Kim, who looked like a model in her boots, designer jeans, and cute little sweater jacket.

The door flew open and in walked a militaristic woman who introduced herself loudly as the expert we'd come to see. She shook hands brusquely and immediately ordered Kim to the examination table. After the examination, we reclaimed our seats, and as she was to join us in discussing next steps, she slid her chair farther away from us and thumped down in her seat.

Abruptly she communicated that Kim had a type of cancer that was difficult to treat. "A killer," I heard.

"This type of cancer likes to come back, usually within the first two years."

She told us she had looked at the pathology slides and was recommending a different chemotherapy protocol, which they were currently using with some success in more advanced stages of this type of cancer. She would contact Kim's doctor in San Francisco to discuss her recommendations and would be happy to see Kim again if this cancer came back.

"Any questions?"

Our prolonged silence and, no doubt, the expression on our faces as if we still hadn't processed the sight of a body falling from the top of a building, gave her an opening to quickly make her departure. Those fifteen minutes we'd spent with her were like a bucket of ice-cold water to the face. No Zen here. Kim still calls her "the Nazi."

Back home, Doug and I were allowed to accompany Kim to the outpatient surgery to put her drug port in and to her first chemotherapy appointment. The drugs were changed to the newly recommended chemotherapy protocol, and she would receive her treatment every three weeks as an outpatient.

Kim was angry. Her life had gone off the rails, and though we told her this was just temporary, she was understandably miserable anyway. As her treatments continued, she lost her thick chestnut brown hair and had to deal with the extreme side effects from the drugs she was on. She moved back home but continued working at her unpaid internship. She came home later and later, spending weekends with friends. I sat on the edge of my seat, ready, just in case she wanted to talk.

She kept telling us that living with us was not the way she wanted to live; we weren't her people, her community. It soon became clear that all she seemed to want was to be left alone and talk on the phone to "her people." After tiptoeing around in the minefield for a few months, one evening Doug raised his head at the dinner table as if from sleep after she made a particularly nasty comment. "When are you going to stop throwing your mother under the bus, Kim?"

After checking my email one night, I did a search for the term *sarcoma genetics*. That was the entrance to the rabbit hole that is Google.

While paging through the results, a few searches from where I started, I saw "Li-Fraumeni syndrome" appearing repeatedly. Ignorantly, I clicked on one of the links, then I clicked on another, then another. Then it "clicked."

Li-Fraumeni syndrome is an extremely rare autosomal genetic defect. *Autosomal* means that either the egg or the sperm had the defect; that it is inherited. If you are diagnosed with Li-Fraumeni, you have a defective p53 chromosome in every cell of your body. The reports continued,

> It predisposes you to multiple cancers; the most common types include osteosarcoma, soft tissue sarcoma, leukemia, breast cancer, brain cancer and adrenal cortical tumors. There is an increased risk for melanoma, Wilm's tumor (a type of kidney cancer), and cancers of the stomach, colon, pancreas, esophagus, lung and gonadal germ cells have also been reported.

My heart sank.

I learned that the p53 gene is known as the "guardian" of the DNA of the cell. If there are any errors when the cell divides, p53 suspends the process, initiates repair, and if repair cannot be made, it instructs the cell to self-destruct. If the gene is damaged, as it is in this syndrome, the cell containing errors mutates and multiplies unregulated. If the immune system doesn't kill the rogue cell …

I emailed my genetic counselor that evening, asking if I had been tested for this defect.

The next day she responded that indeed with the new information of Kim's diagnosis of sarcoma and given my own history that *now* I certainly met the criteria for the genetic testing for Li-Fraumeni syndrome. I had learned a long time before that genetic testing was not something that was done willy-nilly: You had to meet criteria. For example, there had to be a reason to test for the BRCA 1 and 2 mutations. Not everyone is tested for all known mutations—that would be expensive and unnecessary, even unethical.

I was tested, and by mid-March, Kim and I met with the genetic counselor and the medical geneticist, where we learned that indeed Li-Fraumeni syndrome was what I had.

"Finally," they said, "You have the answer as to why you have gotten so many cancers and benign tumors."

While this was the mother lode for them, all I could think of was this meant that my daughter might have this genetic defect, and if she did, she'd inherited it from me. I didn't really spend much time thinking about which parent I might have inherited this from. They did mention that I might have a "de novo" mutation, which would mean that the mutation occurred at conception and neither parent had the bad gene. My head was spinning.

Kim had her blood drawn for the test and went off to her internship. I drove home, trying to get my head around the implications of this news. I was horrified to find out the why of my cancers only because my daughter had been diagnosed with a very large stage III tumor. Why hadn't I been tested sooner? How many tumors did you need before you qualified? At that point I was in the teens of tumors! Had I been tested earlier, simply because I had multiple cancers, maybe Kim would also have been tested and monitored closely. Then she could have been diagnosed with a pea-sized tumor rather than a mango.

This new diagnosis created more grieving not just for my life and my daughter's young life but also fears for my 19-year-old son's and my siblings'. I immediately realized that this news could affect every person that I loved. My entire family could be destroyed with cancer. Where else was a family smote? My mind went back to the story of Job.

Thoughts fired through my head like bullets from an automatic weapon as I continued to crawl home in rush hour traffic from the city. I remembered they said that there was a chance that I had a de novo mutation which meant that the defect would have occurred at my conception and therefore for the first time in me. How bizarre, I thought, that my life might have been preordained from the moment of conception. I was getting a headache.

I rationalized that right now all we knew for sure was that I had this mutation of the p53 gene: "A heterozygous change from C to T at nucleotide 13346 resulting in a 'nonsense mutation' at codon 196 in exon 6 of my DNA." The conclusion said that this mutation was "deleterious to the subject's health." I would have to look up the word *deleterious* when I got home.

Over the next few weeks, I felt overwhelmed, buckling under the weight of it all, too tired to do more than scuff across the floor, walking into walls, really.

"Mom, you need to take care of yourself," Kim was constantly saying. "Mom, you never stop."

"Mom, you never modeled balance. This is why I am always so stressed."

"Mom, I need you."

"Mom, it's none of your business."

"Mom, we can't have you getting sick now."

I wanted to curl up in a ball in a cave … and then what? The cave was as far as I could get. This was my life right now, take it or leave it.

As Kim's treatments continued, she bounced back more slowly and was easily tired. She maintained her commitments in the city and commuted there most days, returning late at night, exhausted. She arranged to spend time with her friends at her treatments, making tiaras, playing cards, being the Little Miss Sunshine of the chemo ward, as only Kim could be. The next day she typically recovered at home, usually on her cell phone. She came out of her room for dinner, when she was there, her dinner needing to be reheated.

She had to become a warrior, and on some level, I was now her enemy. One night she asked me if I thought her cancer had come back. She was lying on the floor, hairless and ashen-faced, and felt that her belly was distended and hard.

"Can't you feel the mass? Do you think it has grown back?"

I felt around to the best of my ability, and told her that what I thought she was feeling was the scar tissue from the surgery. She had just had the first of many follow-up CT scans. I told her these feelings of fear were normal. I told her my post-scan theory of walking the plank of a ship, waiting to see if you are executed or spared. She closed her eyes, turning to stone.

"Could you leave now? I just want to be alone."

I said OK and walked out of her room.

All I wanted to do was hold her, cradle her in my arms, and comfort her. But she just kept pushing me away. I wanted to feel like a mother and not just an experienced cancer patient, a warrior, a problem solver. I was at a loss as to what to do. Finally after fifteen minutes of wringing my hands, I knocked on her door and opened it. She was curled up on the bed, not on the phone for once.

"What?"

"Can I just hold you?"

"Yes."

I crawled into her bed with her teddy bears and Elmo. I wriggled myself in next to her, put my arms around her, and gently pulled her to my chest. She began sobbing from the depth of her being, and soon after, so did I. I felt the hardness of our armor begin to soften and then melt away with our tears.

For the first time in more than a quarter of a year we cried until there were no more tears, not saying a word. None were needed.

I realized that I was now Demeter, mourning for my daughter, and that my daughter for that brief moment had returned from Hades. All those years *I* had been Persephone, cycling through the underworld on a regular basis through the process of death and rebirth. But even though I had my own experience of the events that had just unfolded, this experience was hers and needed to be hers alone. She was now Persephone. I was there to help, not live her experience. Kim needed a mother who could be what *she* needed. I had to stop being the mother that perpetually needed, like my mother.

Maybe getting cancer for Kim allowed her to get out the axe. All the things that had been bothering me about her behavior toward me, the feelings of not being heard, not being seen, not being valued, were exactly the same for her. I needed to see her still needing me. There was now no doubt that our relationship to each other was changing. It was going to have to.

Kim's test results were positive for Li-Fraumeni syndrome, as we suspected. She seemed too overwhelmed with the immediacy of her situation to share her feelings about this.

I was so sad. But then I thought, *Would I have not had her if I had known?* I couldn't imagine a life without her ever being born. I thought about all the parents who have children born with inherited genetic defects. How many defects are not yet identified? Is this natural selection at its finest? It didn't seem to get any worse than having the p53 mutation. Although it was really a mutated tumor-suppressor gene, could it really be *the cancer gene*?

If I thought about what Kim's life might be like, that she now had something like a 100 percent chance of getting breast cancer, that her life might be like mine, I just wanted to die. But then I thought, *I lived—sometimes it has even been great. Maybe things won't be too bad.* I went on like this for weeks.

Kim walked in the procession for the conferring of her master's degree wearing red boots under her black gown and a shocking pink wig with silk butterflies attached flying around her head. Even with her low blood count from the chemo the day before, she looked vibrant, youthful, and so full of life, on the precipice of the beginning of her career. Doug and I didn't know most of her friends in attendance, each so different, representing the diversity of the city of San Francisco. Kim planned to celebrate this accomplishment with her new family, in her own style. Doug and I congratulated her and drove home.

In July, Kim and I had our scans on the same day. A week later, on my 53rd birthday, we would receive word of the results at our appointments with our respective oncologists. Kim was now finished with chemo.

Both of our scans were clear, and we went out to lunch to celebrate. Earlier in the week, we'd finally found out that Brad tested negative for Li-Fraumeni. After holding my breath for a month I was jubilant. Now we had a trifecta of good news and my birthday dinner was truly a celebration for our whole family. We toasted with flights of sake at Ozumo in San Francisco.

I had to discount that sharing scans, oncology appointments, and a bad gene was now the new normal, not to mention a macabre way to bond with my daughter. But I thought, *It's a hell of a lot better than some of the other options.* We were still alive and able to continue the untangling, redefining, and refining of ourselves and our relationship with one another and with the world. Who thought I would live to 53? And each month and year that Kim makes it will truly be a gift to be cherished—especially if the gift that is my daughter is her own person, separate and rooted to the earth in her own way.

CHAPTER 31

THE VIEW FROM THE MOUNTAINTOP

OCTOBER 2009–JUNE 2010

I finished all the prerequisites, completed the training, performed hours of practice teaching, was tested, and became a "Seven Spiritual Laws of Yoga Teacher." I never had any intention to teach yoga. It is a wonderful practice for integrating the mind, the body, and the spirit. I felt much more grounded and was toned and in great physical shape. One of the challenges of my life was to become disciplined and have a routine. But much to my detriment, practicing yoga and meditation had to be scheduled and this wasn't a top priority during Kim's treatment. It certainly would have helped, if only I had thought about it.

I continued singing, and we hosted another karaoke party for a group of Doug's co-workers. In between yodeling and oompah music, the teams of Munich, Berlin, Dresden, and Frankfurt competed for the top karaoke group prize at our own Oktoberfest. Guests wearing alpine hats and lederhosen or dirndl skirts chugged from beer steins. Doug wore a Nordic tribal outfit with a wolf cape. I was dressed in "über-chic"—military boots, liquid leather leggings, a bullet collar, white wig, and long *Matrix*-style coat. Doug got a kick out of it when one of the young attendees, almost thirty years our junior, commented to him, "She's a keeper."

Many times during the evening, people asked why we had such a professional karaoke system. At some point, later in the evening, my answer to this question became "I'm thinking of maybe starting a nonprofit." The party was such a success that the wheels started turn-ing in my mind. *Why not bring this kind of experience to people who are being treated for cancer, their caregivers, and support personnel? What a great way for people to be in the present moment and remember that life can be really fun even in the midst of cancer.*

The following week I called one of my friends with whom I used to sing in the choir. I told her what I was thinking about doing and asked her if she knew anyone who could sing and who would want to form a karaoke group. I was envisioning that we could sing a cappella (with-out accompaniment), and then as a karaoke group we would get people warmed up so they were encouraged to do it themselves. We had to sing well enough not to embarrass ourselves or be too painful to listen to, but not so well that we would intimidate people or make them afraid to sing.

My choir friend introduced me to Ellen. Like most of us, Ellen wasn't a singer, but as it turned out, could sing. She had a master's degree in piano performance and pedagogy (a fancy word for teaching methods and psychology). She had been a college professor and *could* play the piano to save her life. She was currently working as an accompanist to several opera companies and classical vocal performers. I wondered why she would want to join my little ragtag group.

Ellen was reserved and, not surprisingly, nervous at first about sing-ing. I soon learned that Ellen's only daughter, Jennifer, had died very quickly only a year and a half before, at age 24, from a particularly vicious type of leukemia. Ready to venture out with a baby step, Ellen was attracted to the idea of the nonprofit, but more important, she was interested in the technical aspects of a cappella singing. She decided to give us a try.

Once we enlisted a soprano who could blend, we started working on music arranged for women's four-part a cappella. Under my direc-tion we began practicing twice a week for an hour and a half each time, learning traditional barbershop songs. I sang the low part. Ellen sang a little higher. My choir friend sang the lead, or melody, and our soprano sang the high part.

Ellen was always on time. She came ready, having practiced at home, dressed and made up for an outing. I usually had just tumbled out of bed or the shower, pulled on yoga clothes, and skipped the makeup.

It took us quite a while to master a tune, our own group dynamics soon becoming the most challenging part. Ellen was interested in phrasing and musical dynamics, wanting to closely adhere to the instructions such as *forte, pianissimo, staccato* and resolving a held note in a swell to diminishment. I had wanted this endeavor to be fun, but within three months this was no longer the case. The lead proclaimed that my vowels didn't match (blame my New Jersey accent), my voice was dark (I had always heard that it was rich), and I didn't breathe in the right spots (I was suffering from allergic asthma at the time). I felt beaten up.

Ellen soon felt comfortable enough to start commenting on the technical aspects of the piece. I had to spend many hours reflecting on the ego of artistic performers, what I owned and what wasn't mine, and how to improve the group dynamics so that I could get back to the goal of having fun. I learned that to sing well a cappella, the four parts have to vocalize the vowels the same way, although there is no one right way. The group needs to breathe as one being, again with the time for breaths being negotiable.

Finally, though, we were making beautiful harmonies. Sometimes during a song, the pitch, tone and intonation was so perfect that it felt like we were singing with the choirs in heaven, my body would shudder, and I would get goosebumps. I would look over at Ellen. We'd smile at each other with our eyes, knowing we were one—although we were criticized for it by the lead singer. She said we should never look at each other. We decided to ignore her. After many months we were ready to perform.

We performed our first "show" at the Wellness Community, now known as the Cancer Support Community. I packed all the equipment into the truck, and with the help of the husbands unloaded it all and set it up at the center. I presented my prepared talk about the journey of cancer from diagnosis through not knowing how the story will end. I had no experience in giving a presentation to a large group, and I had certainly never sung in front of one. I knew I was nervous when my mouth felt parched and I required many breaks for water. I think I drank a gallon.

We had chosen a popular song to sing that fit with each section of the talk. We sang "Help!" We sang "Blowin' in the Wind" in three-part harmony. During the karaoke portion, sometimes the rest of us were backup singers for Ellen and several times I sang the lead. I think we sang eleven songs with accompaniment besides the two we sang a cappella to open the show. The hit of the night was my rendition of "That's Life" à la Frank Sinatra, complete with fedora.

Everyone seemed to love what we did and we received a standing ovation. Then it was time to implement my plan to get everyone up to sing. My mission was similar to the ending of Dr. Seuss's *The Grinch That Stole Christmas*—all the Whos in Whoville singing together after the Grinch has done his worst. Soon, the village of the Cancer Support Community was singing and celebrating, despite the "Grinch" of cancer. People had their chance to shine individually, to be in the spotlight and give voice to their experience by choosing happy songs, sad songs, or songs of hope. It was great fun, and our mission was accomplished. We had succeeded in bringing some joy to Whoville.

One of my former therapists, who was working as a facilitator to a support group at the center, came over to me after the show. "Linda, that was great. Glad to see you are doing so well and that you and Doug are still together."

Yes, that was another hard-won success.

We had to suspend performances during Kim's treatment and recovery, but United We Sing—Together We Can End Cancer nonetheless became incorporated as a nonprofit. Jacqui signed on as the CFO and Clara as the corporate secretary. Once Kim was finished with treatment later in the year, we renewed our efforts singing and raising funds for cancer research.

Over that next year, Ellen and I became very good friends. She'd grown up in the Deep South, so both of us had regional accents. ("That makes us special," I said.) We were the same height, the same size, even born the same year within a few days of each other. We both loved to read and watch independent films and discuss them. She liked yoga and loved the outdoors.

We had so much fun singing together. Some nights when Doug was away, I'd invite her over to sing karaoke. That was when she reintroduced me to pot, something I hadn't tried since the incident after Dave died. She was a connoisseur of marijuana. I was tentative at first, afraid of going over the cliff again. Two hits later—*wow*—for the first time in months I wasn't worrying. It was like the top of my head was numb—nothing bothered me, the mind chatter stopped. It felt great. To absolutely everything, my response was *Ah, who gives a shit!*

Under the influence, one night we sang the entire collection of the Rolling Stones, worse than Mick. Another night we sang sixties one-hit wonders, and another night drug songs. We harmonized, taking turns singing melody. I had a hard time scrolling through the now ten thousand songs on the machine. The pointer on the mouse moved like water sloshing out of a bucket. I would usually forget what song we were originally looking for in the midst of scrolling and we'd laugh our asses off. One time she must have brought a particularly powerful joint—either that or she wanted to sing alone—because I couldn't sing. I just stood in front of the microphone with my eyes closed, hitting the tambourine maybe once every sixteen beats. I had a great time nonetheless.

One day she gave me a baby pot plant as a gift. I had no idea what to do with it. She said she would coach me. I potted it, mulched it with chicken manure, set it up on the hill in full sun, and watered and cared for it like an infant. What the hell was I doing? My husband told me we had gophers in the yard again that year, and after running up the hill to check my pot plant, I saw they had taken out the squash. The tomatoes were next. I called up our pest control service for them to take care of the gopher problem.

When the guy came over to deal with the gophers, he commented, "I like your herbs on the hill."

Rather than responding with something like You know my daughter has a medical marijuana card, I went *hmmph*, thinking, *Who gives a shit what he thinks?*—and this was without smoking it! I haven't and never will become a pot head, but I have definitely experienced the benefits of medical marijuana. Unfortunately, before a year was out, I had to stop smoking it—it bothered my lungs too much.

Ellen helped me to get out of my head, but I also knew I needed to get grounded. Though I had proclaimed the year 2010 to be a year of adventure and connecting with nature, I hadn't had much of a chance to do that. Ellen asked me if I would be interested in hiking. I thought, what a great way to connect the body and soul to the great mother earth. After purchasing all sorts of what I deemed necessary equipment—a camelback, fanny pack, BPA-free water bottles, hiking shoes, hiking socks, UVA protective clothing, hats, a pedometer, and corn-free energy bars, we went on an easy hike.

It was during these hikes that we really got to know each other. I learned that since her daughter's death she believed her life was over. In contrast, I believed that with all the traumatic events and never really being an empty nester, my real life hadn't yet begun.

Hiking gave Ellen a venue to discuss her grief and her daughter's death, the details and all the regrets. She watched me sob without comment on the top of a hill when I released my fear that my daughter might die. We talked about our families, our husbands, our disappointments. She told me that she didn't care if she died. Then we discussed the irony of her being friends with me, who spent most of my life fighting to live.

On one of our more strenuous hikes, while quietly focused on moving forward, I thought about Li-Fraumeni syndrome. The defective p53 gene is part of the DNA of every cell of your body from the moment of conception. *Wow,* I thought, it seemed that my fate—a fate of getting cancer after cancer—was determined from conception. I passed the legacy of attending the University of Virginia to Brad and the legacy of Li-Fraumeni to Kim. It just broke my heart. But then I would see Ellen and imagine her grief and think, *Well, Kim is still here.*

Continuing in the spirit of adventure, in the spring Ellen and her husband, Jim, joined Doug, Brad and me for a white-water rafting trip down the twenty-one-mile south fork of the American River. The spring melt of the Sierras was particularly good that year, from the heavy precipitation of the winter, the winter of tears.

We spent a wild day roaring down class III and IV rapids with names like Hospital Turn, Satan's Cesspool, and Troublemaker. Our navigator adeptly instructed us to paddle hard left, paddle back, and stop as we careened down the river getting soaked by the thunderous splashes. When another raft collided with ours as we were making the turn through one of the rapids we had to rescue a young boy who fell off the side of his boat. Fun ceased for a few minutes while the right side of our raft had to "sit hard right" as Jim and I oriented ourselves to the emergency.

I screamed, "What are we waiting for?" and then we yanked the boy up and over the side of our boat.

The day was filled with laughter, hard work, and lots of *yee-haw*s. I realized that, beyond the thrill of experiencing the river, man versus nature, all of me was focused in the present moment. There was no time to ruminate on the past or worry about the future. There was only the now, and I was an active participant, not a spectator. This gave me hope.

Ellen and I laughed, and every picture taken by River Raft Photos that day showed each of us with a smile.

One Saturday, several hikes later, we decided to try hiking the Juniper-Pioneer-Summit trails loop of Mt. Diablo. Somehow we misread a trail sign, and that sent us descending and then ascending a thousand-foot elevation change through Mitchell Canyon.

"If this is listed as a moderate trail, then what could *severe* mean?" I said to Ellen.

Using all those large muscle groups climbing back up was about as aerobic an activity as you can imagine. Man, was I out of shape. Smoking cigarettes and pot wasn't helping, either.

While making the ascent for our course correction, I started panting for air on the hot, dry, sunny trail and hearing the whine of some desert-loving bugs in the background, but amplified. The distance we still had to go just to get back on course was daunting. Frequently, Ellen and I had to stop, using the excuse of taking in the scenery, soaking up nature, taking a sip of now-warm water.

As we slowly moved forward, my inhaling and exhaling became deep gasps. I was getting dizzy and my front teeth started getting numb. I started feeling very emotional. *Was this due to an accumulation of carbon dioxide in my blood?*

After taking yet another stop to look at the scenery, I found focusing on the ground immediately in front of me helped. It was not unlike living in the present moment. If you thought of the challenge ahead, you just wanted to die. In my head I heard, *You can do it, you can do it.* I thought I could use this as a tool, use the rhythm of the words over and over like a mantra. Now I had to find a way to deal with regulating my breath.

Looking over to Ellen, who was using a walking stick made from a birch limb, hunched over, making her way forward inch by inch, I told her, "You look like an old hag." Together we laughed between choking coughs.

Continuing to ascend, I realized that if I concentrated on exhaling more than on inhaling, my breathing settled down a bit. I tried watching the ground in front of me, thinking *You can do it,* and breathing like a version of Lamaze—deeply inhaling, then slowly exhaling to the count of four steps. It worked—before I knew it, I was reenergized. I shared my finding with Ellen.

"Good for you," she said.

Was it chemical mastery, mind over matter, focused attention?

My body is amazing, I thought.

Later in the day we sat at the top of Eagle Peak. If we'd had a flag we would have placed it there. From our vantage point we could see San Francisco, the Sacramento River delta, and the snow-topped peaks of the Sierra Nevada. Here we were, on top of the world (at least locally), two mothers, one grieving for a daughter no longer here and another for a daughter fighting for her life who, if she made it, would never be the same. We were triumphant crones, teenagers, pot smokers, philosophers, singers, inhaling the perfume and the stink of our fume-filled life, exhaling, post-processing. I had many revelations on that peak as I considered the geology of the millions of years it took to create such beauty. If there weren't earthquakes, torrential downpours, floods, rushing rivers, gale force winds, and volcanoes, the view would not have been the same. All the powerful forces of nature were necessary to create the magnificence of the landscape.

I thought about my life. If I hadn't had the volcanic mother I had, I wouldn't have become so strong or learned how to survive. If it weren't for the earthquakes of my childhood, I would never have learned to be vigilant, a sentinel. I wouldn't have become a nurse. If I hadn't married Dave, I wouldn't have learned about unconditional love. I wouldn't have had Kim. If I didn't have Kim, I don't know if I would have lived when Dave died. If Dave hadn't died, I wouldn't have gone from being a nurse to becoming a CPA. I wouldn't have met Doug. Then I wouldn't have been supported as I had been, with the best medical care, the freedom to not work and to explore all the avenues of healing I desired. I knew without a doubt that I had a loyal, unconditionally loving partner who was as strong as a rock—not perfect, but perfect for me. And Brad never would have been born.

I knew having Brad and Kim, most of the time, was the only thing that kept me going. If I hadn't had my first breast cancer, I never would have found the second. If I hadn't had the breast infection and learned that they didn't get clean margins, I probably would have had a recurrence of a very aggressive cancer. If all of those things hadn't happened, I wouldn't have been so relentless in pursuing the cause of my symptoms, which resulted in finding pancreatic cancer at an early stage. If I hadn't been monitored so closely, the small lung cancer would not have been detected.

I wasn't yet sure where Kim's large tumor fit in all of this, but maybe, someone in the medical community will learn something because of it. Maybe the criteria for testing for Li-Fraumeni syndrome will change. But in any event, this was now part of Kim's story, the story of a powerful woman whose father died, whose mother struggled with life-threatening illnesses, and who was now recovering from treatment for her own tumor, diagnosed at age 28. I already knew she was amazing. It didn't matter that I didn't know all the things she would do.

All this had happened, and all of it was good. I felt a sense of humility that I had lived long enough to understand it all. I felt blessed to know that if these things had not happened, I wouldn't have been the person that I was at that moment. Neither would Doug, Kim, or Brad. I didn't know what the future would bring, but I knew I had to have faith and trust that it would also be good, even if not readily apparent.

Exuberant and exhausted, we made our way back to Ellen's car, six and a half hours after we had begun. As we took the blind switchbacks down the mountain at breakneck speed, the Allman Brothers on the stereo, I said to Ellen, "I want to have a party, a goddess party." She looked over at me with a raised eyebrow that said *continue.*

"Let's celebrate the circle of life, celebrate the maiden, the mother, and the wise women—the cycle of death and rebirth. What do you think?"

"Sounds good to me."

I sent out e-vites with a beautiful picture of Gaia (the daughter of Chaos), mother earth herself, to the women-only party. It would be at my house, outdoors, on the Saturday after the summer solstice. Everyone was instructed to come dressed as a "goddess," whatever that meant to them, and bring scarves for swirling, twirling and to prepare to really let go. We were going to celebrate being women—powerful divas, Gagas, and real goddesses—and do it with song, of course.

Feeling inspired by the project, I decided to paint the picture of Gaia that I had found on the Internet for the invitation to use as the backdrop for the karaoke stage on the back deck. In the picture, Gaia was emerging from the earth with her shoulders as the mountains, her head covered in flowers, birds, and butterflies. Rays of white, teal, mauve, and yellow light radiated from her head. Her loving gaze was toward the virgin horizon, as if just her intention was enough to create the beauty of the earth. A river began at the nape of her neck and flowed down to the life-filled oceans that were her one breast. The other breast was inhabited with the animals of the forest. I went to an art supply store and bought a five-by-four-foot canvas and decided to paint it in oil to maximize the experience of all the colors.

After struggling to fit the canvas into the back of the SUV, I picked up Ellen and we went off to a craft store to buy party supplies. There we bought flower garlands and sprigs for the wreaths that guests would make for their heads. I selected twenty-four spools of satin ribbon in red, pink, blue, green, yellow, orange, and purple to cut into lengths to decorate the tambourines I was giving as party favors. We searched the store for floral tape and spools of wire for attaching the ribbon. After filling the cart with all the supplies, we waited on the long checkout line, exhausted, having spent all this energy creating.

Over the course of the next couple of weeks, I blocked out the painting, began to lay out the base colors, then the figure of Gaia herself. As the painting was taking shape, one day Ellen came over for rehearsal.

"Do you think I could paint one little corner of this painting?"

"Absolutely!" I said.

After I'd finished Gaia's face and head of flowers and started blocking out the animals, I asked Ellen when she wanted to start her corner. She said, "I don't want to ruin it." I didn't push. That was one of the great things about our relationship. Nothing was forced, everything was accepted.

We practiced some duets. Coming from the world of classical music, Ellen didn't care for pop. In song, she was a jazz and blues gal; I was the blues rocker chick. We intersected at the blues. Like a couple of teenagers we practiced the karaoke versions of the Cranberries' "Dreams," "Sisters" by Bette Midler and Linda Ronstadt, Everly Brothers duets, and "Telephone" by Beyoncé and Lady Gaga.

The plan for the party was that each person would pick the goddess they most identified with from a list I'd selected. The four options were Athena, warrior, goddess of justice and truth; Artemis, goddess of the hunt and nature; Aphrodite, love and beauty; and Hestia, hearth and home. Each goddess group would select one song from each of three categories—Women's Empowerment, Songs of Heartbreak, and Screw Him songs. Then they would get up and perform them—no contests, just for fun. All the songs were ones everyone would know.

Ellen arrived at the party a vision of beauty as Artemis. I was Athena. She had curled her hair. Her makeup was beautiful; she was even wearing eye shadow. She told me she'd spent the whole day getting ready and painted her fingernails just for me. Her dress was a silk-and-lace sheath in teal and brown that her husband had purchased as a gift for her in Hong Kong years before. It had been in storage until the party. She was radiant.

The guests sipped Bellini champagne punch as they made the wreaths for their heads and decorated their tambourines, giggling and sharing stories of their lives. We had an incredible Hestia-inspired potluck dinner and spent the rest of the evening singing, dancing, celebrating each other, our lives, and good times. Our ages ranged from mid-20s to mid-60s, but everyone there was young. Just like the famous cartoon that can be seen alternately as a girl or an old woman, if you looked carefully in each face you could see the joyous, carefree expectancy of the maiden, the loving glow of the mother, and the knowing appreciation of the crone.

At the end of the evening, after everyone else had left, on the back deck under the full moon, Ellen, Clara, Kim, and I, each of us in various states of grieving, did shots of limoncello. We drew from the deck of goddess cards we'd forgotten to use at the party and laughed as we interpreted their meaning, arguing whether they applied to each of us.

Late in the evening, I walked Ellen to her car, where we embraced and wished each other well. Then Clara, Kim, and I shared a group hug and said goodnight. I walked back through the house picking up all the debris, the petals fallen off flower sprigs, the scraps of ribbons, a couple of tambourines forgotten, a flower wreath left behind.

Later in the week, watching the video, I noticed the sparkle had returned to my older, and maybe wiser, eye.

EPILOGUE

APRIL 13, 2011

I'm on a women's tour in Ireland sponsored by the New York Institute of Jungian Studies entitled The Realm of the Goddess: A Women's Pilgrimage to the Sacred Sites of Ireland. I am hoping to connect with the earth and the "crone" or wise woman—the next phase of my life.

APRIL 14

I am finding Ireland to be very magical with the lush green hills about to burst into bloom. The Irish broom brush is flowering in golden yellow. The idea of the fairies, the fairy trees, the beautiful farms with the rock walls, the little cottage homes seen while along the way to and from our sites, look like the Easter bunny is about to come with bouquets of tulips and daffodils. While looking for the crone, I found my child goddess here instead, further confirmed by the etched card I purchased of the elf Fairy Heart. I have reclaimed her. I'm even giggling! I realized that the Goddess—the child/maiden, mother and crone—has always been within me. I can also see her within the beauty and power of each and every woman I have met.

APRIL 19

I found HER! After visiting the Library of Ireland and calling up books about fairies dating back to the 1600s, I decided that I want to get a fairy pin or charm as my souvenir, a symbol of the trip. So today, while I was walking the streets of Dublin looking for a fairy to bring home, I got shivers up my spine when I finally found *my* fairy in a store window. She is a silver charm that wears a red enameled motorcycle helmet, with stars, goggles, and red lipstick. She is dressed in a green skirt and over-the-knee shiny black Christian Louboutin platform boots with their red soles, and crystal-studded garters. Her arms and legs move. I bought her and a chain to hang her from as a necklace. She is *my* charm. She is me—the *Kick-Ass Fairy! She is me whole—with all the parts of me reclaimed. And now I know I have always been a Kick-Ass Fairy.*

Later, in the fall of 2011, after doing some research into what I could do to make a difference, I contacted the Clinical Genetics Branch of the National Cancer Institute (NCI), part of the National Institutes of Health. Even though it was going to be weeks of work, I wanted to participate in the clinical study on Li-Fraumeni syndrome that was just about to start. After speaking with the study nurse about the criteria for participation, I received a large package of information that needed to be filled out. There were booklets of questionnaires to be answered, family trees to be made, medical problems to be described.

For weeks, I pored over the five four-inch binders I had accumulated of medical records, surgeries, pathologies, and lab reports to fill in all the relevant information. I was struck again by how amazing it was that I had lived through all of this. I called aunts, uncles, and cousins to gather data. I called my mother, but she was no help since she did not remember anything. When I finally gathered everything, I sent it all to the NCI.

In November, I had another surgery for yet another lung cancer (making this the fifth primary) in a different part of the same left lung. This one was also small, requiring no further treatment. Once home, I collapsed into recovery. I spent two entire weeks in bed watching all five seasons of *The Wire*.

I knew it was going to be a happy Thanksgiving. I *chose* not to go down into the deep and just be grateful—grateful for my prognosis, for dodging the bullet, grateful for my doctors and their skill and for the technology that they *do* have that can find these little tumors before they kill me. I was also grateful that they could reuse my scars.

Unfortunately, though, by February of 2012, my body went into lockdown mode. I had to start wearing splints for problems with both of my feet (plantar fasciitis), splints for my wrists (carpal tunnel), and immobilizers for my elbows (epicondylitis, or tennis elbow). One night while

I was lying in bed, I thought, *I look like the Tin Man.* I was practically wearing full body armor and thought I looked just like a warrior. I had been in combat whether I was conscious of it or not.

Toward the end of that spring, I joined a pool to loosen up my muscles and joints. I figured if I can't take the steep hill, I will go around it. If I can't go around it, I will blow it up. I knew, after all was said and done, that I was a *CANCERIAN,* but not just in the sense of the horoscope.

I *am* a Cancer Warrior, a fighter with a hard shell and a big heart. Not just a survivor but a member of the *Legion of Cancerians.* I revel in all the *drama* of life, while learning how to live, living to love, and ready to fight another day if I have to. But I am, was, and always will be a *Kick-Ass Fairy!*

In June, right before we left on the plane to go to the NIH in Bethesda, we hired contractors to continue the remodeling of our house, our home. We are continually reinventing our lives.

I know I *will* live to see Brad walk the lawn at the University of Virginia when he graduates from college next year! I believe the best of my life is yet to come.

Really.

ACKNOWLEDGEMENTS

To Family and Friends:

I would not have been able to live to tell this tale were it not for my children, Kimberly and Bradford. Their precious souls, their personalities and interests were the spark that lighted my fire every day. I thank them also for their tolerance and for loving me in spite of my flaws.

My deepest gratitude goes to my husband, Doug, who lives all of our marriage vows every day. You are a great man, honorable, loyal, and have been my Steadfast Soldier. Your unwavering support allows me to soar and your provocation inspires the fighter in me. You have allowed me all and loved me unconditionally. You held me up when I couldn't walk, fed me when I couldn't feed myself—relieved my pain when I couldn't do for it myself. You took it all from me and gave it back transformed. I love you on the cellular level.

I am grateful for and appreciate my parents Bruce and Frances for sharing their greatest gifts, for dropping everything and coming across the country to be there to support me and my family and for being at the top of the list of my greatest life teachers.

During a life of crisis some friends come and go and even family members turn their backs when they can no longer tolerate the crisis. They seek relationship elsewhere. To those friends and family—I thank you for the support and love you just for being you and for what you were able to give, for as long as you did.

To the friends that stuck by me through thick and thin for close to a lifetime:

Nancy, I thank god I didn't listen to my mother. We've walked together through the fire many times. I love you, my heart of hearts.

Clara, my California soul sister/surrogate mother/friend, what can I say? Many times it was only because of your willingness to hold space for me and listen that I was able to face another day. We've shared it all, love, death, joy, laughter and I love you, my Ethel!

My love to Robert, you have been my brother and friend for so long. Thank you for being just what I needed all these years—you—true, kind, and cherished.

For my friend Lyn, you have been such an angel and a prominent color in the thread of the tapestry of my life for the last twenty years. You are so much more to me than a friend. I am grateful for you and our group, The Hidden Assets, Mary, Jane, Kelly and Jan. Our friendships and gatherings and celebrations are the infrastructure that holds together the entire year, year after year. There have been many laughs, the sharing of life's trials as well as good fortune with this tribe. Thanks to each of you for holding up the mirror and helping me to grow in ways beyond imagining.

Many thanks to my friends at book group who offered too many flowers, cards, casseroles and cheer as well as ongoing friendship and help above and beyond: especially Joanne, Susan, Kathleen, Lynne, Leslie. A special shout out to Mary M! Twenty years of thanks to Jacqui, another great teacher, kind, loving and true. I thank you all as well for your support and early critiques of my manuscript.

For the Health Care Community:

During this journey I have encountered and dealt with many physicians. I appreciate them all for their years in training and dedication to their profession and for the challenges they face every day. You are heroes. There are some doctors that I have met who I consider exceptional. Not only are they extremely knowledgeable and current in their fields, but they also connect and see the whole patient, and that has made an extraordinary difference to me while facing extreme challenges. I want to name them here and thank them for being over and beyond the norm. The Exceptional Doctor awards go to (in no particular order):

Dr. Donald McKean

Dr. Margaret Tempero

Dr. William Hoffman

Dr. Henry Ward Trueblood

Dr. Bradford Prescott

Dr. Peter Carroll

Dr. Thierry Jahon

Dr. Roseanne Gorey

Dr. E. Shelly Hwang

Dr. Susana Ortiz-Unda

Dr. Orlo Clark

Dr. David Jablons

Dr. Harvey Young

Dr. Stephen Rothstein

Dr. Matthew Sirott

Many thanks to all the doctors behind the scenes, the anesthesiologists, pathologists, and especially the researchers for their innovation, passion and the hope they give the world. Little by little, they work to make sense of our biology so that someday soon their research may lead to a cure and there will be no more patients with cancer.

Of course I want to shout out thanks to the hundreds of sister/brother nurses who took care of me when I couldn't care for myself. You are angels here on earth! You are now nameless, but I remember your faces. I see you as incredibly awesome—the heroes of all the heroes. I want to give a special shout out to Brian, Anna, Elizabeth and Shane.

I want to acknowledge the psychotherapy community for its commitment and desire to facilitate healing. I accessed your skills often. I especially want to thank the therapists that support the population of cancer patients and their caregivers, usually on a volunteer basis. You are also unsung heroes. I want to give a special shout out especially to Trisha, Erika, Frances, Ron and the many other professionals at the Cancer Support Community of the East Bay.

Hospitals are like a town with many people working separately to create the whole. There are the people that bring in your food tray, the pharmacists, the stockroom people, the transport people, the radiology assistant, the phlebotomist and lab assistants, the admissions clerk, the discharge planner, the medical records person among many more. I've visited your town too many times to count, but I thank you for your dedication and hard work. I want to acknowledge first UCSF Medical Center for being truly a center of excellence in all that they do. I want to acknowledge Stanford Hospital for excellent care. I want to thank John Muir Medical Center for the care its staff provided when times were simpler.

Also, my thanks to all the practitioners of non-Western body medicine I have seen. The acupuncturists, Chinese medicine doctors, somatic energy workers, massage therapists, cranial sacral therapists, myofascial release specialists (shout out to you, Dana). You help to complete the circle of healing that was and still is necessary.

Please see my Resources page for the many books that also helped me on my journey.

The Craft of Writing:
With respect to writing, I took only one English composition class in college. I never gave any thought to being a writer. So besides having many stories to tell, I want to thank all the incredible authors I have read for helping to open a door into other worlds and perspectives.

While I never set out to be a writer, I worked hard to learn the craft. I want to thank Caroline Goodwin, a poet, former Wallace Stegner Fellow at Stanford, and a Senior Adjunct Professor in the MFA writing program at California School of the Arts and a continuing studies instructor at Stanford. She watered the seed of an idea that I could write a book. She encouraged me to ford the stream and bring my story, "a story that needs to be told," into the world.

I want to thank Adair Lara for her humor, for being a great teacher, for hosting a wonderful writing salon, and for the early critiquing of my manuscript. Brave, compassionate and experienced are you. Thank you for helping me to focus on what's important to the reader and to me. You helped me to re-pot the plant and inspired me to not get out the chainsaw.

For members and mentors on my pro team:
Thanks to Alan Rinzler, my developmental editor, for taking me on and helping me to prune and water the tree to encourage it to grow in the

best way. I appreciate your direct sharp wit and wisdom and all the support you've provided since then.

For pruning, I thank Leslie Tilley. Thanks for what you do, and how you do it. It's been great getting to know you. For precision pruning, I thank Nan Fornal for being a bonsai master.

I want to acknowledge special appreciation for Kimberly Glyder, my cover designer, for her patience and stick-to-it-iveness and for wanting to read the book before designing the cover. Thanks also to Joel Friedlander for sharing his knowledge of book design and publishing and helping me to move the ball over the finish line.

Finally, I would like to thank Skye Wentworth, my publicist, for her inspiring creativity and extensive knowledge. Her ideas generated bursts of outright giggles and delight for me. Her long experience in marketing and publicity have been invaluable in bringing this book into the world.

My Furry Friends:
I want to add my love and gratitude for my papillons, Indigo, Sienna, Bailey and Kenyon, for their unconditional love and comfort when a teddy bear just wouldn't do.

Linda Zercoe
September 20, 2013

RESOURCES

Here I have included some of the books that I found the most helpful in my journey. This list contains the editions I have on my bookshelf. In many cases, more recent editions are available, including other formats—print, audio, and/or ebook. A few titles may be out of print, but they can still usually be found through online booksellers.

Alternative Healing

8 Weeks to Optimum Health: A Proven Program for Taking Full Advantage of Your Body's Natural Healing Power, by Andrew Weil (New York: Alfred A. Knopf, 1997).

Anatomy of the Spirit: The Seven Stages of Power and Healing, by Caroline Myss (New York: Three Rivers Press, 1996).

Choices in Healing: Integrating the Best of Conventional and Complementary Approaches to Cancer, by Michael Lerner (Cambridge, MA: MIT Press, 1994).

Getting Unstuck: Breaking Your Habitual Patterns and Encountering Naked Reality, by Pema Chödrön (Boulder, CO: Sounds True, 2005), audiobook.

Heal Your Body, by Louise L. Hay (Carlsbad, CA: Hay House, 1982).

Healing Trauma: A Pioneering Program for Restoring the Wisdom of Your Body, by Peter A. Levine (Boulder, CO: Sounds True, 2005).

Meditations to Heal Your Life, by Louise L. Hay (Carlsbad, CA: Hay House, 2002).

Positive Energy: 10 Extraordinary Prescriptions for Transforming Fatigue, Stress, and Fear into Vibrance, Strength & Love, by Judith Orloff (New York: Harmony Books, 2004).

The Power of Radical Forgiveness, by Colin Tipping (Boulder, CO: Sounds True, 2009), audiobook.

Spontaneous Healing: How to Discover and Embrace Your Body's Natural Ability to Maintain and Heal Itself, by Andrew Weil (New York: Alfred A. Knopf, 1995).

Vital Energy: The 7 Keys to Invigorate Body, Mind & Soul, by David Simon (New York: John Wiley & Sons, 2000).

You Can Heal Your Life, by Louise L. Hay (Carlsbad, CA: Hay House, 1999).

Your Body Speaks Your Mind: Decoding the Emotional, Psychological, and Spiritual Messages That Underlie Illness, by Deb Shapiro (Boulder, CO: Sounds True, 2006).

Eastern Medicine and Philosophy

Between Heaven and Earth: A Guide to Chinese Medicine, by Harriet Beinfield and Efrem Korngold (New York: Ballantine Books, 1991).

Feng Shui, by Simon Brown (London: Ward Lock, 1997).

The Fundamentals of Feng Shui, by Lillian Too. (Shaftesbury, Dorset, UK: Element Books, 1999).

The Tao of Inner Peace, by Diane Dreher (New York: Plume, 1990).

The Web That Has No Weaver: Understanding Chinese Medicine, by Ted J. Kaptchuk (New York: McGraw-Hill, 2000).

Memoirs and Other Literature

Alice in Wonderland, by Lewis Carroll.

Autobiography of a Face, by Lucy Grealy (Boston: Houghton Mifflin, 1994).

Darkness Visible: A Memoir of Madness, by William Styron (New York: Random House, 1990).

Embraced by the Light, by Betty J. Eadie (Placerville, CA: Gold Leaf Press, 1992).

Gone with the Wind, by Margaret Mitchell (New York: MacMillan, 1936).

It's Always Something, by Gilda Radner (New York: Simon and Schuster, 1989).

The Metamorphosis, by Franz Kafka, translated by Stanley Corngold (New York: W.W. Norton, 1972).

Night, by Elie Wiesel, translated by Marion Wiesel (New York: Hill and Wang, 2006).

The Wonderful Wizard of Oz, by L. Frank Baum.

Mindfulness, Meditation, and Healing

Breathe! You Are Alive: Sutra on the Full Awareness of Breathing, by Thich
  Nhat Hanh (Berkeley, CA: Parallax Press, 1996).

Guided Meditations, Explorations and Healings, by Stephen Levine (New
  York: Anchor Books, 1991).

A Lamp in the Darkness: Illuminating the Path Through Difficult Times, by
  Jack Kornfield (Boulder, CO: Sounds True, 2011).

Wherever You Go, There You Are: Mindfulness Meditation in Everyday Life,
  by Jon Kabat-Zinn (New York: Hyperion, 1994).

Philosophy and Spirituality

A New Earth: Awakening to Your Life's Purpose, by Eckhart Tolle (New York:
  Penguin Group, 2005).

Answer to Job, by C. G. Jung, translated by R. F. C. Hull. (Princeton NJ:
  Princeton University Press, 1969).

The Book of Secrets: Unlocking the Hidden Dimensions of Your Life, by
  Deepak Chopra (New York: Three Rivers Press, 2005).

Close to the Bone: Life-Threatening Illness and the Search for Meaning, by
  Jean Shinoda Bolen (New York: Scribner, 1996).

*The Dark Side of the Light Chasers: Reclaiming Your Power, Creativity,
  Brilliance, and Dreams,* by Debbie Ford (New York: Riverhead Books,
  1998).

*Energetic Boundaries: Practical Protection and Renewal Skills for Healers,
  Therapists, and Sensitive People,* by Karla McLaren (Boulder, CO:
  Sounds True, 2003), audiobook.

*Getting in the Gap: Making Conscious Contact with God through
  Meditation,* by Wayne Dyer (Hay House, Carlsbad, CA, 2003).

Goddesses in Older Women: Archetypes in Women over Fifty, by Jean
  Shinoda Bolen (New York: HarperCollins, 2001).

The Hero with a Thousand Faces, by Joseph Campbell (Novato, CA: New
  World Library, 2008).

Inspiration: Your Ultimate Calling, by Wayne Dyer (Carlsbad, CA: Hay
  House, 2006).

Job: A Man of Heroic Endurance, by Charles R. Swindoll (Nashville, TN: The
  W Publishing Group, 2004).

Life, Hope & Healing: Prescriptions from the Heart, by Bernie S. Siegel
  (Chicago: Nightingale Conant), audiobook, cassette only.

*Love, Medicine & Miracles: Lessons Learned about Self-Healing from a
Surgeon's Experience with Exceptional Patients,* by Bernie S. Siegel (New
York: Harper & Row, 1986).

Man's Search for Ultimate Meaning, by Viktor E. Frankl (New York: Perseus,
2000).

*Meditations for Healing Your Inner Child: Become Friends with the Creative,
Playful Aspect of Your Self,* by Bernie S. Siegel (Carlsbad, CA: Hay House,
1990) audiobook, cassette only.

*Peace, Love and Healing: Bodymind Communication & the Path to Self-
Healing,* by Bernie S. Siegel (New York: Harper & Row, 1989).

The Power of Intention: Learning to Co-create Your World Your Way, by
Wayne Dyer (Hay House, Carlsbad, CA, 2004).

Realizing the Power of Now, by Eckhart Tolle (Boulder, CO: Sounds True),
audiobook.

Sacred Contracts: Awakening Your Divine Potential, by Caroline Myss (New
York: Harmony Books, 2001).

*The Seven Spiritual Laws of Success: A Practical Guide to the Fulfillment
of Your Dreams,* by Deepak Chopra (San Rafael and Novato, CA: New
World Library/Amber-Allen Publishing, 1994).

*The Way of The Wizard: Twenty Spiritual Lessons for Creating the Life You
Want,* by Deepak Chopra (New York: Harmony Books, 1995).

Women Who Run with Wolves, by Clarissa Pinkola Estes (New York:
Random House, 1996).

Psychology

Helping the Woman You Love Recover From Breast Cancer, by Andy Murcia
and Bob Stewart (New York: St. Martin's Press, 1989).

Nonviolent Communication: A Language of Life, by Marshall B. Rosenberg
(Encinitas, CA: PuddleDancer Press, 2003).

On Death and Dying, by Elisabeth Kübler-Ross (New York: Scribner, 1969).

Western Science and Medicine

Boosting Immunity: Creating Wellness Naturally, by Len Saputo and Nancy
Faas, editors (Novato, CA: New World Library, 2002).

Dr. Susan Love's Breast Book, by Susan M. Love (Reading, MA: Addison-
Wesley Publishing, 1995).

Insomnia: 50 Essential Things to Do, by Theresa Foy DiGeronimo (New York: Plume, 1997).

Listening to Your Hormones: From PMS to Menopause, Every Woman's Complete Guide, by Gillian Ford (Rocklin, CA: Prima, 1996).

The Biology of Belief: Unleashing the Power of Consciousness, Matter, and Miracles, by Bruce H. Lipton (Santa Rosa, CA: Mountain of Love/Elite Books, 2005).

The Emperor of All Maladies: A Biography of Cancer, by Siddhartha Mukherjee (New York: Scribner, 2010).

The New Feminine Brain: Developing Your Intuitive Genius, by Mona Lisa Schulz (New York: Free Press, 2005).

The Pause: Positive Approaches to Menopause, by Lonnie Barbach (New York: Penguin Books, 1993).

The Wisdom of Your Cells: How Your Beliefs Control Your Biology, by Bruce H. Lipton (Boulder, CA: Sounds True, 2006), audiobook.

Women's Bodies, Women's Wisdom: Creating Physical and Emotional Health and Healing, by Christiane Northrup (New York: Bantam Books, 1994).